Praise for *Nature*

Even in the toxic conditions created by ~~the ~~~~~~
there is health and well-being to be found in opening ourselves to the
web of life. Right now when we need it so much, these authors bring
to our attention many wonderfully useful methods and tools, along
with the stories of how they have been effective. Especially welcome
is the authors' discussion of the value of risk-taking in our hyper-
protective, soul-deadening society.

> — Joanna Macy, author, *Active Hope: How to Face
> the Mess we're in without Going Crazy*

...offers an accessible, research-informed framework for conducting
therapy out of doors, in ways that allow clients and service users to
benefit from the multiple learning and healing opportunities afforded
by open-ness to the natural world. Combining down-to-earth practical guidance, based on the extensive professional experience of the
authors, with thoughtful and critical analysis of relevant theory and
evidence from a wide range of disciplinary tradition, this is essential
reading for anyone undertaking this kind of work.

> — John McLeod, Adjunct Professor of Psychology, University of Oslo

A profound and sensitive exploration of the healing capacity of
nature and how counselors from all disciplines can expand their
practice into the outdoors. *Nature-Based Therapy* provides plenty of
convincing evidence to support the argument that time in nature can
have biological, psychological and social advantages for children,
youth and families. If you have ever felt the need to take your clinical
work beyond four walls, this book will inspire you to step outside, no
matter your client's diagnosis or the weather. *Nature-Based Therapy* is
a tantalizing blend of clinical anecdote, research and social critique
of our disconnection with nature and what we can do to reimagine
therapy as a process of reconnection.

> — Michael Ungar, PhD, Canada Research Chair in Child,
> Family and Community Resilience, Dalhousie University, Canada,
> and author, *Change Your World: The Science of Resilience
> and the True Path to Success*

Written in a unique, accessible, anecdotal and narrative style, *Nature-Based Therapy* gives a real experiential sense of working with children and families outdoors. This book is a timely and pragmatic contribution to the growing literature on taking therapy outside.

— Dr. Joe Hinds, Senior Lecturer in Counselling,
Department of Psychology, Social Work and Counselling,
University of Greenwich, Old Royal Naval College, London, UK

This book offers nature-based methods that help the clinician to expand the lens with which to see, hear, and work with clients to include the natural world in which we live. With compelling research, illustrative case studies, and thoughtful narrative on ecopsychological theory, *Nature-based Therapy* is a valuable handbook for practitioners working with children, youth, and families. It also offers much for educators and parents to ponder about the importance of re-membering ourselves and our children to the natural world.

— Patricia H. Hasbach, PhD, Private practice clinician, professor,
and co-author of *Ecopsychology: Science, Totems, and
the Technological Species* and *The Rediscovery of the Wild*

This book provides essential answers to the question, "But how do I really do nature-based therapy?" The scientific research literature is now clear enough that interaction with nature greatly benefits people physically and psychologically. It's time for the therapeutic community and the broader public to integrate this knowledge into practice. This accessible and visionary book shows us how. Highly recommended.

— Peter H. Kahn, Jr., author of *Technological Nature:
Adapatation and the Future of Human Life*

...explores multiple ways of enhancing wellbeing through case studies that beautifully illuminate the complex and integrated process of healing and change that can be found in nature-based therapy.

— Dr. Christine Lynn Norton, LCSW, CCTP, CET

A fascinating overview of the health benefits of nature therapy, its healing power and how in this modern age, each of us needs nature now more than ever. Read this book. And then redeem this very day by giving yourself and those you care about, a generous dose of Vitamin "N" (Nature).

— Jacob Rodenburg, co-author, *The Big Book of Nature Activities*,
and Executive Director Camp Kawartha & The Camp Kawartha
Outdoor Education Centre/Environment Centre

NATURE-BASED THERAPY

A PRACTITIONER'S GUIDE to WORKING OUTDOORS
with Children, Youth, and Families

NEVIN HARPER • KATHRYN ROSE • DAVID SEGAL

new society
PUBLISHERS

Cover design by Diane McIntosh.
Cover images © iStock.

Printed in Canada. First printing May 2019.

Inquiries regarding requests to reprint all or part of *Nature-Based Therapy*
should be addressed to New Society Publishers at the address below.
To order directly from the publishers, please call toll-free (North America)
1-800-567-6772, or order online at www.newsociety.com

Any other inquiries can be directed by mail to

New Society Publishers
P.O. Box 189, Gabriola Island, BC V0R 1X0, Canada
(250) 247-9737

LIBRARY AND ARCHIVES CANADA CATALOGUING IN PUBLICATION

Title: Nature-based therapy : a practitioner's guide to working outdoors with children,
youth, and families / Nevin Harper, Kathryn Rose, David Segal.

Names: Harper, Nevin, 1970– author. | Rose, Kathryn, 1981– author. |
Segal, David, 1980– author.

Description: Includes bibliographical references and index.

Identifiers: Canadiana (print) 20190096500 | Canadiana (ebook) 20190096896 |
ISBN 9780865719132 (softcover) | ISBN 9781550927061 (PDF) |
ISBN 9781771423021 (EPUB)

Subjects: LCSH: Nature—Psychological aspects. | LCSH: Nature—Therapeutic use.
LCSH: Counseling. | LCSH: Psychotherapy.

Classification: LCC BF353.5.N37 H37 2019 | DDC 155.9/1—dc23

Funded by the Government of Canada | Financé par le gouvernement du Canada | Canadä

New Society Publishers' mission is to publish books that contribute in fundamental
ways to building an ecologically sustainable and just society, and to do so with the least
possible impact on the environment, in a manner that models this vision.

Contents

Acknowledgments

We are inextricably linked to the web of life, embedded in a vast network of relationships. These relationships shape who we are and in many ways contributed to the completion of this book. We are delighted to express our sincere gratitude and acknowledge those who made this possible.

We thank all our human and more-than-human teachers and mentors who have shaped our understanding of healing and nature-based practice. Specifically, we recognize the land and all of her flora, fauna, flows of energy, and cycles; without these, nothing would be possible. Also, we acknowledge the traditional territory of the Coast and Straits Salish People on Vancouver Island, Canada, upon which we live, work, and draw our sustenance.

We thank our clients, past and present, for trusting to share their life stories and to walk with us. We have been profoundly influenced by your courage to face and overcome obstacles, as well as your willingness to explore your ecological selves. As a result, we have grown personally, and our understanding of this work has expanded.

We thank our colleagues in adventure therapy and ecotherapy fields whose work has informed and inspired us. Special thanks to those who invested time to review sections of this manuscript and provide substantive scholarly and critical feedback: Denise Mitten, Gary Stauffer, Tony Alvarez, Kaya Lyons, Will Dobud, Alison Gerlach, John Scull, and Katie Asmus. Also, thank you to our associates at Human-Nature Counseling and community collaborators who provided direction, support, and encouragement for this project along the way. These contributions, big and small, improved our focus, fueled our effort, and ultimately improved the content of this book.

From Nevin: Love and appreciation to my wife, Jocelyne, for your strength, support, and companionship. Gratitude for my original nature-based research assistants, my kids, Isaac and Stella, for your passion and spirited presence in my life. Cheers to my colleagues past and present, for your influence and inspiration. And thank you to my academic mentors, David Robinson and Keith Russell, for introducing me to the potential of asking hard questions and the influence of the written word. Last, a big thank you to my parents for raising a feral child in the boreal forest.

From Katy: Sending gratitude to my husband, Spencer, for his constant love, support, and steadfast belief in our nature-based work, along with my two boys, Ira and Oakley, whose exuberance and curiosity for the world inspire me every day. I'm also grateful to my parents for being the most incredible role models in raising a healthy family. Thanks to all my teachers who mentored me down the path of ecopsychology, and to the many community champions who have supported our vision at Human-Nature and helped us to develop and deliver the accessible nature-based programs that provide inspiration for this book (Power To Be, Shelley Brown, Monique Moore, Mary's Farm).

From Dave: To my partner, Beca, whose love is unwavering and keeps me growing and showing up fully for the world. To my parents for taking me out of the big city at an early age and fostering my love for the natural world, and to my family and friends who support a shared vision for a nature connected and life serving society. Also, appreciation to friends/colleagues Duncan Taylor and Hilary Leighton, who have generously taught me so much and continue to walk by my side in our endeavors to offer transformational educational experiences, and to Mike Simpson for his enduring friendship and inspiration to continuously strive toward making the world a better place.

Notes to the Reader

Not all who wander are lost.

TOLKIEN

Who Might Benefit from Reading This Book?

Our intention in writing this book was to share our ideas about the potential of nature-based approaches to healing and to hopefully inspire professionals across a variety of human service and educational fields who are working with children, youth, and families. We have read many academic books about outdoor adventure approaches in education and therapy, as well as highly engaging mainstream books about the benefits of connecting with nature. Some of these seemed overly academic and others quite light and entertaining. We aimed to create a book influenced by both writing approaches, even though we recognize that our approach will not satisfy everyone. We were undecided about the depth of research and theory to include versus stories and ideas for practice. As the chapters came together, and our colleagues gave feedback, we identified core elements and content that stayed near the middle ground we sought. At times, we felt lost. Lost in the immensity of trying to capture all that this approach to therapy has to offer. Lost in the literature of "who said what" and "what evidence do we have to say that?" And lost, at times, in our confidence to provide something of value to you the reader. If we take Tolkien's adage to heart, it will all be OK, as we accepted to go on an adventure and wander along in our efforts to share the work we truly believe in.

We hope that early childhood educators, youth workers, community youth leaders, teachers, social workers, counselors, psychologists, psychiatrists, occupational therapists, and a range of professionals in the human service field can find the materials, ideas, and activities we include helpful to their work. We hope this book inspires you to implement more nature-based approaches into your practice, and if you want to dive deeper into the material presented, we have left a breadcrumb trail throughout with our references. We did our best to provide theoretical support for the practices shared, as well as enough evidence from research to satisfy the rigor needed to represent the work fairly and justify our recommendations. So, whether you are a counselor wanting to take clients outside into nature for their weekly 60-minute sessions or a youth worker utilizing parks and greenspaces for relationship-building, group work, or psychoeducational activities, we encourage you to find and use the parts of the book that will work for you.

Chapters and related sections are set up to be read front to back; however, you be the judge of how to approach it. The book begins with broader narratives suggesting why we need nature for therapy and how it is portrayed in the research as beneficial. We locate our practices among other outdoor and ecopsychological approaches and then explore practice more in depth through case examples and personal experiences. We hope these examples and activity explanations offer you plenty of material to explore. Topics from certain chapters may draw your attention more than others; however, while each chapter can be read independently, they are all linked through cross-referenced content, theoretical assumptions, and research evidence, while covering a wide variety of issues, populations, and contexts. In short,

- Chapters 1–3: provide the philosophical and theoretical map for the practice terrain we explore
- Chapters 4–11: provide knowledge, skills, and evidence to guide you into the terrain and direction on design and delivery of your own nature-based practice

We hope we have created a book that can provide practitioners with guidance, program administrators with evidence and justification for practice, and readers new to nature-based therapy ideas with the encouragement and confidence to join us in moving your practice into nature.

What Do We Mean When We Say Nature?

We recognize that what we describe as nature throughout this book may be seen and read as uncritical universal claims—such as "nature is good for everyone" and "nature is healing." We do not ignore the fact that by design we are all nature, and nature is everywhere. Well, that is how we perceive nature. The *Oxford Dictionary* and Wikipedia, however, still define *nature* as "other than human." These definitions perpetuate the belief that nature is just the physical world of plants and animals and the features of Earth such as beaches, mountains, and rivers. This definition excludes human or human creations and dichotomizes our relationship to nature: being nature is

You didn't come into this world. You came out of it, like a wave from the ocean. You are not a stranger here.
ALAN WATTS

other than human. Derived from the Latin *natura*, the word *nature* originally meant the essential or innate quality or disposition of something. If we pause and consider this from a therapeutic standpoint, we are trying to create the circumstances for our clients to achieve this quality of being: to rekindle their vitality and find their core qualities and disposition. This fulfillment of one's potential can be realized through an improved ecological self that begins and ends with a deep meaningful relationship, as Alan Watts suggests above, as being not just in nature but as nature.

Blending Indigenous knowledge with the physical sciences, botanist and member of the Citizen Potawatomi Nation Robin Wall Kimmerer[1] describes human relationships with plants as that of family, or "kin." Her thesis is grounded in knowledge systems of First Nations across North America who relate to other living things in this way versus subjecting plants and animals to the title of "it." "It is a tree" is more likely to lead to a tree being chopped down without gratitude than "She is a tree." While a very simple premise, this approach has had an impact on our work and our clients' relationships with the land. We see this as more than a narrative shift, but in fact a relational one.

We are, however, trying to isolate our practice well enough to provide useful definitions, structure, and process as a therapeutic approach in nature. Nature, as it will be described in this book, is the primary venue and medium for our practice. While in some ways our writing will echo the dualism inherent in speaking of nature and humans as separate, although we also work with our clients toward their reunion with nature in the establishment and strengthening of their ecological selves. Our combined professional experiences include over fifty years as outdoor educators, wilderness guides, youth workers, facilitators, and counselors. Much of our work has been undertaken in nature, albeit in differing ways. References to *wilderness* versus *nature* do not suggest distinct differences to us but rather nuanced ones. We try to focus on nature as a place for healing that is primarily not human-made, and generally nearby, close to where we and our clients live, work, and play. Wilderness, as opposed to nearby nature, in our terms, is just going farther out from urbanized, populated, and manufactured spaces. You might say "more natural" or "wilder" than the city park or town greenspace context.

Within this understanding of nature and wilderness, we still recognize how these terms may be contested. Reading early (and recent) Western literature, nature and wilderness carry Romantic notions of sacred and healing spaces, Judeo-Christian overtones of human "dominion over" nature (as seen in modern Western resource extraction growth economies), and colonial impressions of *terra nullis*, or empty land, which was to be filled up and civilized with settlers from homelands. In turn, the Romantic notion of nature and wilderness as sacred healing spaces ignores the fact that people get lost and occasionally die due to environmental exposure, that environmental crises are real, and that many are left homeless due to environmental catastrophes, war, and economic collapse the world over. These realities make nature as healing space seem ridiculous to espouse across populations and contexts. Biblical ideas of nature being for human dominion and use, and that "wild" is opposed to "civilized," has obviously led to many of the aforementioned global environmental and social crises. Last, and very relevant to us and our work, global colonial projects tend to ignore First Nations. Wilderness was described as those uninhabited places, suggesting "untouched" and "unused" nature, which is ridiculous considering the travel, hunting, harvesting, and settlements of First Nations. What a settler may have considered wilderness in 1800 was simply home to those people whose Nations were already long-established.

What Does It Mean to Do Nature-based Reconnection Work on Traditional Indigenous Territories?

This book was written with strong intentions to improve the lives of children, youth, and families through what we believe is one of the most accessible and affordable paths to healing. Nature-based approaches are becoming more common and offered in education, community, and therapeutic settings. We see the trend and know also that we want to avoid the trap of calling this innovative, unique, or some form of emerging panacea in light of our privileged Western locations and viewpoints. We need first to recognize that although humans connecting with nature for therapy is the main theme of this book, we are generally participating in these activities on unceded and traditional territories of First Nations whose deep connections and relationships with the land are still maintained today. We also recognize that local and First Peoples around the globe have maintained strong ties to the Earth as a healing place, as well as the basis for their cosmologies. We want to be clear that we try to engage in practices that are culturally appropriate for us, and for our clients, and do not engage in ritual or practices of other cultures. Cultural appropriation is a real and harmful practice, especially so when there is a deep craving by so many to reconnect with nature and rediscover their sense of belongingness to something greater than themselves. There are ways to learn from the more-than-human world, and across cultures in a good way, without appropriating, and in our experience, doing so helps to facilitate a strengthening of the sacred bond Kimmerer describes and thus more willingness to bring about a world that is harmonious and life-sustaining for all beings. So, while we who are privileged as benefactors of the colonizing project of Canada are discussing connection with the land, we acknowledge our social location and privilege. We recognize that we live, work, and play on the traditional territories of the Coast Salish people, known also by the colonial name of Vancouver Island, British Columbia. It is important for us as practitioners to honor this reality and to think deeply and act appropriately about our work relative to the land.

Connecting people with nature has been a significant part of our careers, and we hold strong beliefs about the health of our planet and its relationship to human health and well-being as well as environmental well-being. We each have our own ecological stories of the role nature has played in our lives and how it now defines and influences our professional careers. While we utilize our relationships with nature for therapy, we also need to remain mindful to the suffering of the environment and the people of the land. Without this *social and ecological justice perspective*, we would do no more than perpetuate the Western colonial practice of benefiting from the consumption of others' natural resources: a hollow and short-sighted approach to healing in our minds.

Are We Addressing a Modern Western Problem?

We also recognize that the use of nature for therapy is primarily a modern and Western middle- to upper-class phenomenon. The number of people currently displaced from their homelands globally is beyond anything ever experienced in history. Human migration, driven by social and environmental conditions, includes conditions unbearable to most who read this book. Environmental change due to global warming, wars, an ever-increasing competition for resources, and the negative influences of the global economy have created these circumstances. What we have seen and experienced in our work, however, is that connecting with nature is a conversation we hear more often, and we see growth in the research literature building the case across academic and professional disciplines.

While the content of this book may suggest themes and concepts applying to all humans, we know this work is not for everyone (as therapists or clients). We have described nature-based programs and interventions for individuals, families, and groups. These are contextualized relative to client backgrounds, experiences, needs, and interests. We don't assume what we offer can reach across all diverse populations. A telling experience from colleagues a few years ago illustrated the need for our field to improve its understanding of culture and diversity. A group of young new Canadians (recent immigrants) were participating in a service club's recreational program and were asked if they wanted to join in an outdoor experience trip to the Canadian Rocky Mountains. When the trip details were described, these youths said that the idea of going to the woods, carrying all their possessions on their backs, sleeping under tarps, cooking on small portable stoves, and learning to deal with the conditions of living outdoors sounded an awful lot like the refugee camps where some of them had lived, often for years. As practitioners, and with this book as simply one reference, you will need to find ways to appropriately assess and meet your clients' needs, whether in nature or not.

Core Elements of Nature-based Therapy

While nature-based therapy may manifest in various ways, we provide here the core elements of our practice. This list may serve now as an advanced snapshot of our philosophical orientation and how it influences our practice.

- Practitioner's relationship with nature
- Nature as co-therapist
- Full-body engagement, play, and risk
- Restoration and regulation
- Bonding and belonging

As mentioned above, we are not prescribing our approach to practice but, rather, simply sharing our approaches to therapy. We will also be transparent about what we see as the major benefits, and potential limitations, of the nature-based therapy approach.

Disclaimer for Practice

This book is not a substitute for professional training and qualifications. Therapeutic work carries with it significant professional obligations and responsibilities. Taking your practice outside further increases your liability and needs to be undertaken with the knowledge and competencies required to do so ethically. While you may be inspired to try activities and approaches suggested in this book, you must also take responsibility for ensuring the health and safety of your clients, that professional codes and standards are not compromised, and that you meet regulatory bodies' approval for your work. We assume readers will utilize this book relative to their type and level of training and the mandate of their organization or practice and will complement the helping skills they have already developed. Neither the authors nor the publisher assumes any responsibility for any consequences of action taken as a result of the information contained in the book. Names have been altered and story details combined in our case examples to ensure that client confidentiality is maintained. In some cases, clients gave permission for their experiences to be disclosed in ways they may recognize; however, we still altered the case enough to ensure anonymity.

I believe that there is a subtle magnetism in nature, which, if we unconsciously yield to it, will direct us aright.

HENRY DAVID THOREAU

1

An Introduction
to Nature for Therapy

A child grew up in a small northern community. Population 600, and 59 degrees north; that is, just south of the border separating most Canadian provinces from Alaska, Yukon, and Northwest Territories. Being inland and that far north, in the heart of the boreal forest, it was quite cold and dark through the winter months, and –40 degrees was not uncommon. One of the many wondrous aspects of winters there was the presence of the northern lights, also known as aurora borealis. For the child, these electrically charged particles entering the Earth's atmosphere were not a scientific phenomenon but rather a spectacular hypnotic dance of some other-worldly spirits.

I (Nevin), the child, would join my friends in the neighborhood, bundled up in enough warm layers to protect ourselves from the frigid cold, to go find the perfect snowbank, with front-row seats, and to back flop body depth into the fluffy white stuff for the show. In doing this, our bodies were cocooned into the snowy surface of the Earth, thereby providing us further insulation. Another aspect of this wonderful activity is that those many layers covering 98 percent of your body to prevent frostbite included your ears and, hence, your ability to hear. The snow cocoon further dampens any noise, and unless there is wind, a cold winter's night contains very little sound to begin with due to the big soundproof blanket of snow. So, the stage is set: warm, cozy, and primarily left with the sense of sight for the spectacular show above.

The show, an evening with the aurora. Now, trying to remember back 40 years, what was it like as a child? What do I recall? How much of it will be a mash-up of images, feelings, and stories amassed since then? What of it is driven by nostalgia for the past? I do have clear memories of happiness from watching dancing yellowish-green flares, smoky apparitions shivering and swerving along to some unheard orchestra. The trees that far north do not grow tall, and there is minimal light pollution, so when the aurora was really showing up with vigor, the majority of our visible sky could be involved. Compared to the seventeen-inch television screen we had (with only one channel), this "show" was clearly without equal as a childhood distraction. There is plenty of wildlife viewing in the north, so it was not uncommon to come across bears, wolves, and moose, even in town... but the northern lights held the crown for best entertainment to us kids. When the solar wind brought bigger flares to Earth, we could have a really amazing stretch of nights when most kids were out there watching, and a few adults too. Occasionally the rarer colors appeared, the purple-red-blue and the very rare red—which I know now has to do with differing gases showing up at different altitudes. Reflecting on this experience floods my body with emotions and thoughts and triggers memories of my family and community life as a child. I would likely put the northern lights at the top of my fondest, and probably most impactful, memories of my relationship to nature. I can say that now, decades later, although active thoughts of the aurora were not highly present for years after leaving the North. I did not pine for the northern life, and the south offered me, as a young man, many more diverse experiences and opportunities, socially and educationally. When I began working as an outdoor guide in the early 1990s, I was fortunate that my work took me to beautiful places in nature, and around the world. It was in facilitating the experiences of others in nature whether students, clients, or customers (context specific), on canoe trips or adventure travel trips in other countries, when my own memories of discovering nature and my awe of its grandeur and scope were fully rekindled.

Not to fall prey to simply romanticizing nature, I can say that my relationship to nature became more of a subject to reflect on when I was held responsible for others' experiences in nature. What experiences would I want to create for a client? What are their needs? What are their current and past experiences of nature? And so on. As I reflected more on my own childhood, and by actively engaging in my own personal and professional development as a leader of outdoor experiences, I can say with some confidence now that I had spiritual experiences with the northern lights. My attraction to, and awe of, the northern lights at 7 to 10 years of age was uninformed. I didn't then inquire with science teachers or the relic called the encyclopedia. I simply wondered: What are they? Why are they? And yes, who am I in relationship to them? Now, the 7-year-old did not articulate it like that, no, not a chance. And those questions probably wouldn't have gone over so well at home or at school either! My now-improved understanding of nature-connection—although it still grows every day—would suggest that I was having existential inklings, or at least a child's version of those thoughts. I believe now that, in those moments of awe, I felt connected to something much bigger than myself. Maybe I sensed I was nature—and that nature was not something outside of me. I was physically embraced by the bed of snow; I was often in a near trance state; and I too danced and shivered with the aurora, until, of course, a parent yelled out into the frigid night, "Nevin, get inside. It's bedtime!" It's not easy to theorize as to how these early childhood experiences have contributed to who I am in the world. I can say that I truly believe in the power of the human-nature connection and have strong beliefs that our ecological identities can be nurtured through positive experiences in nature and that these experiences carry the potential for health and well-being. We have chosen to include some personal stories throughout this book to increase your sense of who we are, as relationships form the basis of healthy communities. So, let's hold this first childhood story in contrast to the reality that many young people today share, growing up in cities with limited nature contact, even sometimes without the experience of seeing the night sky due to light pollution. In his book *The End of Night*, author Paul Bogard[1] paints a bleak picture of what this loss means to our health, well-being, and, on a deeper spiritual level, us as humans in relationship to the Earth.

We will discuss some of the significant human and environmental crises being experienced today and how those relate to our work in nature-based therapy. Rachel Carson, American biologist, conservationist, and author who advanced the global environmental movement, wrote, "The balance of nature...is a complex, precise, and highly integrated system of relationships between living things which cannot safely be ignored any more than the law of gravity can be denied with impunity by a man perched on the edge of cliff."[2] Carson spoke of the balance of nature as a fluid state, with ever-shifting properties, and not something that can be tallied, organized, or controlled. She spoke out with courage and conviction in the early 1960s to warn the public of egregious acts against the environment through the use of chemicals in agriculture and desires by governments and corporations to control nature. Carson's work was a catalyst for change, and a movement of inspired activists and ecologists has followed as advocates for nature, with success in some areas, but in total, further environmental devastation has occurred in the last half century. This degradation often goes unnoticed from generation to generation as change is measured against what one knows in their own lifetime. Peter Kahn, psychology professor at the University of Washington, termed this phenomenon *environmental generational amnesia*.[3]

Today, scientists around the globe agree that climate change and environmental degradation have been primarily caused by humans and the situation is getting worse. Scientists have dubbed our current era the *Anthropocene*—in that we live with conditions created by our own hands and that this era is marked geographically by human alterations to the planet. Specifically, they argue that the advent of atomic weapons (and their fallout), plastics, and other human products have now left indelible evidence of their existence in the global geographic record. If left to its own, nature would find its equilibrium across its diverse ecosystems and reclaim its full health, in spite of our intrusions. The absolute truth remains that humans depend on the health of the planet, on nature, which sustains us as a species, but nature as a whole surely does not depend on, or need, us humans. Ecopsychologists and those writing on deep ecology have posited that the reality of our current situation has led to a cultural "dis-ease" and disconnect that underlies the prevalence of mental illness in Western societies—with increasing incidences of anxieties, depression, suicide rates, etc. This book is not written from an environmentalist perspective. It is, however, written partially in response to the current deteriorating condition of human health and well-being, as well as how the state of human health relates to the health of the planet. We will do our best in the following chapters to promote nature for therapy as antidote to the ever-increasing mental health issues experienced by children, youth, and families. Nature-based therapy, as a practice, is informed and guided by nature and natural systems. In return to nature, we also hope to increase ecological awareness and concern for the global environmental conditions that affect us all.

The Healing Power of Nature

The essential thesis for this book is that nature can be an ideal place, partner, and guide in therapeutic practices. In short, what we will describe is how an hour session might look in nearby nature versus an office setting. To make this reasonable for our readers, we need to provide a rationale. To start, let's talk about *vis medacatrix naturae*, which is Latin for "the healing power of nature." Often attributed to Hippocrates, the phrase means, in essence, that left to itself, an organism can self-heal. If we simply consider what is known about fevers and inflammation, or how our bodies mend themselves from cuts and colds, we know this axiom to be true for many human physical ailments. An organism must be given the right conditions for healing to occur. In the development of modern medicine and the colleges of human services, we know "do no harm" as the ultimate universal oath of physicians and therapists. This oath is sometimes meant as a moral compass to do something or, conversely, to do nothing, if doing something causes further harm. While ethical debates and moral conundrums arise in this line of reasoning, we would suggest that a "do no harm" approach to many health and wellness issues could be better addressed through direct contact with nature. We could follow Hippocrates, and many ancestors, into the forest and out on the land, if time allowed, to develop our knowledge of the environment through relationship building with her, and to learn her secrets for health. This utopian-sounding approach would actually be ideal versus the pharmaceutical prescription approach to symptoms so often taken today. A walk in the woods may provide health and wellness benefits and yet may not cure the ailment. But alas, we should remember that the second law of therapeutics, well-grounded historically and taught in medical schools, is to "do good." When conditions are right for the client, the safe path would be to walk barefoot on the biomass of the forest floor and trust in *nature as medicine*: allowing nature to counteract dis-ease and facilitate movement toward a desired state of balance. When combined with assessment of the child or family's needs and ecological well-being, and supported with client-focused intentional practice, the woodland stroll becomes a multidimensional, health-promoting experience.

It is within the clinical and educational understanding and skill of the practitioner to align client needs with the intervention in nature and, most critically, to assist in removing or reducing barriers (e.g., negative thoughts and self-limiting behaviors) to allow the individual to recover their own health. Natural healing, green marketing, health-food stores, and "green" car ad campaigns seem to indicate that marketers know full well the powerful attraction humans have to what is "natural." So, what is the attraction to a nature-based approach to therapy, and more specifically, what does it look like? While the practice of a nature-based therapy may take numerous forms, and fidelity may never be achieved to establish this approach as an empirically based therapeutic modality, we will attempt to provide a description broad enough to interpret for meaningful use in your practice yet narrow enough to identify and distinguish it from other common approaches. A promising development occurred during the writing of this book: an announcement was made in the National Health Service of Shetland, in Scotland, that general practitioner doctors will be allowed—and, better, encouraged—to prescribe nature for their patients. The health board decision, as read in the *Guardian*, is promoting health through birdwatching and rambles through the moors.[4] Getting back to nature— just as the doctor ordered. While we are not fans of the "medicalization of nature," we do welcome the field of medicine's efforts such as these to influence health and well-being naturally. On a grander population health scale, significant efforts are also being made to reeducate the masses on the benefits of protecting and spending time in nature. A new edited book, *The Oxford Textbook of Nature and Public Health*,[5] explores the complexities and interconnectedness of nature and health and makes a strong case for local and global public health strategies to improve human health and well-being.

Nature-based Therapy: What's in a Name?

To start, our choice of the name *nature-based therapy* to describe our practice was not easy to adopt for a number of reasons. For the act of sharing our work, a title was needed. We looked to other common names of practice and realized they don't quite fit what we do. So, let's talk about nature first. The notion of suggesting nature as an agent or actor in the healing process seems a bit simplistic when we also recognize we are all nature; that is, we are fully aware that we are composed of the same biological materials as the trees, the rivers, and the bees. The universal "all things connected" ecological story is well-aligned with our beliefs, yet for the purposes of a book, we needed to compartmentalize content to help share it in logical and meaningful ways. We need to be reductionist to the extent we can communicate ideas and practices to you the reader, as well as to make sense of them ourselves in recognition of subtle, and not so subtle, differences they may make in practice. A multi-day wilderness expedition with a group of incarcerated youth, for a very obvious example, is quite different from a one-to-one counseling session with a youth in a nearby park, yet they would both seem to be therapies based in nature.

Are we able to truly connect *with* nature if we are already integral *as part of* nature? Can we heal by simply becoming more aware of our connections to nature? The questions could go on, and to be honest, we do sometimes fall prey to the esoteric and ever-expanding interpretations of this multifaceted approach to healing. The questions and rationalizations we reviewed to name this practice were insightful and interesting, ultimately helping us to focus the organization and content for the book. We have each been employed in fields described as human service work, youth work, child and youth care, residential treatment, counseling, ecopsychology, adventure therapy, wilderness therapy, guiding, and outdoor/adventure and experiential education.

The primary common feature tying our work together is that much of it occurred in natural environments. Nature has also been the central feature in our discussions and descriptions of the change processes we facilitate.

"Nature-based" best identifies our physical location—often nearby nature—for therapy in contrast with office-based or indoors, which is the standard and conventional practice for delivering therapy. This suggests a place and space orientation that are both malleable concepts. We can choose locations and set conditions to create "environments" we think best fit clients' needs and our aims for the session and that can be accessed and utilized in a safe and efficient manner. In doing so, we need to be careful to not adopt a resource-use orientation. We want to portray nature-based therapy not as an expression of using nature as a resource but, rather, joining nature in a healing partnership. This is our ecological position on the relationships we hope to establish between ourselves, our clients, and nature as well. If you agree that we are currently in a time of nature disconnect, then reconnection *with* nature will in fact be seen as a service for one's health and well-being. In this regard, we partner with nature and attempt to assist clients in reestablishing a meaningful relationship with nature that can be mutually rewarding. Increasing one's ecological awareness, or sense of connection to place or nature, can often lead to increased responsible ecological behaviors. It is known that people tend to protect what they love. Preeminent Canadian scientist and eco-activist David Suzuki described in his book *The Sacred Balance*[6] how humans are comprised of air, water, soil, and energy. He eloquently tied environmental issues with each of these elements and left the reader with an increased willingness to care about and protect the environment. We don't lay claim to the spaces we visit or consider them as our home place or office. We do, however, honor our time in these places, as well as recognize those whose lands they are. We also do our best to work toward decolonization through small acts of resistance to systematic social and environmental injustices. For example, we can bring attention to park land managers for the lack of recognition of traditional lands on park signs or ensure our clients are informed of the history of local Nations and their territories.

So, why not simply call this approach nature therapy? As with many therapeutic approaches, a title generally suggests a focus or element of practice to differentiate it from others. Nature therapy could literally imply nature as therapist, or maybe it could be misinterpreted as therapy for nature! We know she could use some after those humans started messing with her! Should nature be described front and center as the essence of our practice, as the lone agent of healing? While the notion of nature as therapist is also well-aligned with our beliefs and definitely in the right spirit of this book, we also recognize the value of intentional and client-centered therapeutic practice that meets the needs of children, youth, and families being served. This means the facilitator plays an important role alongside nature in the process.

There are already therapeutic practices considered to be outdoor therapies. Each by name, and definition, holds slightly different conceptualizations of practice than just being in nature. We will cover some of the more common approaches briefly in chapter 2. The research literature on outdoor therapies is growing and showing positive treatment outcomes, yet the mechanisms of change are hard to identify, and it's even harder to prove they work, let alone how they work. We as practitioners are biased and believe they do work, and we assume those reading this book may believe so as well. Truth be told, much more empirical work is needed to solidly claim efficacy of outdoor therapies. Further, meaningful dialog and research on processes and variables in practice are needed to uncover with more certainty, surely more than we can offer now, as to how being in nature is therapeutic.

Nature as Medicine: A Dose Response

It seems there is now a pharmaceutical response to almost every medical condition and discomfort, and the notion of a *dose response* is pervasive in Western medicine as well as mainstream society. A pill for every ill. A dose is that amount of medication required to treat a symptom or cause of illness. The biomedical industry is driven by measurable, repeatable, and prescriptive use of curatives. As one can

Let nature be thy medicine.

now find "contact with nature" recommended online at WebMD and elsewhere for health and wellness, immediate questions within the industry are how much and for whom is nature a medication? The notion of prescribing nature in a dose is a bit tongue-in-cheek, yet also quite troubling as it objectifies nature once again as a resource for human benefit.

We have worked with kids and adults who have been medicated for a wide range of disorders, some physical although mostly social and psychological, such as anxiety and depression. We have had to, at times, monitor or assist in administering a range of medication when working in nature-based programs, especially when on multi-day trips. This has, at times, compromised or at least challenged our ethical position on the use of medications for young people during extended time in our care. We make no recommendations here but can suggest that some youth may benefit from nature-based approaches and not require medication for ADHD/ADD to assist in managing their behavior, specifically for school hours during the week. For those who question this premise, it is based on the dosage and timing of the meds which indicate the time and place for being "medicated" is in the classroom. Many youth coming through our programs have dosages for the morning and noon, but not for the afternoons, evenings, or weekends. At home, parents were also advised they need not medicate during the holidays unless they felt it necessary to manage behavior—indicating that the "problem" is contextual and environmental rather than a "problem" residing within the child themselves.

To be diagnosed with ADHD, a young person has to be exhibiting significant inattention or impulsive/hyperactive behaviors that impair or impede success at school, home, or during play. It is actually hard to diagnose accurately as the symptoms may be caused by other illnesses, influenced by the environment, or related to attitudinal or motivational issues. Further, those diagnosed with ADHD often also have concurrent diagnosable disorders, such as learning disabilities, substance abuse, affective and regulatory disorders (e.g., anxiety or depression), or disruptive behaviors (e.g., oppositional). ADHD is treated with stimulants, usually amphetamines or methylphenidate, and common brand names include Ritalin and Adderall. While hard to get conclusive answers from the literature, we have understood these medications to have side effects including appetite suppression, insomnia, and increased emotionality. Evidence from the 1970s and 1980s showed growth and weight suppression associated with ADHD meds, but this line of research trailed off and all but disappeared over the past two decades. Concurrently, the use of the medication has increased significantly; 1 in 10 young people in the US today are diagnosed with ADHD, according to the US Centers for Disease Control. The evidence suggests that physical growth suppression does not last, and long-term studies show youth using ADHD meds would eventually gain back weight and height "lost" during the period of medication use. One theory is that the appetite and sleep disruption was to blame for the suppressed growth. Logical, but what other costs to a growing and developing body would these disruptions cause? We speak from a critical position on child and youth medication in general; however, these meds have been studied well enough to make solid claims about improved student behavior and "compliance" at school and at home. We will treat the school system to just a bit more critique here and reinforce our belief in how nature-based approaches can easily counter some common practices and misconceptions about the need to medicate kids for the classroom.

Suffice to say that the level of performance stress at school and at home today is higher than ever, and children's social skill capacity is in decline due to screen culture and a decrease in recess and physical education, along with reduced available time and supervision for physical activity outdoors. Further, the fundamental attribution error of thinking something is wrong in children for not being able to sit in rows of desks for hours on end, quietly listening and learning, without fidgeting or getting up to move around, is actually quite absurd! This is not an area we claim any expertise in, although it is surely worthy of further investigation for nature-based therapy. We don't ask our clients to sit quietly in chairs and talk to us. In fact, it is only in recent history, after millions of years of human development, that young people have been asked to sit for 7 hours each day, 5 days each week! We move, and our clients move, and we engage them in open spaces in forests and on the beaches. These environments are less constrictive than the shared yet controlled spaces of school classrooms and hallways. Nature seems to be able to absorb immense amounts of behavior and emotional energy—as well as give it back. In a study by Faber Taylor and Kuo,[7] kids diagnosed with ADHD were found to demonstrate significantly better concentration after a 20-minute walk in a nature park than after 20 minutes walking in a neighborhood or downtown—and with similar effect to that reported for Ritalin. In short, the need for the medications is drastically reduced by the environmental changes alone.

A Story from the Field

We would like to offer an example to try to illustrate the potential of nature-based therapy as an alternative to medication. In doing so, we are opening ourselves up to criticism, and we can accept that. We can also challenge those who have to make decisions about medications to consider the possibility that activity in nature may yet be proven as a dose approach to the same issues (e.g., child success in school). We might also add that, beyond possible negative side effects, about a third of young people prescribed ADHD meds either show no change from using them or that their bodies cannot tolerate taking them.[8]

When working in youth corrections and taking groups of adolescent males on month-long wilderness expeditions, I (Nevin) and my colleagues were able, with consent from parents, probation officers, and doctors, to reduce and eventually take some youth off their ADHD medication completely. In this example, the youth and his parents agreed that the medication may be causing more harm than good. Tony, was able to realize the benefits of nature as a reasonable facsimile to the meds and to again experience his full vitality. The behaviors he was medicated for included the commonly cited inattention and impulsiveness in the classroom, blurting out answers, and moving too much, all of which distracted the other students (who likely would prefer to be moving themselves). Moving? To think, kids who wanted to honor their body's desire to do what humans were made to do, move! Crazy. So, when youth are out on wilderness programs, there is little need to control their bodies, beyond setting and maintaining boundaries to prevent them wandering off in the woods or cutting themselves while splitting wood or chopping vegetables.

Nevin recalls Tony's varied experiences and visceral reactions to changes in environments while reducing and completely dropping his meds for approximately 21 days of the program. Tony, a 14-year-old of small stature among nine other boys his age and older, had been on Ritalin for ADHD for more than three years when he attended the program. He had been in and out of youth court the previous year for breaking curfew and failing a urine test for drugs, and being in breach of his probation landed him on the wilderness challenge program. The program consisted of a two-week ocean canoe trip, a week-long mountaineering trip, a three-day solo experience, and the daily rigors of outdoor travel and living. From the leaders' perspective, Tony was a prime candidate for the program on paper, yet when he arrived, he moved through his days in a state of low energy interspersed with erratic, impulsive behaviors and anger, which led to heated arguments with other youth and the guides or being inattentive with his gear, like ripping the zipper out of his sleeping bag or leaving his boots too close to the fire to dry. Nevin and his co-worker discussed how Tony seemed to be unmotivated and yet frustrated much of the time. It was determined on Day 3 to get permission from his parents and probation officer to reduce and then withhold his meds during the rest of the month to see how he responded without them and to give his body a chance to detox from them. We were curious about his capacity to self-regulate and concerned for his overall health. What we learned was that within forty-eight hours, Tony, in many ways, came back to life. He began eating more and was far more energetic during the day. By month's end, he had gained almost 10 pounds and was much stronger, and we were convinced he had grown in height, although we had no measurement on that. His behavior was still somewhat erratic, and yet it did not interfere with his success, or the group's, while on expedition. We learned how inquisitive and reflective he was, as well as the extent of his energy and humor. Although we saw Tony's full potential as a growing and vibrant young man, we also knew he had to transition back into his home, school, and community, where his impulsiveness got him into trouble. He left the program assuming he would be back on his meds within the week. While the month was a gift to Tony's health and happiness, what was most interesting for us to witness was his increased sensitivity to the changes in the environment.

Tony had a temporary break to grow and experience the potential of his physicality when off his ADHD meds; he also experienced heightened sensory awareness in nature. He first brought this to our attention at mealtimes, when he expressed how much he enjoyed the taste of the food. We are talking about camp food here, although the program prided itself on nurturing youth with healthy filling meals. Tony's taste buds were only the first sense to wake up. He was always looking around, seeking out alternate viewpoints of the local landscape wherever we stopped. When we traveled through forests en route to the mountain we aimed to climb, Tony stayed close to the leaders and was more conversational than usual. Nevin's working theory was that this young man was not so comfortable with the deep dark places we were traveling through, which were in a region inhabited by cougar, wolf, and bear. He remained nervous and fidgety until we gained the alpine area the following day and had climbed up on a ridge above the tree line. At that point, Tony became near silent and walked some distance apart from the rest of the group. He seemed to be scanning the horizon in all directions and happily sat alone when we took breaks. This was all new behavior for us to witness. It was hours later, when we arrived at the summit, that Tony held his arms up outstretched to the sky and in front of the group yelled, "We're on top of the world!" Shortly after, he wandered off and sat by himself, staring off to the southwest, where he correctly identified a distant smokestack of his hometown's local wood mill. When preparing to descend, Tony seemed reticent to return from the summit. He never really shared what his reason was for this during the descent, but observing his summit experience and his quiet time alone suggested to me that he had a deep experience of joy and was wanting to reflect more on that when we, as a group, had to leave. In now retrofitting those experiences with theory, a clearer picture of why nature for therapy begins to emerge.

We believe Tony's story is not uncommon in youth expeditions in nature, especially the physically demanding programs where leaders and participants become a small interdependent community of travelers doing their best to thrive in the variety of environmental conditions.

What was most interesting from Tony's story was his increased mental clarity once the meds were cleared from his system. It is also worth highlighting that this program provided plenty of nutritious food, was quite rigorous physically, and tended to leave participants healthier and much stronger by month's end. His perception of the landscape, colors, sounds, shapes, and even his tastes were heightened in nature. He was also clear off his meds, so we don't want to overestimate the power of nature alone. For many, experiencing this degree of change in such a short period of time is foreign unless they have had a medical procedure or have altered their senses with drugs or medicinal plants. Tony was in a novel environment, with heightened sensory opportunities. His physical and psychological responses to the changing landscapes and wilderness experience over a month have stuck with Nevin for close to 20 years now as a significant learning about our human condition. Witnessing the connections between a young person's development that didn't fit in with behavioral expectations at school and the resultant medicated life the person had to live was, unfortunately, not uncommon in working with young people involved in the criminal justice system.

What we now understand theoretically about nature-based practices seems more obvious, but we didn't have the language for it years ago. What Tony was experiencing through his senses could be explained through biology and pharmacology. What he was experiencing in the forest and on the ocean was a heightened awareness of potentially dangerous environments, and after the state his meds created was cleared, he paid closer attention. While simple evolutionary devices to protect us from dangerous environments may not need theoretical or empirical research to support, we can say that it is not as common as one would think. Probably half the youth on these expeditions were not afraid of the environments and activities that could harm them. Their person-in-environment awareness was not highly tuned, only improving after considerable time in nature. The most salient teaching from Tony's story was his summit experience. The wide open and very exposed ridge hike up to the summit was for him a steep solitary march where he created distance from others and hardly spoke a word. This was noticed by all youth and yet not criticized or commented on.

The summit was an achievement in Tony's mind and, by his yelling and throwing his arms in the air, obviously one of significance to him. One element of attention restoration theory we will cover in chapter 3 is that of *extent*, or being a part of or connected to something greater than oneself. Tony was extending his arms upward and outward, a near universal expression, argued to be at an evolutionary level, of oneness, connectedness, and unity with something greater than ourselves.

Medication is a complicated aspect of client well-being and not one to be trifled with. We have offered the above example to share our beliefs about the healing power of nature and that, in some cases, it can reduce the need for medication. How does the notion of a dose become of interest to us? In 2011, at a Healthy by Nature conference we all attended on connecting children with nature, UK physician and leading physical activity proponent Dr. William Bird shared preliminary results of a study of diabetes patients and the stabilizing of blood sugar through a novel intervention: walking in nature. While not exactly blowing our socks off, due to our already strong bias for nature-based work, what was intriguing was his idea of a dose response he described in the study. If the biomedical industry has an ability to cite intervention research for a specific condition that has resulted in positive outcomes from a dose of X, then the appeal and uptake as a practice will be more significant. Unfortunately, the biomedical industry is also heavily influenced by Big Pharma. We imagine that the competitive pharmaceutical companies are "beavering away" (Canadian for "working tirelessly") at the formulation of a nature drug. Surely it can be manufactured, no?

The distinctiveness of nature-based approaches from conventional clinical or medical approaches to health and well-being surely lies in the environmental effects. Whether one-to-one or in small groups, the natural surroundings are present, and the time in those environments is where the exposure or intervention model of research could be established. This is not the first time it has been suggested, but we also recognize the inherent difficulties in real-world research when trying to control for, or in this case even define, the intervention. The type, timing, and strength of the dose would need to be established. Dr. Bird was suggesting twenty-minute walks in a natural greenspace, primarily in urban settings. This is an approach more likely acceptable in the bio-medical community because physical activity has been well-established across fields of study as an approach to health and well-being. We have national health-promotion programs established with interventions across media, schools, public television, and radio, encouraging active lifestyles through exercise, sport, and recreation. They recommend two to two and a half hours of moderate to vigorous physical activity each week for Canadian adults and a full hour of moderate to vigorous activity daily for children and youth.

So, let's imagine we could get clients walking at a moderate pace for twenty minutes, a condition we should be able to achieve without too much difficulty, considering we may not access an office setting and would like to move away from the busyness of the parking lot to find a private place to talk. A walk to the site of our session may accomplish part of the client's recommended activity for the day. Now just add a natural setting. As we mentioned earlier, nature is hard to describe and define as a research variable. Is it a question of how much natural versus human-made elements are visible? What do the walkers see? What landscape features are present? What type of weather are they experiencing? What is the walking surface? We often rely on studies with stronger conclusions, and yet those are often completed in labs, not naturalistic settings. Research "in nature" becomes logistically and methodologically difficult to pull off. What is easy to agree on are the benefits of being in nature versus human-made spaces. However, much of what we argue for is lost in research translation from lab-based controlled studies that attempt to prove nature-based theories. Suffice to say, we would happily accept a recommended dose of nature for our clients and for the general population. We have seen here in British Columbia several movements to get people out walking in nature, often informed by a research evidence position. The David Suzuki Foundation has run the One Nature Challenge or 30 × 30 for a number of years now. It recommends thirty minutes of walking in nearby nature for thirty days, with the hopes of developing a year-round habit. The BC Parks Foundation has implemented the Healthy by Nature "Outside & Unplugged" walk series, which is led by local health-care practitioners to encourage and educate families (using research evidence) about why nature and exercise are important for health. These initiatives would both be considered evidence informed, and both organizations rely on the research but do not necessarily prescribe a dose approach; rather, they encourage a lifestyle shift to increase nature connection.

We may need to responsibly ask, in the near future, the questions of what type of nature, how much, and for whom. As with a dose response approach, we would also need to consider how much is too much. Exposure to extreme weather and temperatures can be harmful, yet so can a dark forested path to someone who is anxious about closed spaces, has experienced an assault in a park, or is a returning war veteran who has experienced trauma in unfamiliar environments. A level of sophistication not yet present in therapeutic or educational literature has been found to support this line of thinking in outdoor therapies. With an ethic of care, we need to be cautious in our approaches and ensure client safety and meaningful practices, and to abandon our methods when they are not helping. Without guidance from practitioners before us or telling research behind us, the nature-based therapy approach is ripe for development as a modality. While not fans of manualized and prescriptive practices, we are definitely open to the research-practice explorations that will improve client care and outcomes.

The Right Dose of Nature:
How Much Is Enough?

So, let's stick with the idea of a dose for a minute. If we were to promote a dose of nature for therapy, we would need to clarify what a minimum exposure to the natural world might be to benefit health and well-being. In North America, health promotion organizations, doctors, and exercise scientists all suggest a minimum of at least thirty minutes of moderate to vigorous levels of exercise daily to maintain physical health. This approach to health is fully endorsed by the biomedical community and has a large amount of empirical support. This is also not a very difficult fact to accept, considering the human body was designed to travel the equivalent of a half marathon a day (~22km). Humans were designed as hunter-gatherers, and that would require considerably more significant physical effort than many expend today in our modern technologically advanced and convenient lives, where we have designed ourselves into sedentary beings. Truth is we are capable of so much more physical exertion and do not move enough. We were made to move, and move often, yet today we mostly sit and stand and sleep. Thirty minutes of moderate to vigorous physical activity seems a stretch to achieve for some in our hurried world, yet it should be easily achieved. So now how do we go about suggesting a dose of nature, knowing it is not just for physical benefits? What duration of nature could be appropriately suggested for human health and well-being? What intensity would we recommend? And how could we monitor, or even expect, adherence? Some inactivity in nature is very healthy for one's mental well-being and to reduce stress and recover from attentional loss. If we can imagine the doctors well-informed of nature-based approaches to health and well-being, we may hear someday, "Well, Mr. Johnstone, your son appears to be in good health and has a great reserve of energy. I strongly recommend you take him out for at least two good rips around the park and at least one tree climb each day to ensure he can manage all this pure energy. I'd also recommended fishing or another slow activity you can do with him to also provide space, while outdoors, for his inner explorations and adventures. Get him to find a place to sit quietly, and if that is not easy, make a game of it. Nature-based games are now reporting higher positive outcomes than prescriptions of the past!"

It would be simplistic but acceptable to suggest adding nature to the current thirty-minute dose of daily exercise. Emerging research has begun to support this notion. A recent Finnish investigation with over 2,000 participants confirms this, concluding, "Nature provides an added value to the known benefits of physical activity. Repeated exercise in nature is in particular, connected to better emotional well-being;"[9] the research is once again emphasizing that it is being outside that brings additional health benefits.

Health researchers Barton and Pretty reviewed ten "green exercise" studies and explored the question of what is the best dose of nature in exercise.[10] Their findings suggest both short- and long-term benefits. Self-esteem and mood were most improved with short durations of green exercise (e.g., 5 minutes) regardless of age, gender, intensity, or other variables assessed. Both factors diminished but remained positive over longer periods for outdoor exercise but declined with growing intensity of activity. That is, the best results were for light and continuous outdoor exercise. Again, this sounds like what our bodies were best designed to do: be active more often, but don't overdo it. From a nature-based therapy perspective, we do not often engage in vigorous levels of activity but do find ourselves moving often through our sessions, whether hiking on a beach or in the forest, with low to moderate levels of physical engagement.

Other notable results were that all types of green spaces produced positive results; water seemed to increase benefits; and the greatest impact seemed to be with the younger participants and diminish with age. Barton and Pretty concluded that exercise in nature is a "readily available therapy with no obvious side effects."[11] However, we must always acknowledge that elements in nature can be harmful to human health (bites, stings, allergies etc.) and that there may always be some people for whom the experience of nature creates anxiety and fear rather than being restorative. For example, we have seen in the last couple of years a growing concern for Lyme disease (carried by ticks) that has parents pulling their kids from summer camps and outdoor programs. It is the benefits of time spent in nature that we believe clearly outweigh the risks, real and perceived, that may require public education, and proper risk management, for the masses to be fully realized.

There is a call to address the growing epidemic in the Western world of chronic health issues such as obesity, cardiopulmonary disease, and diabetes. Nature-based activities were identified as well-positioned to promote health, family connectedness, and psycho-spiritual growth.[12] However, the authors also concluded that health and well-being will be improved when programs have specific objectives, build participant confidence, and are challenging and, above all, fun: "Ideal programs should offer both physical activity and ecologically meaningful nature experiences."[13] Fortunately, these criteria are also key descriptors of many outdoor programs. With a growing body of health-related evidence, the argument for increased time and activity outdoors gains strength,[14] and strategies to make it happen become clearer. We can only expect that these trends will include an increased openness to and desire for nature-based therapy approaches.

Prescribing a particular dose of nature is in many ways almost the antithesis of our personal beliefs, philosophies, and lifestyles. However, the current path our global society is following demands a packaged approach that measures inputs and outputs. Promoting a dose of nature clarifies the minimum time exposure people should be outdoors and seeks to highlight the socioecological benefits this natural, accessible, and free health remedy can have for everyone.

2

Outdoor Therapies:
A Choice of Paths to Follow

*If the path before you is clear,
you are probably on someone else's.*

Joseph Campbell

The diverse practitioners, theorists, and therapists contributing to the growing body of knowledge in outdoor therapies come from a wide variety of educational fields and professional backgrounds as opposed to from one specific field, such as social work or counseling. We have read the literature broadly and dialogued with our colleagues internationally and can state that there are few consistent definitions that capture outdoor therapy practices. Even specific forms of outdoor therapy organized by business models, collective research agendas, and professional gatherings may claim more distinct definitions of practice yet are not often accurately representing consistent practices across programs and practitioners. Hence, and in response to Campbell's adage, our path forward is not clear. There remains significant variability, such as intervention length and type, populations served, the skills and abilities of staff and therapists, the mandates of the organizations, and a host of other economic, philosophical, and logistical influences that result in practice differences.[1] That said, a growing body of research in these related fields is gaining increased attention in the health and therapeutic sectors. Rather than fill the chapters with references, we will let you go exploring on your own, and we suggest the empirical works we cite as a starting point. Now, what is nature-based therapy, and what are the core elements of practice? You may be getting a sense that we are not going to simply provide an exclusive definition as that may limit the potential of this approach for you. What we will do is unpack the ideas of nature-based therapy throughout the book and hopefully answer more questions you have along the way. We hope you can find ways to incorporate some of these ideas into your existing work and context with children, youth, and families, as well as to adapt and develop them further for all our benefit.

We have located what we are referring to as *nature-based therapy* in the current opus of related literature and a range of practices we are familiar with. In doing this, we believe nature-based therapy could be found under two umbrella terms that attempt to capture similar therapeutic modalities for the sake of description, definition, and classification. Those who have chosen more specific definitions have done so either to further establish their particular approach, to differentiate their practices as unique, or to serve certain populations. While not going into the conversation too far, we acknowledge the benefits of narrower definitions, which often lead to an increasingly prescribed practice, which can then be empirically tested and gain status as evidence-based. This is a coup in the mental health and addictions treatment world in North America as it provides a significant pathway for funding and increased recognition. As mentioned before, our approach is quite diverse and would be hard to meet the standards for manualization in its current form—so we can leave those developments and research to those who need to pursue it.

Two common practice terms in the literature and related fields are (1) *ecotherapy* (growing out of the philosophy of environmentalism and psychology, and later ecopsychology) and (2) *adventure therapy* (growing out of outdoor and experiential education). Within these two more generic terms a host of therapeutic approaches have been identified, sometimes grouped together suggesting similarities and at other times seemingly desiring to be isolated and exclusive by definition. There are also numerous practices surfacing by names quite similar but with very different aims and practices. One example is a Western take on *Shinrin-yoku* from Japan, an ancient practice of nature connection that has roots and influence from the Shinto religion. American outdoor educator Amos Clifford[2] has recently published a book on forest bathing, describing the practice as mostly synonymous with forest therapy and Shinrin-yoku, and has even started the Association for Nature and Forest Therapy Guides. While we are happy to see more nature-connection literature reaching mainstream audiences, we question, and caution, the use of *therapy* in the title because Clifford describes forest bathing as "a more casual experience among the trees, unburdened by expectations, oriented to simple pleasure," although suggesting forest therapy be undertaken "with an intentional goal of some type of healing best done with a trained guide."[3] Here we have to make a clear distinction in that what we are proposing in nature-based therapy is to be facilitated by qualified and registered practitioners who are held accountable to professional associations in the human service field (e.g., American Association of Social Workers or Canadian Counseling and Psychotherapy Association). While our practice may lead to general health and well-being improvements along with addressing underlying distress and psychological issues, we do engage in similar activities described in the forest bathing book. These fuzzy lines between a number of practices with similar names make for a hard path to clearly mark. Our influences and the bodies of scientific and theoretical literature we draw from are in the realms of ecotherapies and adventure therapies; we will provide a brief overview with key elements from each of these as they relate to our work in nature-based therapy.

Ecotherapies

To begin, ecotherapy has been depicted as those therapies that bring to therapeutic practice an ecological perspective.[4] This means therapies that go beyond the office walls and one's own social ecology but also engage in thinking and relating to the natural world, thinking about environmental conditions and crises as well as human-nature relationships. Ecotherapy practices have been described and developed in response to Western culture's disconnect from nature, connected to the environmental movement's growing concerns for the planet and a slow eye-opening to the links between human and environmental health. A major paradigm shift in the natural sciences has occurred over the past half-decade, which has seen a rise in evolutionary and systems thinking (aka ecology). An attempt is being made to better understand the intricate connections between all living things versus the process of modern Western science (i.e., Cartesian) that reduces the whole to its parts, in which to then study and objectify the elements in isolation from each other. The links between human mental health and more recent effects of climate change—including erratic and catastrophic weather events—is being propelled forward as a significant and rapidly mounting issue. Hayes and colleagues[5] have provided the term *eco-grief* to capture the negative mental health effects of climate change. We can say, in all honesty, that waking up to the effects of wildfires here in British Columbia can be drastic and leave lasting anxiety and fear in those experiencing them. Over the past few summers, we have experienced the apocalyptic muted-gray skies and burning red orb of the sun, often for a few days straight. This envelops your world, and living on an island, with a number of large fires burning, is not comfortable. These ideas will become more mainstream in literature and media as more examples of erratic weather occur (e.g., raging tropical storms, wildfires, drought, species loss).

One ecotherapy practice that may be the easiest to explain is *horticultural* or *garden therapy*, in which a relationship is built between client, therapist, and the plants/nature they care for. This ecotherapy can take place in community or privately owned garden plots or in residential treatment settings that include these practices. Near where we live, and still within the city limits of Victoria, Canada, there is a therapeutic program called Woodwynn Farms. The farm is a therapeutic space for people experiencing homelessness, substance abuse, and mental health issues. The farm activities see clients and staff working to overcome meaningful challenges as a community, like ensuring daily farm chores are done and that healthy food is grown, prepared, and shared with gratitude at every meal. Clients are held accountable and also valued in a community for meaningful contributions to the whole. Their individual thoughts, attitudes, and actions can change, allowing them to reclaim their rightful place in the broader community. Involved in growing food, flowers, or trees, participants are engaging with biological systems, observing the integration of parts in the greater whole of life and recognizing their place in the more-than-human natural world. While nature-based therapy isn't specifically integrating gardening and the cultivation of living things, the practice does include sharing the knowledge of natural biological systems and integrates notions of conservation, species identification, and permaculture, in part bringing biology to therapy.

Ecology has been the rogue science in that it is based on foundations counter to traditional scientific study. In fact, ecology was once dubbed the subversive science. We believe that the notion of interdisciplinary thinking and being, and recognition of relationships and connections over the objectifying of individual parts, will likely be seen as the norm in the near future—and reductionist science may be seen as a regrettable phase of our growing up as humans. While we will speak to the power of metaphors in nature throughout the book, gardening has an obvious and powerful metaphor of caring and nurturing relationships, commitment, and provision of key nourishment necessary for healthy and sustainable growth. Horticultural therapy has been used successfully across populations, from children struggling in school settings to war veterans dealing with PTSD. For military personnel who have been trained to take life, the process of therapeutic gardening, especially with hand tools and in quiet locations, has proven to be helpful in their healing through the nurturing of life. Sylvia Westland details numerous successful outdoor veterans' programs in her recent book *Field Practices*,[6] where farming, equine, and outdoor activity programs are described relative to the successes they have experienced with trauma and recovery for this underserved population.

Animal-assisted therapies are also quite commonly described as an ecotherapy approach for their direct contact with nature through engagement and relationship building with another species. Equine-assisted therapy is one approach that has grown in popularity and has a fairly well-established research base,[7] suggesting positive benefits for therapy. While not central to our practice, taking clients to farms or to ride at an equine-assisted program has been undertaken, and we can acknowledge the potential. The sensitivity to which the horse responds to the subtle nervous system changes in a relating human provides incredible feedback to the client and experiential teaching on how to come into regulation and right relationship with other living beings, human or not. The engagement with animals quickly eclipses an anthropocentric approach to conventional therapies and can bring deeper recognition of one's preferences and beliefs about care for the environment and others, and communication from animals is often more direct, whether subtle or abrupt. Animal-assisted therapy includes domesticated animals such as dogs. Dave's dog, Eidel, a very sweet-spirited Nova Scotia Duck Toller, has provided clients with another being to relate to and opportunities for comfort, sharing, and leadership. In essence, Eidel has been a co-facilitator in a therapeutic process with clients. The possibilities for contact with other sentient beings is common, and we will encourage engagement with animals as a meaningful contribution to the therapeutic process.

The broader body of ecotherapy research and theories falls under the umbrella of *ecopsychology*, a term that describes the greening of psychology, an idea that has been around for a quarter century, although we would not consider it a part of the mainstream vocabulary in North America. We do recognize professional affiliations and the territory of naming professions. For this, we avoid the adoption of eco-*psychologist* as part of our titles. Any therapist taking an ecological approach in their practice may find themselves self-identifying as an ecotherapist. This does not, however, mean that they even engage actively with the outdoors. Some have a conventional office-based practice yet engage clients in processes that bring awareness to their place in, and impact on, the natural world through assessing one's ecological self and addressing global environmental issues and a host of other human-nature topics in their sessions, which could just as easily be done indoors. Nature-based therapy would also meet these descriptions of ecotherapy. We occasionally practice indoors, yet those sessions are often chosen strategically for engagement, particular issues requiring assessment or "containment," or as you may assume, during nasty inclement weather. We will speak more to this in chapter 4 but for now will move on to a second type of outdoor therapies, the adventurous ones.

Adventure Therapies

Adventure therapy is another common term in the literature covering a range of therapeutic approaches.[8] These include wilderness therapy, bush adventure therapy (Australia), outdoor behavioral health care (USA), adventure-based counseling, therapeutic adventure, *friluftsterapi* (Norway), and outdoor recreation therapy. The term *adventure* provides the most obvious distinction from a nature-based or ecotherapy approach. Adventure carries with it notions of risk and undetermined outcomes. When engaged in adventure, we do not know exactly what will happen; the results of the intervention are not predetermined. This unknown factor can be seen or experienced in the activities, outdoor travel and living, or the facilitated adventure experiences during therapy. Much like ecotherapies described above, some practices of outdoor therapies overlap with adventure therapy by definition and in practice, including what we are presenting as nature-based therapy.

We recognize and own that even compartmentalizing ecotherapies and adventure therapies this way, under the term *outdoor therapies*, may not be acceptable to some of our colleagues who are working toward tighter definitions for their specific approaches. We encourage them to carry on, as we are trying to simplify the name games and allow those new to the work to get a better understanding of how programs may identify themselves or align with certain practices. James Neill, educational psychologist and adventure therapy researcher from Canberra, Australia, shared the following on an international listserv conversation regarding "the name game" in adventure therapy, after stating that *adventure therapy* was by no means settled upon for the field:

> The most commonly mentioned terms so far are:
> "therapy" & "therapeutic" "adventure" & "adventure-based"
> whatever is chosen will get simplified in the big wide world e.g.,
> Adventure Based Therapy → [tends to degrade to] Adventure
> Therapy → [tends to be abbreviated as] "AT"

> The label would also get adapted for other linguistic uses e.g.,
> "adventure therapist" seems to be less linguistically and
> cognitively taxing than "therapeutic adventure practitioner" or
> "adventure-based therapist"

In other words, we can adopt "Adventure Based Therapy" or "Therapeutic Adventure" or "Therapeutic Outdoor Wilderness Challenge etc. Therapy," etc. because they seem like more accurate terms but "Adventure Therapy" has already become more widely popular at least in part due its linguistic simplicity and utility. Adoption of more complex terms offers the promise of more exact semantics, but will the supposed gains in semantic precision sufficiently outweigh the practical loss of linguistic utility and the broader popularity of more simple terms?

(Excerpt from a listserv conversation on adventure therapy in 2004.)

Interestingly, this listserv conversation was 15 years ago, and the definitions name-game carries on today for many in the field. In our minds, it is not necessary. We believe that practitioners need to clearly identify what their practice is comprised of and call it such. If you do brief solution-focused therapy for couples, then describe it as such and, equally important, rely on the research and theories that support that practice. What has been seen in adventure therapy for decades is a reliance on the research of the "field" and a borrowing of outcomes to bolster programs that may or may not even be doing the same things. We have also seen an extension, or stretching, of the research from other fields to justify programs and practices, even when substantially different. So, can we identify with any accuracy what adventure therapy is?

Core practices defined in adventure therapy have been described as including active kinesthetic participation, experiential learning pedagogies, connection to place, challenge/risk, eliciting eustress, generating of metaphors, a blending of therapeutic practice with psychosocial learning, and an alternative entrance to awareness.[9] How these practices show up in a variety of settings and contexts could be a study and text in itself, which would benefit the field immensely if someone were to take that on. While not unanimously agreed upon, *adventure therapy* as a generic term seems to have been loosely adopted internationally, as James Neill suggested above, for its simplicity and utility, although it likely doesn't serve all practitioners in accurately describing the specific context and activities of their approach. A triennial gathering called the International Adventure Therapy Conference brings together researchers, theorists, practitioners, and students on this topic. What has been clear to us in attending these gatherings is that if you think it is hard to organize and label your practice locally, you can multiply that by ten trying to capture the diversity of approaches to adventure therapy internationally. For us, the term *nature-based therapy* is the closest we can get to describing what we do, although we can connect much of our practice to the philosophies, theories, and core elements of both ecotherapy and adventure therapy.

Our practice manifests in alignment with many of the approaches and activities described in the literature of adventure therapy. We engage our clients in activity, in places and spaces that elicit particular responses based on client needs (e.g., time at the beach to "decompress" and reduce anxiety versus a strenuous hike uphill to gain the view and assist in "getting back into one's body" or for "shifting a perspective"). We research locations, seek out and meet with local knowledge keepers (i.e., elders, historians, naturalists, educators, local guides) who can help us learn and engage with the places we conduct our work. By helping our clients connect with place, the experience of the session has greater potential to stick, and the likelihood of the client returning to that natural place on their own increases, thereby creating a lasting effect. In this regard, *nature-based* means place-oriented and relational: in nature, and with nature.

Many of our activities include an element of risk, be it physical, emotional, social, or even spiritual risk. Along with risk, the environments we travel in and the activities planned often provide clear and unambiguous feedback as well as natural consequences. Knowing rain is called for during a session leads to discussions and planning with clients about possible environmental conditions, appropriate clothing, and other details related to client care, client preferences, and desired experiences for that session relative to assessed client needs. If the client(s) ignore the planning stages and choose, for example, to not bring decent traction footwear on a trail that is known to get muddy, they may end up having to deal with less stable footing or slipping as a result. Such an experience may be a learning moment but can also be a window to connection: I (Katy) recall a joyous 9-year-old running with glee down a muddy slope in flat sneakers, only to end up plowing headfirst through the mud. He rose from the fall with belly-filled laughter, covered head to toe in mud. As we shared laughter at this incident, we reflected on how flexible he had been when coping with the accident compared to a more usual response of frustration and anger. Again, the metaphorical potential nature affords us is immeasurable and beyond what any reference book on the topic can help a therapist. In this case, and for the metaphorically challenged, a client making sound informed decisions about self-care (e.g., footwear choice) can provide better *stability*, *support*, and *positive outcomes*, all which provide access to conversations about those aspects in their day-to-day lives. Further, we need to recognize that our clients will have varying relationships to nature. We don't immediately know how individuals or families will respond to nature-based therapy, so we consciously invest in assessment and articulation of clients' ecological identity and preferences to better identify appropriate session focus, locations, and intensity.

Adventure therapy also allows for movement in and out of the therapeutic space. A therapeutic space is experienced when the environmental and social conditions are appropriate and designed for therapy. For example, when out on a trail hike with a client, you as therapist may engage in a social conversation that leads to personal insights, which can then be explored through client-counselor roles. When does therapy occur? Is everything that transpires during a sixty-minute office-based counseling session considered therapy? Or are their times when the "work" of the client is being done and other times when we are being relational, reflexive, and ethical practitioners supporting our clients in other ways? When working in nature, the therapeutic space, or frame, as some call it, depending on practice, is not a stable entity. Rather, the frame is malleable, as are the roles of the therapist. A certain comfort may need to be achieved for those trained in traditions that do not encourage or allow variety or creativity in the therapeutic process. We will discuss the ethics of practice related to more finite aspects of therapy in nature in chapter 11. For now, suffice it to say that nature-based therapy allows for shifting roles on behalf of client and counselor. This flexibility is not just practical but may be required to practice away from the office setting. For the office-based counselor who maintains therapeutic space via set office hours and consistently spaced counselor and client chairs, this concept is one of the hardest to grapple with. One also has to give up on the notion or assumption of clients as broken, helpless, and in need of constant protection. Clients spend time outside during the other twenty-three hours of the day you saw them, and to move outside of the office for therapy, in our experience, is sometimes a bigger challenge for counselor than client.

For those who struggle with the idea of taking your therapy practice outside, we encourage you to read Martin Jordan's *Nature and Therapy*, in which he shares his own process of shifting his conventional practice of office-based psychotherapy to an outdoor environment.[10] He carefully outlined his process and addressed many possible barriers or perceived limitations to practicing outdoors from his training as a psychologist. Dave and Nevin met Martin at an International Adventure Therapy Conference and really enjoyed his thoughtful and cautious approach to taking therapy outdoors, even though we found ourselves challenging his conceptions of practice by explaining some of our work, which he saw as a bit maverick yet exciting. Unfortunately, Martin left us too soon, dying shortly after his book *Ecotherapy: Theory, Process and Outcomes* with Joe Hinds had been published.[11] We view Martin's book, and the follow-up theory publication, while primarily addressing one-to-one adult counseling, as companions to our present book, in that we cover different territories of practice—a child- and family-centered approach—and a reflection of walking different paths in our experiences, employment, training, and influences.

Our nature-based approach provides a shifting therapeutic frame and creates new and unexpected options, sometimes called adjacent possibilities, not available indoors, for both client and counselor. This fluidity in the therapeutic frame mentioned above is central to adventure therapy in that the activities and environments are dynamic and can also provide alternative entrances to awareness. By this, we mean that individuals and families are unique entities, and regardless of our assessments and best planning, we do not know how each and every intervention or session will go. We too are along on the adventure. We cannot begin to understand what exactly allows for personal insights, meaningful change, and growth that is sustainable in those we walk with. Nature provides far more opportunities for exploration than office-based or residential therapies than we can comprehend. We openly admit that what we share in this book is really just a starting point for many, and for us, in terms of recognizing what is yet to be learned. We are the first to admit *not knowing*. By pushing ourselves to produce this book, we hope to encourage others to explore nature-based approaches and further to report what you learn across fields of practice. It is only through this dissemination of knowledge and practice that nature-based therapy's full potential will be realized.

Wilderness therapy, identified in the literature as under the adventure therapy umbrella, is of significant relevance to us as practitioners and theorists as we have all worked in programs that would fall under this name. Wilderness therapy has been described as a clinical treatment model taking place in remote and less inhabited places with field guides and therapists managing groups of youth for days to months straight. While many models of wilderness therapy practice exist, considerable amounts of recent research have been supporting the practice in general as a viable alternative to adolescent residential treatment settings. This approach is an out-of-home treatment for youth experiencing behavioral, substance use, and mental health issues. In our perspective, this option, out-of-home, should be considered only as an absolute last effort, as we believe strongly in family-based interventions and the role community can play in a client's life. The ecological reality of being separated from community and increasingly embedded in the natural world is a key aspect to setting the stage for wilderness therapy. Wilderness therapy provides ample opportunity for participants to engage in more intense social dynamics, discover new aspects of self, and engage intimately with changes in self, others, and the environment. Obviously, the skills needed to lead in a wilderness environment are significant, as well as the many logistical and support systems required for a successful and safe trip. The point of sharing this relative to nature-based therapy is to show alignment in the elements of wilderness therapy we try to create in nearby nature settings and suggest how you can too.

Outdoor self-propelled travel and group living are core daily practices of wilderness therapy. These activities come with inherent hardships and rewards. While nature-based therapy does occur outdoors, and often away from public places and marked trails, it is not often undertaken on overnight or multi-day expeditions. That would demarcate the shift from nature-based therapy to wilderness therapy. That said, there is much to gain from understanding the wilderness therapy process, which can be translated and used in nature-based therapy. One issue we have raised with the term *wilderness* will be given full treatment in the next chapter. In short for now, we acknowledge and mostly agree with criticisms of the romantic, colonial, and biblical notions of wilderness and point out clearly that when we use the term *wilderness* we are talking about the less or uninhabited places, usually remote, or a considerable distance from towns or cities where one feels "away" or "out there." We know this word can be problematic, just as *adventure* is to some of our colleagues who describe their work as adventure therapy although their practice doesn't engage the risk/challenge/adventure concepts.

Does Contact with Nature Work? A Research Snapshot

A growing body of evidence suggests the detrimental effects of limited contact with nature is linked to increases in childhood obesity, depression, learned helplessness, reduced attention spans, and resulting lower social and motor skills. These are significant health effects in most domains of one's life, and obviously all are interconnected and suggest that when positive change occurs in one domain, it can have carry-over effects in another. Just spending time in nature, even in a state of inactivity, has been shown to improve recall of information and reduce stress. In the past decade, there has been an explosion of new books on the topics of nature and health. We have read many of them. What has been depicted well is the broad range of research that is pointing to contact with nature as a meaningful and necessary part of all of our lives. If keen, again look to our reading list at the back for some catchy titles like *Your Brain on Nature* and *The Nature Fix*. What we have chosen to include for research herein is not comprehensive, nor is it from a selective review with tight inclusion criteria. We have selected research studies that are assisting us to further our understanding of why nature for therapy. We also include research that is relevant to our theoretical orientation and practice.

Biologists have recently gone so far as to assume that a fundamental shift in children toward preferences for sedentary activity and electronic media has occurred. We don't buy that. It just feels like giving in or, worse, giving up. Recent electroencephalography (EEG) clinical work has shown the negative effects of video gaming and other tech-addictions on the brains of children and youth. Thankfully these effects have been reversed through therapeutic approaches—primarily planned reduction of use, or abstinence in some cases, which has been taken up by family activities and outings—hopefully in nature![12] Reduction in children's gaming, for example, could lead to an increase in the time they play outside, which could presumably increase their level of physical activity, which then could increase appetite and potentially healthy eating, improved sleep, more stable blood sugar levels.... While this example is a shiny "perfect world" scenario, we like to envision a cascade of events to follow a shift in the way our clients experience the world, especially when in the natural world. EEG research has also been used to show the restorative properties of time spent in nature.[13] In a study comparing moderate exercise in indoor and outdoor (natural) environments, researchers found that exercise in both environments produced increased cognitive performance but that the outdoor environment also contributed to significantly higher meditative and relaxed states. The gains in these two states were also found to be retained long after the outdoor exercise, suggesting a latent and not just state effect—meaning the benefits of outdoor exercise are lasting, although the researchers point out, presently, that further studies will need to be completed to identify how long benefits are realized.

Another approach to brain research trying to understand the different effects of viewing nature versus human-made environments is relevant to key practices in nature-based therapy. Korean researchers utilized, in this case, functional magnetic resonance imaging (fMRI) to monitor research participants who were shown rural landscape images (e.g., mountains scenes) or cityscapes for two minutes at a time followed by rest breaks.[14] Cityscape viewing led to higher levels of stress as indicated by increased activity in the amygdala, the part of the brain generally indicating reactions to adverse stimuli. The amygdala response from the cityscapes was also associated with anxiety and impulsivity.

Whether these findings are due to a learned or socially conditioned response or whether they are evolutionary is hard to tell, although these studies provide yet another indication of the compatibility between human and natural places versus less-natural-built environments.

Reconnecting children with nature has demonstrated a countering effect to many of the above-noted health and behavioral problems, either through viewing nature, being in nature, or participating in activity in nature.[15] Some theorists have suggested time in nature is a critical factor in healthy emotional, cognitive, and spiritual development of young people. A recent Canadian study suggests spending time in nature is a protective factor for mental health in young people.[16] The researchers were able to identify that as little as a half-hour spent in nature each week reduced girls' prevalence of psychosomatic issues by 24% compared to their peers who spent no time in nature. Issues addressed in this study included depression, irritability, bad temper, feeling nervous, difficulty sleeping, and dizziness, as well as head, stomach, and back aches. Even just the perception of the importance of connection with nature was found to reduce the prevalence of heightened psychosomatic issues in both boys and girls. This large and nationally representative study provides a snapshot of the important role of outdoor play and nature connectedness in the promotion of positive mental health. Another recent national study in Canada, commissioned by Nature Conservancy of Canada (NCC)[17] suggested that the majority of Canadians (94%) now recognize (i.e., have the knowledge) that spending more time outdoors is beneficial—needed to counter the amount of time we spend in built environments—for their health; however, they also responded that they don't make the effort to get out (i.e., not changing behaviors). Most said they are happier, healthier, and more productive when connected to nature, yet 74% said it's just easier to stay indoors, and 66% indicated they spend less time in nature now than when they were young. This is a classic behavioral change issue and one that most North Americans are faced with. Are we too lazy, too distracted, too busy to get outside more often for our health and the health of our families? In response, NCC also announced a $750 million campaign to inspire Canadians to explore their relationships with nature, while also ramping up their conservation efforts to protect wild spaces and launch environmental education projects. Sadly, more than 80% of the survey respondents worry that accessible natural areas will not be there for future generations. This discomfort reflects what the ecopsychologists have been suggesting for decades: human and environmental health and well-being are intricately related and need to be addressed concurrently.

British researcher Tim Gill published a paper in 2014 outlining what benefits contact with nature had for children that had been demonstrated empirically in the literature.[18] He chose to complete a systematic literature review to identify specifically those papers that met strict criteria for inclusion; in this case, he sought studies with rigorous methodologies, numbers of studies to support specific claims, and an assessment of the quality of each study. As an independent researcher, Gill was funded by the London Sustainable Development Commission to answer the question of what empirical support exists for beneficial claims of child contact with nature. His inclusion criteria, to help understand the context of his search, was that studies had to be about children 12 and under; take place in woodlands, urban green spaces, and outdoor and "wild" spaces near urban areas; and be published in English and undertaken in developed nations between 1990 and 2011. A report such as this is ideal for governments, communities, or organizations to make decisions about policy and practice. So, what did he find?

Gill reported on 61 studies, and the range of benefits included mostly health benefits (physical activity, mental and emotional health, healthy eating, and motor development), well-being (quality of play, psychosocial health), cognitive benefits (scientific learning, environmental knowledge, language and communication skills), social skills, emotional/behavioral benefits (self-control, self-confidence, self-awareness), and ethical/attitudinal benefits (concern for the environment, connectedness to nature, sense of place). While hard to share all of the benefits in this brief overview, it is fair to say, from Gill's review, that it was easy to see which claims of benefits were well supported and that his overall conclusions below also had ample support:

- Child contact with nature leads to pre-environmental beliefs, increased feelings of being connected to place, and increased environmental knowledge

- Residing near green spaces is associated with increased physical activity
- Mental health and emotional regulation are improved for children with ADHD and children in general
- Outdoor play increases motor fitness in preschool children

This review should not conflate being outside with these child benefits. There were certain caveats that were also analyzed from the 61 studies to complete the picture of how these benefits are realized. Without these distinct factors, it is easy to misrepresent the research, and as researchers, we understand there are myriad limitations to this study, as well as many we utilize in this book. We interpret research findings cautiously as we recognize not all environments, programs, or practitioners are the same. Tim Gill identified that the qualities of outdoor environments mattered: differences in landscape, tree and plant cover, ambience, and size. He also left readers and researchers with numerous questions yet to be answered, such as, Is there an adult influence? Do repeated visits increase effects and benefits? How do benefits vary across age groups, cultures, gender, ability, and socioeconomics?

Further to Gill's broad findings above, the following studies briefly illustrate the breadth of a growing body of research tying health and well-being to contact with nature for children specifically. Often the need arises for nature-based therapy practitioners (or any other therapeutic approach for that matter) to identify and articulate evidence for their services and programs to ensure their viability, funding, and reputation. This can allow practitioners to purposely express how the work they do can have impact, grounded in empirical understandings:

- Creativity has been shown to increase with time spent playing outdoors and with decreased adult involvement or supervision.[19]
- Children report green playgrounds are more restorative than artificial or built playgrounds.[20]
- Children engaging in "green exercise" have lower blood pressure than when engaging in standard exercise.[21]
- Well-being and resilience were found to improve for children from challenging backgrounds after participating in a nurturing outdoor program.[22]

- Positive effects on stress, attention, competence, and supportive social relationships were found across age groups in a study of green schoolyards.[23]
- Utilizing the outdoors in a "nature kindergarten" nurtures deep connections with the natural world.[24]

The literature now holds a very rich and clear story in support of reconnecting humans to nature and the innumerable applications across health, education, and therapy. Practitioners can position themselves in alignment with the extant research to better represent the services they wish to provide. The research will continue to contribute effectively to the further development of our related fields by asking innovative questions and exploring areas of programming that have yet to be researched. For example, Dalhousie University social work professor Michael Ungar suggests that one of the most significant outcomes of unsupervised and creative play in natural spaces is resilience.[25] While speaking at an International Adventure Therapy Conference, he defined resilience as the capacity to navigate (with available resources and knowledge) as well as negotiate (and influence that which is provided) the world you experience. He discussed the dangers of overprotecting children during their development in comparison to the potentials of children participating in adventure therapy activities. While fully supportive of outdoor play and its inherent risks, he also cautioned that the perception of risk is still too high in parents and the general public to fully conduct research and better understand why. The idea of studying children, unsupervised and taking risks, would not likely be approved by many university ethics committees either, as academia is also embedded as part of today's risk-averse society.

While it is assumed to provide significant benefits, to what extent parents, educators, health workers, and mental health prevention and treatment professionals can incorporate nature into their practice is indeterminable. A general impression is that some is good, and more is likely better. Although parents often face barriers of time, access, and cost in meeting many of the perceived needs of their children, reconnecting them with nature may serve as a simple and cost-effective prevention strategy. Parents are a significantly influential facet in the health and well-being of children. We have written this book primarily for an audience that is serving children, youth, and families, although parents are just as capable and welcome to engage its ideas and materials. Our rationale for this stems from the amount of parent-oriented literature that already exists. We will also reiterate that taking on new practices often requires training and the development of new skills and qualifications. Hopefully you will seek support and advice from those already practicing to assist you in your development.

In the following chapters, we will blend our theoretical position with practice informed by research and trial in the field, interwoven with case examples and contributions from our colleagues. Again, we do not prescribe a practice, nor do we claim to have a complete theoretical model to back our work. We have combined what we have found works best in our practice, for our clients and contexts, nothing more. As readers, you may take what you need, leave what you don't, and hopefully are able to see prospects to bring your practice into nature. And even if you don't become a nature-based practitioner, we hope you can further develop your own ecological self and nature-connection and be able to provide guidance and ideas to your clients to practice for their health and well-being.

3

Why Nature-based Therapy
for Children, Youth, and Families?

The earth has music for those who listen.
GEORGE SANTAYANA

Introduction

Many of our colleagues and clients feel better when we take our practices outside. One of our aims in writing this book is to share our convictions for the capacity of contact with nature to assist in the healing process. We are at risk of being accused of simply suggesting a return to an earlier and more primal way of being in the world. We can point out that, as a species, we have become more detached from nature than at any time in our collective history. If we don't pay attention to the negative effects of urbanization, technification, and an increasingly unstable climate and deteriorating ecological health, we may find ourselves even further away from human health and well-being. While Spanish philosopher and humanist George Santayana offers his advice above to pay attention and listen to the Earth, he was more famously quoted saying, "Those who cannot remember the past are condemned to repeat it." Let us not lose track that we are collectively participating in a larger movement here to address and reconcile global ecological and social crises as well as human dis-ease accompanying them. Even in our review of the research and literature associated with nature-based therapy, we read messages and hear calls to action that have fallen on

43

deaf ears for decades. We need to look back and pay attention to our collective pasts to better inform our work as we move forward.

We need to accept some level of responsibility in writing this book to help you as reader understand some of the core reasons for this approach, and how it works. To do so, we will first establish why we believe nature-based therapy is an ideal modality to address personal, family, and societal issues. Our rationale includes a brief review of research outcomes from similar and related practices, and the theories that help explain how it works. The theory of nature-based therapy, as exciting as that sounds to read about, is simply our field's collective best guess at this point. By chapter's end, you will recognize that there is also much we don't know. In fact, during our time writing, we have found new and innovative research being published suggesting alternative explanations as to how our practice works. We hope we can convey this with as much excitement as it brings us.

The definition of *health*, as stated by the World Health Organization (WHO) in 1946, goes beyond just the absence of disease or infirmity, suggesting that health is the "complete state of physical, mental and social wellbeing." Other definitions commonly include the ability to adapt and function under changing circumstances. In short, health could be the ability to manage and optimize participation in life, be it through relationships, employment, education, recreation, or other aspects of daily life. While the dominance of the biomedical model's influence on psychological treatment (e.g., DSM) in many nations carries on today, alternative approaches (e.g., mindfulness) are becoming more commonly accepted and utilized for health promotion and therapy. Participating in outdoor activities either alone, with family, or with others contributes to engagement across domains—physical, mental, emotional, and spiritual—and may be considered an ideal example of a socioecological model of health care, for people and the planet. Care for the Earth, care for others, and care for self are intertwined in one's ecological self. In describing the awakening of our human role in the web of life, renowned physicist Fritjof Capra stated, "Over time the experience of ecology in nature gives us a sense of place. We become aware of how we are embedded in an ecosystem; in a landscape with a particular flora and fauna; in a particular social system and culture."[1]

Capra suggested that learning about nature and developing a deeper sense of connection to the ecological system that provides us with life make it more likely children will grow up with a sense of responsibility to all living things and systems.

Nature-based therapy, in this regard, could be described as an ecologically sound approach to therapy. In more practical terms, this integral approach would be classified as a complementary approach to the biomedical model and to health promotion in a more general way. Why, after a century of technological advances across society, are we now proposing going "back to nature" for therapy? What has changed in the lives of humans that would call for this stepping back toward a simpler relationship between humans and the environment that sustains us all? What is current in the minds of the population that can support our conversation about the value of nature? What is it that hasn't already been suggested in nature writing and the philosophies across cultures for millennia? Are we only now recognizing how far removed our daily lives are from the lives of our ancestors who were deeply linked with nature, sacred places, and other species? These questions are of importance to us and many other researchers interested in health and well-being. The literature we have drawn on crosses a spectrum of disciplines from urban planning to forestry to deep ecology. While we do not provide a comprehensive review of the literature that supports our theses herein, we will dip in and out of it and share what we believe may be of importance to you, the readers.

How Did We Get Here?

More than half of the 7.6 billion people on Earth now live in *urban* settings, and on average, many nations have greater than 80% of their populations compressed into large towns and cities. Within these communities, urban development slowly consumes vacant lots and wooded areas, and human access to nature and natural areas is in decline. Even cities with progressive park planning are finding urban densification is limiting human contact with nature in significant ways. In North America, we currently spend almost 90% of our days indoors and another 5% in our cars. While that may seem outrageous, you only have to track your activities for a week to come to the same conclusion: apart from your holidays, unless you work outdoors for a living, you too are likely spending considerable time indoors. With this in mind, the majority of people, at least in Canada and the United States, will be living and spending their time predominantly in *built* rather than *natural* environments. Does this matter? Research seems to suggest it does, and we think so too. Since you are reading this, we assume you may also be in agreement.

Of note, at the time of writing this book, there were more than 65 million refugees worldwide, many displaced from their homelands and living in unsafe and unstable places such as refugee camps and temporary housing. As the global diaspora continues due to political, religious, economic, and environmental factors, we want to be clear that we are not writing about connecting to nature as a global panacea to the world's problems and for all individuals. The nature-disconnect dialog in current mainstream literature is primarily a modern Western and middle- to upper-class conversation. Suggesting connection with nature for therapy to groups or individuals across cultures and contexts would be insensitive, and we want to reiterate that our recommendations need to be relevant to your region, culture, and population served.

We assume readers will primarily be dealing with clients, students, and families in schools, community, private practice, and social service settings. Under the right conditions, nature can be a healing space and provide respite and rejuvenation to those living under difficult circumstances.

Rates of mental and physical health problems for those living the hurried and technologically driven modern lifestyle are rapidly increasing and could be argued as epidemic. The negative impacts are seen most critically in children and youth during their developmental years.[2] North America has witnessed a near meteoric rise in internalizing mental health issues such as depression and anxiety, as well as lifestyle diseases including obesity and diabetes. Urban populations are now living longer, and medical advances have reduced infant mortality and infectious diseases. We have also seen an increased global burden of negative mental health effects, mood disorders, and a reduced ability to deal with, or buffer, life stress. Further, whether linked with health issues or as a result of societal or parental influences, research has identified a steep increase of narcissism in youth over the past forty plus years. While not wanting to cast dark clouds over our introduction to nature-based therapy, we do recognize and experience, on a weekly basis, some of these trends effecting children, youth, and families. We will extend the conversation related to mental health throughout the book and locate the role that this approach may play in tackling current issues. Case examples will address anger, self-regulation, depression, anxiety, ADHD, grief and loss, and declining social skills, among other issues. We will also share how nature can address these issues through the design and facilitation of accessible opportunities for children and families to connect more deeply with themselves, each other, and the Earth within a supported therapeutic space. Research providing empirical support for the benefits of nature-based therapy will be woven throughout, but again, we do not claim to provide exhaustive coverage of the literature, but rather we focus on content that provides guidance to the practitioner.

We know, in North America, that 1 in 5 youth have been diagnosed with mood or behavior disorders such as depression and anxiety. Reporting of these disorders is generally conservative, that is low, due to the stigma of reporting and because many young people have "sub-threshold" symptoms in that they do not meet the full criteria for diagnosis. Growing and developing children seem to suffer the most from the effects of urbanization, rapidly growing technification of our lives, and a significant increase in sedentary lifestyles, often coupled with entertainment and distraction. TV, once the devil in the living room destroying our children's minds in the '70s and '80s, is hardly an issue compared with today's access to screen time for gaming, YouTube, Snapchat, and other social media. We now see uninterrupted access to screens of all kinds and an increasing child disconnect from nature, and outdoor activity in general. On many fronts, therapy and pharmacology have been increasingly offered as antidote to these significant societal lifestyle shifts and subsequent ill health, yet we also know that many children, youth, and families are underserved.

While not suggesting all childhood issues are due to a nature deficit, we do hope to address what we see as significant change in human-environmental behavior experienced by many in modern Western societies. We believe the exposure to and growing dependence on screen time, especially in children and youth, can be addressed in a cost-effective and generally accessible way. Following Santayana's sage advice above, we have listened to the music the Earth has offered, and we propose options for different situations: individual counseling, group work, family settings, and school-based approaches.

A simple internet search yields thousands of sites for programs, services, and items for sale to help you connect with nature. The notion of reconnecting with nature has recently become common in educational and community settings, although without a patterned or common approach or theoretical grounding. While often heard, seen, and generally accepted as a good idea, the actual practice of nature as therapist has not yet been critically challenged. In fact, *contact with nature as healer* has, in our minds, become near cliché. Popular books have attempted to comb the research to provide some theoretical understandings of why nature is healing. While this is positive and helpful, most become long literature reviews of scientific studies and leave little to work with on a day-to-day practical level. We have also found many hands-on books about nature-based activities and building human-nature connections, which we use in our own work and trainings and recommend to colleagues, parents, and friends. What we haven't yet seen, however, are neither well-supported therapeutic practice descriptions nor clear directions about how a practitioner can integrate nature as co-therapist in their work with children, youth, and families—most have been aimed at psychotherapy with adults. It is worth noting that many Indigenous and conventional healing practices that include human-nature relationships are not widely shared and, therefore, are mostly unknown to Western practitioners. And so we write with caution that alternate healing ways may seem to be lacking in modern Western society yet are present and in use by therapists and cultural groups. Research has shown a fairly strong indication that nature can assist in achieving positive social, psychological, and health outcomes with clients, but little has been offered to the practitioner in terms of specific knowledge and skills for practice. The questions about "why nature for therapy" and "how does it work" still need to be answered, even though we have strong biases and do believe it works.

We do not claim to have all of these answers. In fact, we know this is simply a starting point for further research and dialog among practitioners. We hope what we can offer will help, knowing that it may be challenged, advanced, or even dismantled by future research and practice interpretations; we are willing to take the risk. We provide practical applications of nature-based therapeutic work grounded in the theoretical understandings and evidence we have found and incorporated into our practice. The conversation will include theory from adjacent fields of psychology (including neuropsychology), education, and clinical counseling and other conventional therapy practices. Before we dig into the theory which supports nature-based therapy, we share our understandings of what may have happened over time to land us in the situation we now find ourselves, looking to nature for help in dealing with human issues and crises.

Humans and Nature: Trends and Crises

Social psychologist Erich Fromm wrote in his classic book, *The Sane Society*, that as humans alter the world, they also alter themselves, thereby creating many unintended circumstances.[3] Environmentalist and deep ecology author Paul Shepard, following up on Fromm's ideas in his classic *Nature and Madness*, suggested that the Western world's consumptive behavior is creating a lack of connectedness, rootedness, meaning, and self-identity and that this growth leads to insanity of greed, ambition, and in essence, a form of madness. He goes on to suggest that modern Western society has not entered into a mature stage of development relative to its relationship with the natural world.[4]

While arising from complex issues, Shepard's thesis is simple: humans have stalled out in their development; we have become stuck in adolescence—that place where exploration and boundary pushing are backed by a well-armed ego and lowered concern for impact on self and others. Youth are more impulsive and seemingly selfish at this stage, and that is fine in the bigger picture of human development. Many advances in human capacity have occurred because this state exists, although it may be hampered in more recent decades through our increasingly risk-averse society. The adolescent brain interprets and enters into risk-taking in a very different manner than that of a child or an adult. As we now know, brain development carries on until mid- to late-twenties, and judgment and self-preservation seem to go hand in hand with those last frontal lobe developments. So, the adolescent brain operates with increased risk tolerance, hyper-rationality for those risk-related activities, and lowered concern for others.[5] This reality originally led to further ranging of human communities into new hunting territories and bolstered bravery in combat defending homelands. In modern times, this reality has led to the breaking of sports records and continually accelerating demonstrations of human achievement in the physical realm at least (e.g., base jumping, squirrel suit flying, triple backflips on a motorbike...). Shepard's thesis was most critical of this stalled development in that it has resulted in atrocities against mother nature in general due to the lack of rootedness or connection with nature, and a failure to reach mature and elder/mentor stages as a society. While pursuing the ultimate possibilities of achievement, including financial success, many adults have carried on within a stage of adolescent development where the achievement model equates to conquering, regardless of human or environmental costs.

The teaching of basic food production and local knowledge of flora and fauna, let alone excursions into wild nature, are often considered novel and unique experiences. Further, we are also now witnesses to the gravest conditions of global environmental health, from species and cultural extinction to climate change and deteriorating air quality and food security issues. While not hard to rationalize, or demonstrate, poor environmental health has been linked to poor physical health. Harder to legitimize is the relationship between ill environmental health and its negative effect on the human psyche, ill mental health. Ecopsychology theory depicts our psychological health as intricately related to environmental health. We may yet come to accept the links between current global environmental problems and increasing rates of mental illness as a society. Was Eric Fromm correct fifty-five years ago in suggesting that a significant cataract in the universal vision of our relationship to nature may have caused us to go insane?

With an apparent cultural "forgetting" of modern Western society's earlier relationship with nature, and possible evolutionary preferences being denied, it is easy to conceive that we should be taking action to restore our relationship with nature from a psychological and health perspective. If our societal madness has detached us from an equitable and beneficial balance with our environment, what is the antidote, and how does it work? If contact with nature, as simply proposed here, is an antidote, and a key in the context of nature-based therapy, what theoretical support exists to articulate it?

Urbanization and Technification

Current trends of denser urban settings and dwindling green and natural spaces have resulted in reduced access and exposure of children to nature. Regarding child and youth development, this reduced access has been clearly linked to obesity and diabetes, whereas increased contact with nature has been seen to benefit children's overall physical and mental development.[6] Other findings examining children living in urban settings, with access to parks and nature spaces, showed those who consistently played in nature during recess performed better on motor skills tests than others who played on a traditional playground; nature contact improved motor fitness, enhanced attitudes toward increased physical activity, and positively affected social, emotional, and cognitive development. What is made clear in the literature is that natural play spaces which engage children in active and dynamic play produce a wide array of physical, social, and emotional benefits through increased imaginative play and creativity along with increased levels of physical activity.[7] Naturescapes are design elements attempting to bridge the gap between modern playscapes and more natural physical areas, especially where wild nature is not accessible. These manufactured spaces may take the form of increased variability in topography, forested areas, boulders, logs, or gardens. The literature reviewed suggests natural elements added to schoolgrounds and local parks act as a catalyst for child development and well-being through increased affordances for creative and risky play. All good for us too as we seek possible locations for sessions relative to our clients' levels of ecological engagement. (See chapter 4 for ecological assessments.)

Less than 10% of Canadian children and youth are currently meeting the recommended physical activity guidelines; a recent national *Report Card on Physical Activity* graded their overall physical activity levels at a D-.[8] These disturbing Canadian trends were reflected in report cards across 38 countries[9] and increase the probability of childhood disease and insufficient fundamental motor skill development and decrease the probability of children being physically active adolescents, and consequently as adults. This fact is easy to connect to the current crisis in childhood sedentary behavior and related lifestyle illnesses of obesity and diabetes. A growing body of evidence shows the positive relationships between outdoor time + physical activity = decreasing sedentary behavior and increasing levels of fitness.[10] The built and natural environment's effect on health and well-being is influenced by complex interactions of infrastructure and social factors. Human interaction with more natural environments provides an overall benefit to mental health; increases levels of physical activity and the potential for, and actual; fundamental motor skill development;[11] reduces anxiety and boosts psychological well-being;[12] and reduces behavioral symptoms associated with attention deficits in children and youth.[13]

To summarize, significant evidence now demonstrates the physical and psychological benefits of children simply playing in natural spaces, whether physically active or not.[14] While showing a fairly strong body of evidence for positive benefits of spending time in nature, Gill still called for increased "early intervention and prevention initiatives from the health sector."[15] This review highlighted increased benefits of more *playful* engagement with the environment, encouraging use of natural spaces and features of the environment that allow for free play, exploration, and child-directed play and learning.

Some Theoretical Explanations of Why Nature?

We wouldn't want to make claims for our nature-based approach, even with the supportive research outcomes, without also providing explanations of how nature is contributing to the positive therapeutic outcomes described earlier. To embrace theory provides us with guided intention in our practice and rationales for our methods, and whether proven to be true in the long term or not, they also are exceptional tools for teaching and training outdoor therapists and leaders about using nature as a co-therapist (which we will explore in chapters 7 to 11).

Attention Restoration

If you work with children, youth, and families, the following experience may sound very familiar. You are working indoors, let's say at a school or residential treatment center, and someone is unhappy, getting frustrated, and leaning toward an impulsive outburst, and the need for intervention from you as leader or facilitator is imminent. The first need is to ensure everyone's safety, and the easiest resolution is to ask someone, preferably not requiring any force, to go outside with you. We are not simply suggesting all will be well once you are outside.

You step outside and walk with the youth to a bench under a tree. "It's pretty chilly out here; winter's coming," you say to the young person. She takes a second to pause and pay attention, long enough to notice it is cold out. This minor distraction, and intentional guidance toward the temperature, engages the young person in sensory awareness and shifts her thinking away from the crisis and, instead, to the surroundings outside. Does it dissipate her anger? No, not completely, but the flow of negative energy has been interrupted. Bodily she recognizes that her cheeks are cold to the touch and the wind is blowing softly, adding to her chilled state. You may then mention how the leaves have begun to change colors as fall marches on, another effort to engage her mind in nature's presence. While sensory awareness is not a novel concept to a youth worker or therapist, doing it outdoors has a distinct added advantage: nature can help replenish necessary resources to deal with stress and difficult situations. One critical resource is attention.

Indoor built environments, and many human activities within these spaces, are not what we were evolutionarily designed for. Most North American homes are built with straight lines (e.g., walls and window shapes), artificially consistent distances (e.g., evenly spaced stairs of 7¼ inches in height), and numerous materials that reduce air quality (e.g., paints, glues, plastics). Natural environments, in contrast, do not have straight lines, provide diverse topography to negotiate, and not always, but often, provide sunlight and clean air to breathe. Activities indoors may include screen time for work, life management, or entertainment, most often the latter. On average, young people are spending 50 hours or more each week staring at some form of screen. The environment and activities are taxing our abilities to think straight, are draining our attention, conditions hard to operate effectively in, let alone be our best selves. Smart phones, use of computers and screens in school, YouTube, and other social media are quickly speeding the lives of our children up through the sheer volume of materials shared. Time to be quiet, reflective, or even alone have been diminished significantly.

Couple these technological influences with life stress due to personal or family crisis, health and behavioral problems, limited community resources, and restricted access to natural outdoor spaces, and you have a significant recipe for disaster. Attention is needed to make sound decisions (executive functioning), manage our behavior (self-regulation), and process new experiences (reflection). Without this resource, we are truly at the whims of our instincts and baseline selves, often not our best selves. This critique of humanness is not new. John Dewey, education philosopher and to some the granddaddy of experiential education theory, suggested that it is a human endeavour to define and describe one's subjective experience of life.[16] He claimed that the unanalyzed world does not lend itself to control and that, by nature, humans desire to constrain some of the unpredictability and, in doing so, create and maintain a separation from nature. In short, if the natural order is very complex, and we are simply a part of it, Dewey believed the human mind needs to rationally protect itself by creating distinctions and distance. Time in nature can restore our attention and concurrently reduce levels of stress. The late Stephen Kellert, professor of social ecology at Yale University, suggested that "our inclination to connect with nature also addresses other needs: intellectual capacity, emotional bonding, aesthetic attractions, creativity and imagination, even the recognition of a just and purposeful existence" and that these benefits may provide an antidote to the pressure and what he called the "relative unattractiveness" of the modern world.[17]

Attention restoration theory (ART) provides some guidance for us in explaining how time in nature can replenish the necessary attention for executive function and self-regulation. The idea of human consciousness as an ongoing depletion and replenishment of attention was first theorized in the late 1800s but only more recently taken up as an area of research. When we are forced to work to pay attention—think of that hard-to-understand lesson in school or maybe reading an overly theoretical book—we are using our *directed* attention. When our attention is overtaxed, we become irritable and mentally tired, lose concentration, and make more mistakes. Another type of attention is *involuntary* and does not result in attention fatigue but rather can restore our resources for directed attention and dealing with stress. To engage involuntary attention usually requires a change in environments, and here is where our preferences for all things natural kicks in. Nature seems to be idealized as the preferential environment for improvements to attention. Around the world, being in aesthetic natural spaces is often sought for solace and pleasure. Harvard professor Edward Wilson dubbed this *biophilia hypothesis*, or the love of life (or all living things).[18] Being in nature provides stimulus to engage our involuntary attention. Seminal researchers in ART, Rachel and Stephen Kaplan, have broken the theory into four fairly easily understood constructs: Being away, Fascination, Extent, and Compatibility.[19] Further research in ART has extended the number of constructs and how they fit together, as well as developed measures of the perceived benefits. We will describe these briefly and include examples of how these constructs can be intentionally planned for and show up in a nature-based practice.

Being away is a conceptual versus physical transformation, although it often includes being in a different place, whether unique or familiar. When one is removed from their daily routines and burdens, and the necessary directed attention demanded of them, they perceive a shift in how they feel. Holidays are the ultimate example, and a physical manifestation of being away. The person, however, who chooses to continue working via cell phone, laptop, internet, etc. while on holidays may not fully experience the sensations of being away. A practice example that easily illustrates being away is when a family takes part in an overnight or multi-day therapy program. The shift from parental routines of home into a simplified way of living and traveling on the land (or just staying at a campsite) can be considerable in terms of where they focus their thoughts and subsequent energies.

Fascination has long been associated with involuntary attention, and hence the relief from directed attention, that which taxes our cognitive processes. This can occur without fatigue and carries the sensation of relaxing the mind and increases reflective states. One only needs to think of sitting and looking into a fire or listening to a babbling stream to grasp the concept of fascination. Moments of fascination can easily be aligned with reflective activities and allow for clients either to have mental space for themselves or to leverage the attentional restoration and engage in difficult conversations. In running month-long trips on Canada's west coast, which usually included at least two meals each day cooked over beach fires, Nevin found the fireside conversations, especially the ones after dark, to be the most effective time for group work to occur. The adolescents he worked with in the justice system were often quite guarded emotionally and did not share their personal worlds openly. Fireside chats were most often the place where they took risks and became more confident articulating their experiences of family strife, negative life circumstances, and trauma. It likely resonates with most readers that when staring into a fire, with most of the world shut out by darkness, your ability to think lucidly and share without pretense is heightened.

Extent relates to the sensation of being a part of something bigger than oneself, of interconnectedness of the elements, and of the possibilities of exploration, learning, and growth. One example of this is our bodily reaction when reaching summits or attaining views of large open landscapes, sunrises over the prairies, or the afterglow of a sunset across a body of water; those moments when your brain is consumed with the beauty or immensity of the environment, and your relationship to it. With arms stretched up and out, as if to embrace the world, we recognize, possibly subconsciously, that we are a part of something greater than ourselves. This can, of course, happen in micro-environments as well. One such example is when we have taken youth to have a close look at the rainforest floor with magnifying glasses. If you take one square yard of rainforest floor and examine it as an archeologist may— with the greatest attention to detail—you can find hundreds of living things; most will be new to you. Some clients, and not always the children, have been overwhelmed with the biological diversity discovered. It is in these moments of awe, when they experience extent, that an exceptional space takes conversations into meaning-making and self-exploration on a personal level. Seeing the clients' awe in the micro-immensity of the forest floor, you might ask, "I wonder what we can learn about the day-to-day world we live in from this?" or "What advice do you think this snail might offer you for what's troubling you?"

Compatibility speaks to the alignment between individual desires, environmental patterns, and actions required to match these all up. Understanding this construct, we choose our locations and activities appropriately relative to what is *compatible* with our clients. Chapter 4 will discuss an ecological assessment that allows us to identify pre-existing relationships to nature and outdoor experiences, skills, and interests. Truth is, clients who come to us for nature-based counseling have some understanding of what they are seeking and often a positive bias toward the benefits of being outdoors. Still, what we may yet learn is that a client has never lit a fire or that the client's outdoor skills are exceptionally developed, and yet they express a desire to benefit from developing a mindful approach to being outdoors. Having started to map out an ecological identity allows the therapist to better choose locations, activities, and objectives for sessions regarding compatibility between client and nature. As practitioners, we do not yet know with any level of sophistication how clients will respond to being in dark forests, standing near a cliff edge, experiencing an open prairie wind or hail storm, or even having a sunny day at the beach. These all will provide unique encounters to clients in relation to their lived experiences, evolutionary preferences, and influences of cultural, social, and economic forces.

Research across multiple fields is confirming the necessity of connection to nature for our health and wellness. In the literature related to child and family functioning and how our practice of nearby nature can help, research suggests that life stress can be buffered or reduced in children through simply living in proximity to nature[20] and that exposure to forest environments can reduce cortisol levels, pulse rate, blood pressure, and sympathetic nerve activity.[21] These are but two examples from a rapidly growing body of research, especially prominent in the past decade, that suggests that contact with nature offers much more than just the restoration of attention. In 2018, Danish researchers Schilhab, Stevenson, and Bentsen conducted a detailed systematic review specifically looking at attention restoration theory.[22] They identified, analyzed, and clustered studies supporting contact with nature benefits, such as improved working memory, attentional control, visual attention, vigilance, impulse control, processing speed, and cognitive flexibility. These researchers also found growing support, but currently less well evidenced, for improved delay of gratification, reduced aggression, and improved logical reasoning abilities. While nature contact seems to be an ideal activity to assist with cognitive and behavioral problems, debates still remain over what exact processes are at work, and what conditions specifically bring about these results. One argument exists for a burden, or cognitive fatigue, to be present for restoration to then occur when in nature—which seems reasonable and in alignment with our work and experiences. Another is that some studies put participants in natural spaces to test restoration, while in other studies, they just look at nature on screens indoors. Research utilizing nature instead of just images has shown better outcomes— again, the idea that real nature experiences work better than virtual ones seems logical to us.

In an effort to share this research with college students in an environmental health course, Nevin used a method common to some studies in Schilhab and colleagues' review. Students were subjected to a 15-minute lecture, with images, of the state of environmental destruction and social inequity in the world. This intentionally intense and depressing presentation was followed by a cognitive processing test called the digit span forward. Students were read a series of random numbers then asked to write them down. Four more sets of random numbers were given and written down, although each series became longer by one number (i.e., 4, 5, 6, 7, and 8 numbers). Following the last series, students folded up their answer papers, put them in their pockets, and headed outside. Nevin then led the students up a hill to a nearby woodland area for a slow and quiet nature walk. Entering an open area within a grove of large trees, students were asked to stand in a circle, take deep breaths, and participate in a very short guided meditation intended to relax their minds and bodies and to seek a connection with the forested area. Immediately after the guided visualization, they repeated the cognitive test with a new set of random numbers. The nature-connection portion of the class described occurred within 15 minutes of the digit span test taken in the classroom. Rather than just lecturing on ART in the classroom, the intention was to have students experience the process themselves. When asked, students expressed feeling more relaxed and at peace when in the forest. What they were not prepared to hear, nor did they perceive in the activity, was that the calculated difference in their scores showed a 20% increase in accuracy outdoors. In four years and with more than 100 students, only a few had ever scored better indoors than out.

ART stemmed from the early work of psychologist William James, who depicted types of attention as being less taxing on cognitive and emotional faculties and even possessing restorative properties. These properties were attributed to interesting or unique situations in which the individual is engaged but does not require concerted effort (i.e., directed attention) and experiences a reduction in mental fatigue.[23] Rachel and Stephen Kaplan integrated theoretical understandings of stress with the restorative properties of natural environments and suggested that stress can be prevented or reduced through the restoration of directed attention.[24] This "healing power of nature" is reiterated throughout the ART literature as vitality enriching and capable of restoring mental health. Another closely related yet less explored attempt to understand nature as restorative is psycho-evolutionary theory (PET), which describes nature's ability to reduce stress. This suggests responses to nature are adaptive human traits that may be genetically determined, hence, evolutionary. Swedish researcher Roger Ulrich's take on attention and restoration was different from that of Kaplans.[25] Ulrich built PET on the assumption that humans' immediate responses to nature are actually pre-cognitive, that being emotional and more aligned with affective processes, as opposed to ART, which is described as a cognitive process. PET suggests humans relate to specific conditions that produce restorative experiences. A long-standing academic debate has ensued between ART and PET theorists, which is of little concern to us in our practice; both provide solid working theories for nature-based therapy. ART: attention is restored in compatible natural environments and improves numerous cognitive functions. PET: people have emotional responses to natural environments that they then may respond to cognitively in positive or negative ways. Both help us to understand our work and to teach others why it works. What's important to note is that both theories suggest we have evolutionary responses to nature, cognitive and affective, and that nature can restore resources necessary for vitality in life.

Theory of Affordances

The theory of affordances was originally coined by J. J. Gibson as a learning theory of human relationships with objects and spaces.[26] Almost 80 years ago, he was studying air force pilots' capacity to perceive distances and accuracy of targets from fighter planes in World War II. His studies shifted toward more laboratory and day-to-day situations but always focused on the human-environment interaction. He was interested in how, often kinesthetically, humans adapted or adjusted their choice of actions and physical performance to successfully negotiate environmental conditions. When we consider how we choose to move clients out of the office and into a variety of environments, the theory of affordances speaks volumes. Our clients have increased opportunities for action and experience in a dynamic versus static environment. Gibson's work was considered interactionist in that human responses were influenced by information available in the environment.[27] Further, affordances were reasoned to be not just about stimulus-response, as was much scientific research in the '50s and '60s, but were instead argued to be about responses to new environments, differentiating characteristics in environments, and perceiving and acting upon them; in short, learning is about improving, and "of getting in closer touch with the environment."[28]

What we can take from Gibson's work is that our clients can both perceive and discover an environment relative to their abilities and constraints. Their abilities may include physical fitness or flexibility while hiking up a rough root-covered section of trail or sense of balance when crossing a log over a river. Abilities may also be how well one perceives distances, such as when throwing rocks into a lake or how far a walk may take at a set speed. Constraints, in the environment, may be overgrown trails covered in thorny blackberry stalks or a high tide preventing passage around a headland on the beach. Affordances describe the human as agent and environment as situation processes (agent-situation). From a practitioner's perspective, picture yourself in a conversation going nowhere with a young client while in an office talk therapy session. Now imagine the two of you sitting beside a stream with a small rock waterfall. These two settings couldn't be more different. One "affords" opportunities for attention restoration, quiet reflection, and distraction, distraction from the difficult conversation sitting across from the therapist. The calming and meditative sound of the water burbling and splashing over the rocks leaves the young person in a positive mood state, and a conversation can eventually take place while both, sitting side by side, gaze into the mesmerizing movement of the water. The easiest way to engage with the theory of affordances as a practitioner, or researcher, is to think about human-environment interactions and what elements may "afford" the client. Asking questions of the site for each session can stimulate new ways of exploring environments as well as allowing clients to answer those questions themselves. What does this environment allow you to do? Or, what does this environment ask of you when we are here, or travel through it?

Spiritual Dimensions

When nature-based therapy is implemented with intention, it can be utilized in ways that facilitate improved relationships with the natural environment and with others. These outcomes can be enhanced through an appreciation of the uniqueness of the experience. Meaningful experiences in nature have the potential to be unconsciously equated with what Carl Jung referred to as *sacred space*, which is central and vital for our individual and collective health.[29] We have observed, and heard from our clients, that nearby nature and wilderness therapy experiences have included deeply meaningful aesthetic, archetypal, or spiritual/transcendent aspects. Awareness of and openness with clients about the potential of sacred spaces, spiritual dimension of self, especially in young people, brings recognition to clients that something important may be happening to them and that being intentional about creating sacred spaces may become a meaningful process in their healing and their lives.

German theologian Rudolph Otto identified how most religious or spiritual experiences—he referred to them as *numinous*—are comprised of three components: mystery, terror, and fascination.[30] Combined, these elements can be achieved in the majesty of nature, and we find them in activities such as climbing or trekking in the mountains and paddling oceans and rivers. The combined beauty, potentially over-whelming power (weather, viewing of large open landscapes), and evolutionary attraction of nature makes it an ideal venue for spiritual experience, which may be an unavoidable benefit to those who par-ticipate. The leader/therapist's awareness of their client's spiritual di-mension may assist in preparing the client for these experiences. For those new to nature-based approaches, it should be an area explored in assessment and intervention because natural environments, and time spent in nature, have a tendency to accentuate spiritual aspects within individuals.

As a society, we are waking up to the need to re-experience the spir-itual dimensions of nature. Spirituality is one dimension of human existence often left out of the modern health and well-being conver-sation. We as humans—in our modern Western world—are trapped by highly individualized thinking and have, in many ways, diminished our spiritual selves. Classic and contemporary literature on nature has re-peatedly described our connectedness to nature as a journey or expres-sion of soul. If intentionally facilitated nature experiences might assist in taking us beyond our usual human experiences and open us to the numinous, assuming spirituality is a meaningful contribution to one's health, then we propose that our innate desire to connect with the more than human world may be central to our re-engagement with spiritual-ity, leading toward increased maturity, spiritual health, and well-being.

4

Making the Choice
to Take Therapy Outside

Some people feel the rain; others just get wet.
BOB MARLEY

Formal counseling and psychotherapy traditionally takes place indoors, whether with individuals, couples, families, or groups. An office, with four walls and a closed door, provides a consistent, reliable, and contained space within which people can be comfortable knowing that their conversations and experiences will be private and they will be safe. Further, clinicians often personalize their space with comfortable furniture and inspiring messages/pictures (often of nature), and they may even have a cup of tea waiting by their client's seat. These details enhance the client's ease and sense that the therapeutic relationship is nurturing, attentive to their needs, and aligned with their values. Choosing to venture outside of the office walls for therapy introduces numerous novel elements into the therapeutic process requiring thoughtful consideration when determining who might benefit from this approach. As illustrated by Bob Marley's lyrics above, the varying ways that individuals may perceive and respond to the outdoor experience (along with internal responses) need to be assessed for best practice.

As nature-based practitioners, we certainly hold biases that being in nature is more often the preferred location for our clients and ourselves.

Likewise, most of the referrals we receive from the community are seeking our services specifically because of our unique approach of meeting clients outdoors. For these individuals, the four-walls approach has either failed to engage them in the past or possibly even prevented them from willingly accessing services at all. Most often, the schools, parents, or individual themselves recognize how being in relation with the natural world may be a powerful resource for their well-being. This differing perspective opens up the possibilities for novel approaches. As American philosopher David Abrams suggested in the *Spell of the Sensuous*, when we leave indoor built spaces, we are actually entering into more direct and unencumbered contact with nature, and thus we are in a sense moving "inside" of mother nature rather than moving to the "outside."[1] This notion flips the commonly held belief that we need to "get outside" on its head—in that case, our therapeutic approach involves helping clients go more fully "into nature."

Despite the mounting research regarding the benefits of being in direct contact with nature, we still need to ask ourselves who thrives outside and, likewise, who may benefit more from the predictability and familiarity of an office environment. This chapter explores some important questions in order to help a practitioner in making these decisions. Further, it introduces the concept of an assessment of one's ecological self as the foundation of our session planning, as well as an examination of the different environmental considerations for choosing the location of service.

Who Thrives Outside?

When making the decision to head outside with clients, we often ask ourselves who will be invigorated or increasingly engaged in therapy by being in the wonders of nature versus who may need the containment and familiarity of an office setting. We have found that a combination of a client's (1) history, motivation and interest to go outside; (2) goals for therapy; and (3) mental and physical health are the key pieces to the puzzle. We'll explore each of these factors with examples to better illustrate how they contribute to the ecological assessment and the planning for client sessions.

Client Motivation and Interest

The decision to take the counseling practice outside lies in the basic interest of the client—just like any other specific modality, such as art or somatic therapies. Most often, families who seek out our services have been drawn to us, or referred to us, because they have expressed an interest in the nature-based approach. Therefore, the provision of nature-based therapy is a response to that request, rather than a case of counselors suggesting to clients that meeting outdoors is a good idea.

Often a referral to our services has been made by school counselors or psychologists who know the needs of the client and suggest that being outside will help them to better engage in therapy. Parents often express that their children are happiest outdoors, thrive when they are in nature or being highly active, and struggle to focus indoors—a pretty obvious example of an ideal client and not far off the truth for many children at school. The parents have a clear sense that their children or youth would be more motivated to engage with a counselor when simultaneously engaged in activity and exploration in nature. If parents are unsure about the best approach, then we often suggest they ask the client whether they would prefer the initial meeting to occur in an office or outside.

We have also found that the motivation for seeking alternative counseling options often comes from past negative experiences with office-based services. Some examples are cases where children have shut down in therapy due to their discomfort (e.g., refusing to speak), have been unable to build a positive therapeutic relationship with the clinician, or felt that they were being put on the spot and refused to return. There are many children or youth who have difficulty making direct eye contact, to whom such intense connection feels unsafe, and for these kids, the chance to slowly build relationship while walking side by side, playing, or co-examining a wild mushroom or a slug can greatly enhance their sense of safety and ability to open up. We have found that taking these clients outdoors and introducing them to a completely different version of "therapy" can help break down barriers and build bridges. Specifically, the alternative context helps to "disguise" the counseling and turn down the volume on common misconceptions that helpers are challenged with, such as "the client as broken and needs to be fixed," "therapist as expert," or "therapist as the center of the process." Counteracting these misconceptions helps reduce the stigma associated with visiting a counselor. Chapter 7 will further describe the benefits of the outdoor approach and discuss how we confront dominant narratives and stigma, and bolster alternate stories with our clients and nature as co-therapist.

An illustrative example of the positive impact of taking therapy outdoors was Justin, age 10, who had previously been through numerous forms of interventions, including individual and intensive family therapy and psychiatric assessments. He still had an unclear diagnosis of the problem. This boy was really struggling to succeed in school and relate with peers, and he had frequent meltdowns with his family, which made it difficult for them to function normally. When psychologists or psychiatrists interviewed him, his common response was to hide under chairs or inside his shirt, refusing to answer questions. Justin's parents were desperate and worn down when they reached out for our services. After the family stated his love of animals, we agreed that a good first meeting location would be a local therapeutic farm, which was both private and contained. As Justin stepped out of the car and caught sight of the llama grazing in the field, he was immediately at ease and eager to explore the farm with his parents. He engaged directly with the therapist (Katy), asking and answering questions, and connected with the animal friends who inspired him—including cats, chickens, and even worms. At the end of the first session (just sixty minutes), Justin's parents said this was the most they had ever witnessed him engage and open up in counseling; the sense of relief on their faces was palpable. Justin was more than eager to book another session at the farm, and over the course of therapy he was willing to explore concepts of self-regulation, boundaries, and his emotional world.

Client Goals for Therapy

It is usually clear when someone is motivated to be outside, and we have found following their lead to be most effective. However, it is important to take their therapeutic goals into consideration. For example, if a family is needing intensive crisis support, such as developing a safety plan for their child's extreme behaviors, being in an environment with fewer distractions may be beneficial. Likewise, if a youth who is experiencing intense social anxiety or isolating depression needs a high degree of privacy to talk about personal struggles, meeting in a quiet and controlled environment may be a better choice. Finally, if a client is experiencing psychosis, or is working on resolving relational trauma, and if taking the therapy very slowly and somatically is important, then again an office environment may be preferred, at least at first, for the containment it provides. We'll cover the issue of client confidentiality and other ethical concerns related to protecting clients while working to maximize results through nature-based therapy in chapter 11.

It is also important to be flexible with shifting between indoor and outdoor locations as goals and needs change. Having an indoor office space available to your practice means that you can be responsive to those needs. For example, sometimes holding sessions indoors at the beginning of the counseling relationship allows for an orientation to what outdoor therapy will involve. This would be appropriate for a client who is interested but quite nervous about meeting outdoors and needs to build more safety and gather information first. Some counselors may want to initially meet with just the parents in the office for information sharing, understanding family and historical trauma, and goal setting. This introductory session also serves to orient them to what to expect in nature-based therapy, as they may be less comfortable with being outside with the play and experiential approach than the kids are themselves. It is also advantageous to have an office space available for other specific reasons throughout the course of therapy, such as case planning, parent check-ins, specific psycho-education activities involving paper and pen, or providing comfort when choosing to avoid inclement weather.

We have found that, for the majority of our clients, sessions are greatly enhanced by being outdoors. The therapeutic goals that benefit from the experiential, dynamic, flexible, numinous, inspiring, and varied qualities of wild and natural spaces are numerous. Common goals that clients seek out nature-based therapy for include improving self-esteem, self-regulation, social skills, emotional awareness, anger management, family relationships, and skills to manage anxiety and depression. Many families who choose this approach struggle with grief and loss, social isolation, school avoidance, screen addiction, ADHD labels, and the general feeling that their children do not belong, or fit into the mold required of them relative to societal expectations. Their goal is to find an approach that can help their children's inner light shine through while enabling the child to function safely in the home, school, and community.

Mental and Physical Health

Throughout our years in practice, a diverse group of people have accessed our services with a range of physical and mental health needs. Following the client's lead has been the most reliable way to assess when to head outside. We have found that there are many ways to adapt to people's physical and mental health needs. Power To Be Adventure Therapy Society, a non-profit organization operating in Victoria, BC, has been demonstrating through their innovative programs for the past twenty years how no physical or mental health need poses too significant a barrier to overcome. For example, their programs have taken people with significant mobility issues to summits of mountains in a Trailrider (i.e., a wheelchair with one durable off-road wheel and grab bars front and back that allow for a team to drive/lift/steer the device over difficult terrain). Youth can rise to the challenge of helping a friend access that beautiful view from the mountaintop or travel together in a tandem ocean kayak with outriggers to stabilize them. The organization has spent two decades facilitating nature-based trips for almost anyone and has found ways to celebrate diversity, difference, and ability. We have taken from their inspiring approach a similar attitude and strongly believe that, with enough planning and preparation, natural spaces can be found that meet the needs of most clients. However, discerning what are real barriers that must be addressed versus self-limiting beliefs is a challenging task that requires collaboration and a detailed assessment.

Considerations and Adaptations

Physical health concerns and adaptations: activities and locations based on physical capacity are one of the primary considerations we need to assess. Clients, be they children, youth, or families, must be able to access and safely travel in the environments we choose. Knowledge of medical conditions, physical fitness, and ability to self-motivate and stick to activities when they become difficult is important. Some youth, for example, have plenty of fitness and motivation for more challenging pursuits such as hiking steeper hills or moving through wilder terrain off-trail. The opposite is also possible: a child spending far too much time indoors, gaming and not participating in physical activities, may in fact have quite poor fitness, low motivation, and little to no staying power if the activity becomes difficult. Building a picture of client capacity has to be a conscious and documented process. As the therapist gains insight, activities can be altered to meet the client's needs, session aims, and overall effect of nature-based therapy. An example is the basic use of progressions. A client may enjoy being at the beach. Early sessions may have started with a beach near the youth's home. If a therapist and client agree to engage in more challenging activities, a different location, duration, and intensity of activity can be designed as needed. We are fortunate to have access to marine trails used for multi-day backpacking in our region. Some sections can become ideal places to intensify a beach session; the experience of wilder nature, the physicality of the trip, and potentially the intensity of the affective experience can all be adjusted.

Mental health considerations and adaptations: Client assessments and intake information gained through conversations with school counselors, parents, and others may educate us on previous mental health concerns that we need to plan for. Knowing about previous psychosis, a tendency to run/take off, self-harming, hallucinations, extreme anxiety (to the degree where they won't leave the house), extreme aggression, etc. all require appropriate adaptations. As a general rule, those situations would indicate initial office-based sessions and probably family involvement. Then, through our ecological assessment and ongoing client care and communication, we would take the progressive steps toward nature-based therapy if the client was ready and interested.

Ecological Assessment

An activity inspired by the work of deep ecologist, systems thinker, and Buddhist scholar Joanna Macy[2] involves going swimming in a lake on a clear starry night. The idea is that, as you swim, the lake water absorbs your body while it also reflects the night sky, resulting in the boundary between your skin-encapsulated self and that of the larger cosmos starting to meld. The perception is that you no longer can sense where your body ends and the water begins. This activity is intended to provide an experience of what Norwegian philosopher Arne Næss[3] describes as the *ecological self*: a self that is not restricted by one's physical and mental processes but instead connected and inextricably linked to all of life. This idea of the self being larger than one's own physical body and individual mind, and connected to all living beings, has been articulated by numerous worldviews and philosophies—more recently in the West, through the fields of systems theory and ecology, which focus on the study of the relationships between organisms rather than the organisms in isolation.[4] As practicing nature-based therapists, we have found that assessing the degree to which someone describes experiencing an ecological self can assist in determining whether nature-based therapy is a fit and what activities may be most impactful.

If we are doing an intake for a child or youth client, then often this initial assessment takes place through the parents' perspective. They usually have a strong sense of how comfortable their children are in the outdoors and whether spending time outside is a resource or a stress for them. This perspective will often influence the decision to conduct initial sessions in the outdoors or in the office. With younger children, we commonly arrange them outside, as it is within that context that parents believe their child will best engage. For example, a mother of a 11-year-old boy recently said that when she told him they were meeting a counselor, he responded with anger, but then when she added they were meeting at a familiar local park, he responded, "Well, OK then, that's fine!"—his resistance to the idea of counseling was immediately disarmed. We often find that with older youth it is appropriate to initially meet in the office, and then we can assess their ecological identity and preferences together. An ecological identity is the manner and depth in which one connects to and engages with the natural environment.

Assessing One's Ecological Identity

To our knowledge, there is no formal standardized questionnaire with clinical validity measuring ecological identity. Instead, the utilization of a clinical interview to inquire into both present and early-childhood experiences and relationship with nature is most effective in providing a useful picture. This approach is not new. In fact, we have been using a series of questions influenced by Howard Clinebell's pioneering ecopscyhology book, *Ecotherapy*.[5] Clinebell used a series of questions to help understand client's ecological biography, what he called one's *ecological story*. More recently we have seen iterations of this approach in the work of counselors in both academic and practitioner materials. Some questions we often ask include

- What's your favorite way to connect with nature?
- What were your favorite places to visit in nature as a child, youth, and adult?
- Where do you currently enjoy going in nature?
- How do you feel when you are in nature?
- What activities do you enjoy doing in the outdoors?
- What natural places and beings do you feel most connected with?
- How do you show your love and care for nature?
- (When appropriate) What pains you the most about the current environmental predicament?

The answers to these questions provide the practitioner with a sense of how much nature-connection the person feels, their history of time spent in nature, and levels of motivation to be in nature. We have found that the process of discussing both these early and current experiences can be a powerful intervention in its own right, opening doors to the transpersonal realm of a client's life and sense of meaning.

Why Does Ecological Identity Matter?

Being present and fully aware of the wonders of the natural world is a particular state of being that is not always accessible. Similar to a muscle, being open and receptive requires practice in order to strengthen that state of being. Clients may have had experiences in nature that were frightening (e.g., being lost, alone, having aggressive or intimidating encounters with predators, fire, displacement, natural disasters). Perhaps they had experiences where they were uncomfortable due to environmental conditions and never felt a sense of safety and openness to the magnificence of the natural world. For many people, their social and cultural milieu may simply have not exposed them to quiet and undistracted time spent in wild spaces, such as growing up in inner cities where even outdoor play was limited by concerns for child safety. The thought of spending time outdoors without a particular activity or purpose may simply sound uninteresting, boring, or even uncomfortable or irrelevant to the client. It is our position that if people can move from an adverse or survival mode regarding their relationship to nature into a state of safety and connection, that over time their ecological self will emerge and grow stronger. The more present and connected they feel, the more receptive they will be to receiving the gifts of their relationship with the more than human natural world.

In doing ecological assessments, it can be helpful to understand a person's current relationship with nature in three distinct ways: *averse*, *receptive*, and *connected*. Keeping these relationship stances in mind can guide the types of activities and locations decided on with the client. These distinctions build on the work of Canadian ecopsychologist, conservationist, and environmental educator John Scull.[6] While now retired as a practicing psychologist, he still leads nature-connection walks for the Canadian Mental Health Association in the picturesque Cowichan Valley where Nevin lives. Scull described assessing clients with nature connection questions and divided them into three categories: (1) those with pre-existing negative feelings about nature (i.e., averse or phobic), (2) those with pre-existing positive feelings about nature (i.e., connected), and (3) those who had attended his nature-based sessions (which we are calling receptive). These simple designations provide a starting point for engaging clients in nature-based therapy.

Scull has found that conducting the ecological assessment can be a therapeutic experience itself. He has shared case examples where clients' engagement with the memories of earlier nature-based experiences have led to positive lifestyle and behavioral changes outside of therapy. It is our optimism in this reality—that healing can begin by even imagining or remembering positive experiences of contact with nature—that supports our encouragement for others to engage in this ecological assessment process.

Averse

These clients, with either very limited or negative experiences in nature, are concerned for their safety and feel out of place when in natural environments. They do not see the natural world as offering them anything meaningful and have no desire to change that stance. These clients may have encountered traumatic incidents that have established "wild nature" as a very negative association with their nervous system (e.g., war veterans whose trauma occurred outdoors, which may be a trigger, or in the case of sexual assault that occurred in a forest). It cannot be understated that respecting and honoring a client's survival response is critical so that we "do no harm" in assuming what is best for the client. If we find ourselves with a nature-averse client, then an office setting is most suitable, and we would aim to understand more about their historical, cultural, and familial experiences that have led to this adverse relationship. Using our ecopsychological lens, we may discover very simple and slow ways to introduce vicarious contact with nature (described below) within the office, with the intention of uncovering new helpful resources for the client.

Receptive

These clients have a neutral or positive stance toward nature. They have had limited experiences developing their relationship with the natural world but are open to exploring their connection. They may see the natural world as separate from themselves and focus on its practical uses, rather than being in relationship with or part of it. Receptive clients actually have the most potential for us to offer experiences and meaningful help. They may remain neutral about connecting with nature, or could move toward connection, and we take care to prevent negative experiences in nature that could shift them toward averse.

Connected

These clients have already developed strong connections with the natural world and recognize their own embeddedness and inextricability with nature. Connected clients may have family influences that have brought them closer to nature. They may have lived in close access to nature and already have established pastimes they love in the outdoors (e.g., nature walks, fishing, bird watching, or nature photography), which they can continue and enrich through deeper explorations.

Having an understanding of a person's ecological identity can be useful when deciding on locations and activities being offered to explore. As Bob Marley suggested above, the rain falls on us all, but we need to recognize that not everyone will experience it the same. Meeting people where they are at is a crucial component of developing a trusting therapeutic relationship with clients. For a person with an averse stance toward nature, the counselor can utilize their own relationship with nature to serve as a vehicle for generating interest, and supporting the counseling process. In this case, the person may have an aversion or disinterest in direct physical contact with nature, so going outdoors may not be appropriate, especially to start. Stories about nature, pictures, plants, animals, windows with a view, and even the client's own body and breath may be the focus while in an office environment. These activities can create a bridge for clients to safely start connecting to nature and provide a catalyst to head out of the office. A favorite tool we always have in our office space is a beautiful basket filled with fascinating and varied nature objects that clients can touch, hold, and draw upon for metaphor, self-expression, and comfort.

For a receptive person, nature can now be brought into the session, but rather than working overtly with the client's relationship with nature, the practitioner lets the experience speak for itself (e.g., hiking or walking in the forest, sitting around a fire, noticing interesting plants and animals). The rationale is that the client is still discovering their connection with nature and that the best way to begin this process is to offer positive direct nature experiences that spark curiosity and motivation to continue exploring. Finally, when working with people who are already nature connected, the counselor may choose to center the client's relationship with nature in sessions and provide opportunities to directly draw on, explore, and enhance this relationship. With all three client types (i.e., averse, receptive, connected), building relationships is the central aim: between client and nature, client and therapist, and therapist and nature. It is this triad of relationships, of equanimity in the process, that allows for nature to fully express its role as cotherapist.

Across all three of these situations, practitioners are also holding their own ecological identity at the forefront of their work. Their own nature connection, practices, and personal sense of connection are vital components of effective nature-based therapy. This inextricable connection between humans and the more-than-human world operates in the background, no matter where clients may be in their journey. Thus, we feel that all therapeutic work, whether it occurs in the office or outside, has the potential to be considered nature-based. How it looks depends on the clients' goals and motivations, relationship with nature, sense of ecological identity, and particular environmental considerations, which we turn to next.

Different Ways of Interacting with Nature

Stephen Kellert contributed immensely to our understanding of the vital importance for connection between humans and the natural world. In particular, he helped to elucidate the *biophilia theory* with Edward Wilson,[7] which purports that humans have an innate drive and need to connect with nature that extends beyond our reliance on nature for our physical sustenance to include a "human craving for aesthetic, intellectual, cognitive, and even spiritual meaning and satisfaction."[8] Kellert's in-depth research on the intersections between nature and children and youth explored how three different kinds of contact with nature, (1) direct, (2) indirect, and (3) vicarious (or symbolic), may impact developmental processes.

Direct contact is described as interactions with unmanaged natural environments that are self-maintaining and regenerative, requiring minimal or no human intervention to exist, yet that are still vulnerable to impacts by human activity. Examples include forests, wetlands, meadows, and savannah ecosystems, and a defining feature is that contact with these places often involve spontaneous and unpredictable interactions with flora and fauna. Kellert suggested that local parks, and even a backyard, could provide direct contact experiences when elements of the space are ecologically diverse or with enough diversity and a sense of coherence (i.e., the place seems to fit together naturally).

Indirect experiences of nature still involve actual physical contact but in environments that are highly reliant on human management and intervention: "Indirect experience of nature tends to be highly structured, organized, and planned; it may occur in settings such as zoos, botanical gardens, nature centers, museums, and parks."[9] These indirect experiences may include pets, plants, and other more-than-human natural elements that have been brought into human-managed environments.

Finally, *vicarious or symbolic experiences* of nature are those that do "not involve contact with actual living organisms or environments but, rather, with the image, representation, or metaphorical expression of nature."[10] Vicarious experience can be clearly evident or, at times, "highly stylized and obscure."[11] Examples include stories, photographs, nature guides, personal memories, artwork, and digital representations. In a child's life, the role of teddy bears, other animals, and storybooks and movies full of animated and talking animals provide great examples of vicarious experiences with nature. While anthropomorphized, the characters presented to children are very accessible to their mind and perceptions of the world. Play therapists have long known the value of, and utilized, animal toys and figurines and nature objects to represent real-life characters and situations. As a parent, I (Nevin) learned early with my own children that harder conversations of a personal nature were facilitated more easily through their friends, Cavani the bear and Winter the snow lion. Our engagement by the vicarious means includes found objects from nature, as mentioned above, as well as nature-based stories and poetry, pictures, or film.

After thoroughly examining the research on how different types of contact with nature impact a child's cognitive, affective, and evaluative development, Kellert concluded that "direct, often spontaneous contact with nature appears to constitute an irreplaceable core for healthy childhood growth and development."[12] Further, he commented on how the increasingly common lack of such contact may be considered an "extinction of experience" and how we are still not clear whether the corresponding increase in indirect and vicarious experiences of nature provides enough compensatory influence to offset this reality; "indirect or vicarious contact rarely offers the same degree of opportunity for experiencing challenge, adaptation, immersion, creativity, discovery, problem solving, or critical thinking as that afforded by direct encounters in the natural world."[13] Considering these points regarding the significance of direct experiences in nature, it is even more important that barriers are reduced or removed for children, youth, and their families to receiving such direct experiences. However, despite the potential benefits, not everyone is open and receptive to these wilder environments and experiences. We have found that combining knowledge of our clients' ecological identity with Kellert's three modes of experiencing nature can be helpful in meeting clients' needs and supporting the growth of positive relationships with nature. Table 1 provides a baseline decision tree we use for matching our clients with nature relative to their ecological assessment.

Matching Context to Presenting Needs

The choice to take therapy outdoors depends on many factors, yet, as we have articulated, our bias is that much more can be gained than lost by heading outside where direct contact can occur. With that said, matching the specific environment with client needs is critical to the process. Some additional factors to consider beyond ecological identity and type of contact include level of privacy, type of terrain, proximity to natural spaces, and weather. As mentioned earlier, we live and work in a moderately sized coastal Canadian city with easy access to diverse nearby nature and wilderness settings. This affords us a variety of trails, peaks, forests, parks, lakes, beaches, and fields to choose from for our sessions. Clients can travel to these environments within minutes from their homes, schools, and work. Because clients are not required to travel to one specific office location, which may be inconvenient for them, and instead meet in a natural space near their own community,

Table 1. Ecological identity and ideal clients' modes of experiencing nature.

	Averse	Receptive	Connected
Direct	Direct-averse Not recommended until a safe and trusting relationship has been formed between client and counselor; and client shows interest	Direct-receptive Activities that involve exploring engaging species and terrain in order to build up positive experiences	Direct-connected Activities that emphasize, explore, and deepen the transpersonal and ecological self, e.g., exchanging breaths with a tree, land-based tasks, blindfolded sensory exercises
Indirect	Indirect-averse Activities that start to expose a person to nature in a controlled but not direct manner, e.g., walks on trails, having plants in the office, nature objects, therapy animal	Indirect-receptive Activities that start to explore their connection with nature by utilizing games and crafts that enhance positive affinity and connection	Indirect-connected Activities that utilize metaphor, mindfulness, and other practices to deepen their connection in an intentional way
Vicarious	Vicarious-averse Starting with stories, visualizations, and inquiry for early memories with places, animals, activities in nature. May access counselor's relationship with natural world as access point	Vicarious-receptive Activities introducing nature metaphors, pictures, and stories to support the client in strengthening their connection	Vicarious-connected Activities recounting personal experiences with nature and exploring one's relationship with nature as well as how one's own body is a gateway into deep nature connection

nature-based counseling can actually become more accessible to families than office-based services. Further, visiting nearby nature increases the chances that clients will continue to visit that park, trail, beach, etc. on their own time. Remote wilderness camps and programs, by contrast, do not share this beneficial outcome, in that the clients and families may never be able to revisit them. So, how does the counselor decide where to meet with clients?

Privacy and a Sense of Wildness

We have found that most clients prefer to have their first few outdoor sessions in familiar environments, thereby increasing their comfort. For most people, finding locations for indirect experiences is preferred, including a park near their neighborhood, a favorite beach, or trail. However, an obvious ethical factor to consider in nature-based counseling is the limitations on privacy that are afforded by public outdoor spaces. Therefore, it is essential to discuss with clients beforehand regarding how to handle encounters with other people. For example, will the conversation continue or be paused if others approach? What will happen if either of you encounter someone you know? How do the clients want to respond if they do run into someone familiar who asks about what we are doing? How do the clients feel about encounters with dogs and their owners, and what if a dog comes up to visit?

By previously addressing these possible situations, the clinician is both acquiring consent and reducing potentially awkward moments. Having a plan will allow both (or all, if a family) to be prepared and have a smooth response that does not interfere with the therapeutic relationship or process. Answers to these questions can also help to guide the selection for a suitable location. If someone is afraid of dogs, then the counselor would want to offer locations where dogs are not permitted or are only allowed on leash. If the client is very concerned about privacy, is worried about running into friends, or does not want to be seen or possibly heard, then choosing a nature setting that is further from their own neighborhood, is more remote, or is on a private property would be preferable.

In one illustrative example, an 8-year-old girl and her family were seeking nature-based counseling and chose to meet at a large nature park (with many trails and fields), about fifteen minutes from their home, that was also popular with dog walkers and runners. After the initial greetings and interactive activities, the young girl said that she felt uncomfortable and that the venue was too public for her. She was quite private about her struggles and was already resistant to the idea of "having to see a counselor" in the first place. Even though other park visitors could not hear the family's discussions, the presence of people and dogs coming and going was too much for her to feel safe. Future plans to meet were thus adjusted to more private spaces, including her own large backyard and a private farm that the counselor had permission to use. This case story demonstrates the importance of continually assessing the context and client's consent—as the family had initially chosen the location together, but the child was able to be clear with her needs only after actually experiencing the setting firsthand.

If a family is comfortable being around others in a public space, however, then a familiar local park can be chosen; children generally prefer this because they develop a sense of connection and belonging in these spaces. Many younger children actually tend to be less aware of the presence of others and less self-conscious about being seen acting silly, showing emotions, or playing games. Another telling example involved a 10-year-old boy (and his parents) who chose to regularly meet in an oak woodland that was walkable from his school. While this park was commonly visited by neighborhood people, his familiarity with it and his love for its landscape, plants, and creatures were the motivating factors for his choice to meet there. He was not concerned about running into others and did not feel private about the fact that he met with a counselor—thus he could be fully present with the process within this public domain.

Ideally the nature-based counselor is familiar with the nearby nature locations they choose to take clients and can identify the quieter parts of the park to ensure privacy and confidentiality for most of the session. The initial greeting and check-ins may occur close to the main parking lot before traveling together to the preferred areas for exploration. Because nature often affords wide-open spaces with only birds and squirrels listening, therapeutic conversations may actually be more confidential than in an office space that has various clients coming and going in waiting rooms (and sometimes requires noise machines to create privacy). Further, we have found that nearby nature environments offer different experiences than a remote wilderness setting. Wilderness settings are certainly more conducive to privacy, unplanned encounters with animals, and the aesthetic experience of larger natural landscapes. However, based on the fact that wilderness is often harder to access, and farther away from urban centers, we do believe there is a strong case to be made for choosing nearby nature, so long as there are still opportunities for interaction with varied and unmanicured landscapes.

Motivation and Developmental Factors

As previously discussed, one of the benefits of nature-based therapy for children and youth is the enhanced motivation and engagement in the counseling process. The idea of getting a midday break from school to go run in the woods, or finishing off a long day of sitting in school with a visit to the beach, can be more appealing than the idea of an office appointment with a counselor. Ideally, at the end of the first session, the child/youth should be feeling excited about the process and ask when will they be meeting next. This sense of engagement helps to form the basis of the therapeutic relationship from which change can occur. Thus, matching the terrain of the location to the interests and developmental needs of the child/youth is an important factor to consider. A mismatch in terrain selection may result in disinterest, lack of safety, or an obstacle to the therapeutic alliance.

A wilderness setting often provides a higher level of biodiversity, which is associated with a stronger beneficial effect from contact with nature, a greater chance of encountering exciting or interesting flora and fauna (e.g., birds of prey, great climbing trees, animals to track, and an abundance of easily identifiable wild edibles), and an enhanced sense of adventure when on a trail less traveled. Teenagers, for example, tend to desire and express higher risk-seeking behaviors; their need to be challenged and to find self-efficacy may be better met by a more challenging environment (e.g., more isolated, denser forest, steeper terrain). The objective risks associated with wilderness environments also need to be taken into account (e.g., farther away from medical attention, higher chance of encountering wildlife, greater risk of getting lost if clients get separated). Wilderness environments often are more difficult to access both with the time required to travel there and the availability of public transit. Taking all these points into account, we have found that most of our clients' goals can be accomplished by working in a nearby nature environment. We also tend to stay focused on activities that do not require any specialized training or equipment. That said, to build fires, we teach clients safe knife handling and fire management skills, so these are no longer specialized and can become a regular activity when appropriate.

If it is possible to find accessible areas that offer safe scrambling opportunities (i.e., steep hiking terrain to gain a ridge or height of land), for example, that might be enough to pique the interest of a youth who is seeking adventure and exploring his boundaries/limits. Not all of the client's goals may be achievable in one particular location, and visiting a few others over time may be needed. For example, a session may begin in a local park with lots of open space and familiarity. After meeting a few times and building trust, sessions could shift to an environment with more pockets of forest where the practitioner and client can gain an enhanced sense of wildness. Additionally, a session may take place on a private property where fires or natural shelter building is allowed and where the client will have the chance to participate in collaboratively or self-designed activities with the assurance that only invited family and wilderness creatures will be present.

Weather and Environmental Conditions

Legendary Rastafarian musician Bob Marley's words can be thought of in two ways: literal or metaphorical. We have explored the metaphorical understanding above in that we don't know how our clients will perceive nature and the activities we facilitate, hence the need for the ecological assessment. We should also take Bob Marley's words literally as rain happens, as does snow, wind, cold and hot temperatures, barometric pressure changes, etc. Regardless of how connected clients believe they are with nature, how they really respond to environmental conditions may also require a level of assessment. We need to remain mindful of our own familiarity and comfort/discomfort with adverse weather and environmental conditions and observe our clients' responses. Not all will react in the same way. Although the rain can be seen as a metaphor for life's troubles, some feel it more than others, and can potentially be triggered negatively by it, while those more able to acclimatize and demonstrate the self-care necessary for the conditions barely notice it at all.

While building relationships with our clients, we also gain increased awareness to their preferences and responses to different weather and environmental conditions. Just being a wee bit creative, one can imagine the possible metaphorical interpretations of these situations. Wind may represent instability or change; hot and cold temperatures can be challenges to self-care; winter's early darkness can inspire bringing the family together around the fire for light and comfort. There is very little empirical research to support the role of weather and environmental conditions in therapy. However, if you read broadly across the nature writers and poets, across cultures, religions, and spirituality, you can find plenty of references to human-weather relationships. A clear example from my (Nevin) past includes the mood and tension in groups of adolescent males on wilderness expeditions when the barometric pressure drops preceding a storm. The observations, year after year, were that groups became more agitated and surly as the weather deteriorated. If you think of the properties of an oncoming storm—gloominess, darkness, instability, etc.—the group often appears to manifest these qualities, and you as counselor need to prepare activities and interventions to meet and work with the changing group and environmental climate. (This brings new meaning to climate change.) Not to generalize, nor lay any claims herein, we simply suggest therapists working outdoors need to stay present to weather and the environmental conditions when traveling with clients.

From a very simple perspective, checking the weather forecast will indicate how to prepare for a session and where to go relative to the report. If the weather looks particularly bad, we may call parents ahead of time to get a sense of how the child/parents are feeling about being out in the elements, so that we can make a decision collectively and be prepared. We have often found that clients are still up for the challenge, even when we might not have expected it. It is quite incredible how miserable it can feel to drive in the pouring rain, even for us, and then how fresh and nourishing that same rain can appear when heard and felt from beneath the canopy of giant Douglas-fir and western redcedar.

It is pertinent to acknowledge that we do live in the most temperate climate in Canada. Being a nature-based therapist in Nebraska, California, or Newfoundland, will look quite different, coming with their own challenges, especially in winter. We mostly have to contend with strong rain and wind, not snowstorms and freezing temperatures, although, when there has been snow and ice, we don't avoid the outdoors—our clients (both in individual and group settings) have been particularly excited to engage with the elements, whether building ice formations, throwing snowballs, or sliding penguin-style down a hill. Snow can actually provide many new opportunities for play and exploration, along with the unique beauty it brings to a landscape. Inclement weather such as high winds and rainstorms can also provide avenues for experiences of self-care, thriving outdoors, and, metaphorically, in dealing with life challenges and formidable forces (when appropriate). The fact that our counseling sessions with children and youth outdoors still tend to conform to the sixty-to-90-minute length means that, as long as everyone is dressed appropriately, it can be pretty manageable to maintain warmth and comfort regardless of the weather. Bringing a warm thermos of tea along with you never hurts either. See appendix B for a suggested clothing and equipment/materials list.

5

Nature-based Play, Regulation, and Healthy Neurophysiology

Play is our brain's favorite way of learning.

Diane Ackerman

A s outlined in preceding chapters, a growing body of knowledge and literature now articulates numerous positive benefits for people as a result of spending increased time in contact with nature. Physiological and psychological changes are experienced in nature and explain restored attention and decreased stress. For a practitioner of nature-based therapies, the questions of why such an approach may work and what underlying change mechanisms contribute to healing are still hard to explain. So, we ask, what else can we lay claim to as beneficial to a counselor and client relationship? Play and experiential learning are central to much of our work, and we are coming to recognize the clinical values inherent in our activities that have been practiced but not understood with any level of sophistication in the past. We can admit that experiential learning activities and play often elicit significant shifts in group and family dynamics and assist in the counseling process, yet until recently we hardly understood why. In this chapter, we lean on research and practice insights from somatic psychotherapy and advancements from neurobiology and regulation theory. Specifically, we are indebted to those who have helped translate the complex neuroscience involved in healing trauma into concrete practice applications. The task at hand is to explore the clinical application of play in nature-based therapy as it relates to self- and co-regulation, highlighting the skills and abilities needed to attend to and transform embodied information for the child, youth, or family.

We are mammals. We have mammalian nervous systems, and nature is the ideal mammalian environment. We argue that if you understand the mammalian nervous system, you too will agree that nature is the preferred place for therapy with children, youth, and families. We have found that increased knowledge of nervous system functioning provides a rich theoretical explanation of the complex connections between play, regulation, and relationships. This chapter shares how applying this knowledge in nature-based therapy provides creative and life-affirming ways to enrich your practice and improve potential client outcomes. Application of some of these concepts requires a development of skills associated with client assessment and a level of comfort in facilitating play and experiential activities. As a counselor, you may already have the capacity to design and lead sessions according to an intervention plan, based on assessment, and within your scope of practice and skills. Activities and examples of practice given here may be new to the reader yet are grounded in the same structure and processes outlined throughout the book. Utilizing novel environments and engaging in activities with unknown outcomes may be outside your comfort zone or intimidating to practice, but we encourage you to explore these approaches.

Advances in interpersonal neurobiology have brought forth a more coherent understanding of how to process difficult affective experiences, as well as the critical role interpersonal relationships have on healthy brain development and a *felt sense* of safety.[1] The *polyvagal theory*, as described by Porges,[2] has been particularly helpful in our clinical nature-based practice. This theory informs the differing ways clients' cognitive processes and physical bodies are responding to the present moment, as well as what they carry forward from the past, thus influencing how they respond to stressors in the environment. Polyvagal theory also provides a rich explanation of how socially engaged play can produce transformative learning experiences.

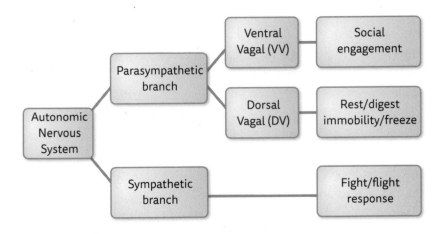

Figure 1. Porges's polyvagal description of the autonomic nervous system

Porges has helped to elucidate how the human autonomic nervous system impacts *affect regulation* and perceptions of safety, highly beneficial knowledge for therapists. According to Porges, "Evolution provides an organizing principle to identify neural circuits that promoted social behavior, and two classes of defensive strategies, mobilization associated with fighting or fleeing and immobilization associated with hiding or feigning death."[3] In more simplistic terms, the autonomic nervous system has two branches: sympathetic (S, fight/flight) and parasympathetic (P, rest/digest). However, the *vagus nerve*, which makes up the primary component of the parasympathetic branch, itself has two distinct components, hence the "poly" in polyvagal being *dorsal vagal* (DV) and *ventral vagal* (VV).

The VV, which has evolved more recently, is a fast-acting, highly myelinated neural web found only in mammals. It extends from the brain to the top of the diaphragm, innervating organs such as the esophagus, larynx, and lungs, communicates with facial muscles, and influences heart regulation. When the VV is activated, you can see the facial muscles engaged in authentic smiles, eyes brightening, and rhythmic relaxed breathing. It is turned on in moments of social connection, and subsequently dampens the fight/flight branch of the nervous system (i.e., aids with regulation) by slowing the heartbeat and lowering blood pressure. Porges explains that "when the ventral vagus and the associated social engagement system are optimally functioning, the autonomic nervous system supports health, growth and restoration."[4] Thus, within the counseling process, it is our aim to work with the VV nerve, the social connection system, as a pathway to aid co-regulation so clients can access and maintain regulated states during our sessions. The second component, the *dorsal vagal* (DV), is an evolutionarily older, unmyelinated, slower, and less nuanced component of the nervous system. It is responsible for states of deep immobilization (e.g., deep sleep, relaxation, rejuvenation), and the neural web of the DV terminates in the pelvic area and viscera/gut. When activated, it is responsible for rest and digest and is also involved in freeze responses to perceptions of life threat.

An individual can experience these neural circuits operating on their own (i.e., sympathetic arousal, VV or DV). However, Porges goes on to explain that these distinct neural circuits can also become fused together in response to contextual demands. For example, if a person is experiencing terror, and their efforts to defend themselves are ineffective (the person is unable to run away or fight), then their sympathetic branch can become paired with their DV system, and the result is a low or hypo-aroused state, with an underlayer of fear (i.e., freeze). This is the state occurring in animals when they play dead or freeze in response to threat from a predator; in humans it is often experienced as dissociation (where one's body and mind disconnect to protect from the experience of pain).

The sympathetic arousal system can also become paired with the VV system (excitement plus connection), as is often the case when people are engaged in playful activities with others (e.g., playing tag, hiding games, team initiatives). This state of play is an activation of hyperarousal in response to a sense of adventure and risk but within the presence of social connection and safety. It is within this powerful form of play that the therapist has the ability to foster healing states of the nervous system. We have found that this task is much harder to elicit with children inside the confines of an office, and hence another reason to practice in nature. Further discussion on applying this concept appears later in the chapter.

So, How Can Polyvagal Theory Be Helpful in Clinical Practice?

A more nuanced understanding of the different states of the nervous system can allow practitioners to better attune to clients' needs by becoming proficient at reading both their own and their clients' presenting neural states. In doing so, practitioners can assist clients to (1) increase their awareness of their own somatic experience, (2) co-regulate intense affective states with the support of nature, and (3) promote healthy development by expanding their "window of tolerance."[5] This process is referred to as a *two-person psychology* by interpersonal neurobiologist Allan Schore, who specializes in right-brain to right-brain affect communication and regulation.[6]

Promoting Awareness of Neural States and the Mammalian Stress Response

Providing children, youth, and families with education regarding their nervous systems has been a powerful tool for us in helping them better understand their bodies' stress responses. The process of tuning in and noticing what is happening in the body can help alleviate the intensity of an experience, promote self-compassion, and facilitate conscious actions to shift neural states. Even children as young as 6 have been taught this model and can benefit greatly from understanding how their nervous system responds to stress in their environment. This provides the children with a meta-awareness of bodily sensations and how those sensations overwhelm when they sense a lack of internal or external safety. Often tuning into one's own embodied experience is a challenging and novel task for both children and adults alike. We have found that, by first tuning into the "outer landscape" (i.e., natural surroundings) and building rich sensory awareness of the smells, textures, colors, and animate shapes in the natural environment, we can assist clients to build the foundational skills necessary to observe their internal environment (i.e., thoughts, feelings, and bodily sensations). Speaking to the importance of teaching people to tune into their senses, Kaya Lyons, Australian pediatric occupational therapist (OT) and director of Active OT for Kids, explains how "sensory pathways are faster neural pathways compared with cognitive pathways as they have direct branches to the emotional areas of the brain. Activating these sensory pathways in a calm and organized manner helps to strengthen pathways which are organizing to the body and linked to positive emotions."[7] She also offers insights from her field of OT, which recognizes that prior to thoughts and feelings are the internal senses of the body. She explains that, in addition to the commonly known five senses (sight, touch, taste, hearing, and smell), there are three internal senses: proprioception (sensations related to muscles and joints), vestibular (sensations related to balance and orientation in space), and introception (sensations related to our internal organs). Lyons claims that by "activating and organizing both external and internal senses it is possible to achieve true integration,"[8] something we have experienced both personally and professionally in our work with clients. Chapter 7 describes how we teach sensory awareness skills in nature, including suggestions for games and activities.

We have developed an accessible and effective method for teaching polyvagal theory by layering these neural states over the *zones of development* model found in many experiential education and outdoor therapy frameworks. The model also supports the *zones of regulation* system, a popular framework for fostering self-regulation often taught in the school system.[9] We teach this framework with children, youth, and families by laying ropes on the ground in large concentric circles, as depicted in Figure 2. These can contract and expand as needed to illustrate and explain changes in the zones depending on how one responds. For example, spending time in the challenge zone allows the

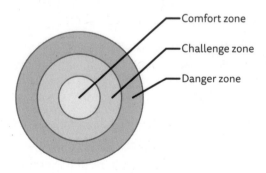

Figure 2. Concentric circles for the zones of development activity

comfort zone to expand, whereas spending time in the danger zone has an opposite effect.

The *comfort zone* (innermost ring) can represent a VV neural state. People in this zone are experiencing a sense of relative safety and comfort, and little activation is occurring. Bodily sensations often include warmth, lightness, ease, relaxation, and expansiveness. The face is relaxed and neutral in color, and smiling is common. A person in this state is calm, focused, and present with the task at hand. In the zones of regulation model, this represents the green zone, which indicates a state of readiness to learn and ability to process information.[10] Examples of common activities that place kids in the comfort zone include listening to music, playing with toys, reading books in bed, being with friends, playing on the beach, exploring outside, and other favorite activities that they find easy and pleasant. It is important to note that what lies within the comfort zone is different for each person and therefore highlights the importance of being attuned to individual responses in order to move toward achieving deeper understanding. This zone is also restorative, representing situations and activities that are resources the child can turn to when under duress. A person is considered to have a regulated nervous system in this state.

In the *challenge zone*, sometimes called the growth/groan zone, the sympathetic neural circuit is activated. The person is experiencing a heightened state of physical activation and is considered hyperaroused. The body is getting prepared for fight or flight in order to address the threat or challenging task. Adrenaline and cortisol pumping through the body are felt through physical sensations, often including energy or tension down the arms and legs, constriction in the chest, sweating, accelerated heart rate, and sometimes tingling in the extremeties. Breathing may be shallow and rapid; the eyes may seem like they are darting around; and the pupils may dilate (i.e., hypervigilance). These sensations are often interpreted as anxiety, nervousness, frustration, silliness, or excitement (the yellow zone, according to the zones of regulation).[11] Some examples of challenge zone experiences might include writing a test, speaking in front of the class, or even getting ready for school in the morning. (Many parents can attest to the increase of stress in the home when trying to get children out the door for school.) Many physical skills and sports (biking, skiing, swimming, etc.) will pass through a period of time in the challenge zone before being considered in one's comfort zone. Very few kids hop on a two-wheeled bike for the first time and take off without any period of nervousness or uncertainty. This state is actually an essential element in high-performance activities (e.g., musical performance, racing, team sports, rock climbing, mountain biking) as it can both energize the body and focus one's mental state on a specific goal.

Importantly, in the challenge zone, the person is able to *concurrently maintain* a VV state of social connection, which keeps the sympathetic arousal of fear within manageable levels. The child may feel uncomfortable and uncertain in this state but is still able to tolerate the discomfort and ride it out toward achieving a goal. A child who is attempting to cross a log on their own has to be able to tolerate the fear of falling when the parent lets go and gives them a chance to maintain their own balance. The more that the child stands on their own feet, the less wobbly they feel, allowing for their nervous system to down regulate. After making it across, they feel success, and with repeated successes, walking across that particular log will be in their comfort zone. If they were to take those skills to a new and perhaps higher and narrower log, the familiar feelings of nervousness and excitement would likely return, and the child is back in their challenge zone, a state of potential learning and growth.

It is important to teach kids and families that if we are not willing to tolerate those sensations of nervousness, and choose instead to avoid the physical and mental discomfort completely, then we get stuck in our limited comfort zone, and it does not expand to include new experiences and skills. Such is often the case when anxiety is in charge and the child manages worry by avoiding any activities which cause uncertainty or discomfort.[12] As we demonstrate these concepts visually by shrinking and expanding the comfort zone rope, we can show that, for a person who rarely leaves their comfort zone and avoids venturing into the challenge zone, their comfort zone circle will shrink over time. For some kids with high levels of anxiety, this shrinking can ultimately result in school refusal and unwillingness to leave the house. On the other hand, if they are willing to tolerate being uncertain or uncomfortable and do not shy away from new challenges, then their comfort zone will expand and grow to include many new skills, opportunities, and friendships. These kids are willing to take risks, knowing that learning from mistakes leads to growth. Many believe that the tendency toward over-protective parenting in our current culture is a contributing factor to the high levels of anxiety and depression in children and youth in North America. The desire to constantly protect our children from potential failure and injury (i.e., from challenge zone experiences) actually prevents them from discovering their own limits, skills, and strengths—and fosters fear and uncertainty rather than resilience. These situations can become feedback loops where kids are looking to their parents for signs of safety or threat and responding accordingly. If a parent's verbal and non-verbal communication to a child is one of confidence and safety, this sends strong messages that moving forward with the task is possible. However, if a parent is unsure and anxious themselves, this can reinforce the child's fears and lead to reassurance and avoidance patterns being strengthened.[13]

Finally, in the *danger or panic zone*, the sympathetic arousal system is engaged, hyper-aroused, without the soothing effect of a sustained VV state. This can look like rage, overwhelm, explosiveness, fear, panic, and lack of self-control (i.e., the red zone in the zones of regulation). Bodily sensations may include difficulty breathing, rapid heartbeat, pupil dilation, sweating, redness in the face, tense muscles, stomach ache, tunnel vision, and lack of bodily control (e.g., hitting, kicking, biting, spitting-fight/flight response). In this state of strong sympathetic arousal without any VV activation, the individual has in a sense "flipped their lid" as Daniel Seigel explains,[14] which means they no longer can access their prefrontal cortex, and their ability to think rationally is compromised by a process of "amygdala hijacking."[15] Only once able to calm themselves down through a process of either self- or co-regulation are they able to engage in self-reflection. This process explains why kids often feel "out of control" when angry, and why we all tend to say things we don't mean or do things we later regret. Most families who contact us for counseling support are doing so because a child or the family system as a whole is experiencing the danger zone all too often in their daily lives.

Further, if attempts are not effective to alleviate the stressor (the individual cannot fight or run away), then the sympathetic system may become paired with the DV and the drive for self-protection may immobilize them. Bodily sensations may include a numbness throughout the body or a sense of a void, stillness, and heaviness (pupil constriction, pale skin, holding their breath). The face may look devoid of affect; muscles around the eyes and mouth may have a flaccid tone; and a collapsed body posture includes the head hung low and shoulders slouched. They would now be considered in a hypo-aroused state (i.e., blue zone in the zones of regulation). This freeze state, or shutdown, can be seen in kids who are refusing to participate, will not talk, or might literally be curled up in a ball refusing to engage. This state can be triggered in situations of perceived high risk, such as a when a child freezes in fear when trying to navigate a steep section of a trail or on a climbing wall, or if they had a negative social interaction and are responding to emotions of shame. Importantly, there is a significant difference between being in a low state of arousal, where a child is seeking to up regulate to reach an optimal state, versus being in a state of shutdown. In a low state, the child is often seeking increased sensory input; in a state of shutdown, their sensory system has reached a level of capacity, and as way to cope, they close down their sensory system and are not receptive. Being aware of these different hypo-aroused states is important as they are in fact distinct neural states. In Table 2 we share our thinking on how zones of regulation, zones of development, polyvagal states and associated behaviors relate to one another.

In our use of adventure activities with groups, we introduce the zones of learning model to clients in order to emphasize that they can expect to enter the challenge zone during the program. We do want them to experience a meaningful level of challenge which can entail moments of discomfort, but we do not want them to be in the danger zone. We are constantly monitoring clients' behavioral and emotional responses to track for signs of the danger zone, and we encourage them to notice when they may be entering that state. This is achieved by not only discussing the different states but also encouraging them to connect with their internal landscape and how their bodily sensations and emotions are responding depending on what zone they are in. This

Table 2. Zones of regulation, zones of development, polyvagal theory, and associated behaviors. (Adapted from the work of Stanley, Kuypers, Vygotsky, and Porges.)

Zones of Regulation	Zones of Development	Nervous System States	Polyvagal Theory	Common Behaviors
Upper **RED**	Danger zone	Hyperarousal	Sympathetic	rage, aggression, panic, overwhelm,
Lower	Challenge zone	High arousal	Sympathetic + Ventral Vagal	hesitant/ tearful, anxious
YELLOW	Challenge zone	High arousal	Sympathetic + Ventral Vagal	hyper-vigilant, playful/silly, excited/ nervous
GREEN	Comfort zone	Optimal arousal	Ventral Vagal	Calm/ connected, ready to learn, present, feeling safe
Lower **BLUE**	Challenge zone	Low arousal	Dorsal Vagal	Bored/ disengaged, tired, unable to think or respond/shut down
Upper	Danger zone	Hypo arousal	Dorsal Vagal + Sympathetic	

approach fosters an atmosphere of self-monitoring and personal "challenge by choice," allowing each individual to identify and ultimately determine which zone they are experiencing for any particular activity.

One effective way to demonstrate individual differences in response to various experiences is to have a group (or family) become a living model by moving their bodies between concentric circles of rope lying on the ground that represent the zones. We call out experiences or activities and invite them to imagine what their sensory and emotional responses might be. With this felt bodily information, they can now physically locate themselves within the zones, either standing centrally in a zone or at the edges between zones. We usually start by asking about less vulnerable activities (e.g., riding a bike, swimming, kayaking, reading, cleaning your room) and then move to more internal topics (e.g., asking for help, speaking in front of the class, getting ready for school, meeting a new friend, family conflict). As the family or group moves in and out of the circles, they get the chance to learn and express themselves in a nonthreatening and nonverbal way and to observe how others have experienced the comfort, challenge, and danger zones in their lives, further normalizing their own experiences.

This activity helps participants to learn more about one another and helps the facilitator to learn about the needs and skills of the group. It helps the group see commonalities and break down barriers for connection. In families, this provides a springboard for open conversation about challenging topics. It can also be a great way for kids to start sharing their areas of difficulty in life, giving them the chance to be okay with all zones and develop resources to regulate between zones. Interestingly, most of our clients will stand inside the comfort zone when asked about playing outside in nature, which is one of the reasons we work with them in the nature-based context: it acts as a resource for maintaining connection within the therapeutic relationships. We also recognize, from a sensory perspective, nature is calming to the nervous system because it rarely overstimulates individuals as its sensory input is well balanced.

Enlisting the help of the parents to suggest activities that they know are challenging for the child can be a powerful experience. Sometimes families are surprised by what is shared, and a child also gets to learn something new about their parents. For example, one mother showed that swimming is challenging for her, but the child never knew and assumed his mother was comfortable in the pool. Now the child sees that his mother tolerates being in the challenge zone in order to do something that is fun for the child. In another instance, where a child was receiving family therapy for anxiety, a parent shared that being within a large group of people is in their challenge zone—a situation that is also an anxiety-producing experience for the child. Parent and child then had a chance for shared conversation about this worry, and it normalized the child's struggle. So often parents keep their own personal vulnerabilities hidden from their children in an effort to protect them from adult problems, in effect alienating them in that shared experience of challenge and discomfort. Developing a common language for emotional and nervous system regulation can help families to navigate mental health issues as a team and to respond to stress with greater empathy and compassion. When a parent models persistence to their children, and can say "Hey, this was challenging for me; I was nervous, but I stuck with it anyways, and this is how I benefited," this offers a very powerful message toward relating to discomfort as something that can be overcome versus always avoided. It also creates opportune moments to describe some resources that helped to manage the discomfort (e.g., I stopped, took a deep breath, and felt my feet on the ground, and then thought of a plan).

Co-regulation of the Nervous System
Supported by Nature

For people to move from their comfort zone into their challenge zone most effectively, the support and scaffolding of a caring other must be present.[16] Thus, the social engagement system must be activated alongside the sympathetic system, so they can maintain their ability and receptiveness to learning in their *proximal zone of development*. If a practitioner is able to first notice their own state, then notice their clients' neural states and assist them to attune to their own embodied experience, this enhanced mindfulness can lead to the possibility for more conscious choices regarding emotional states and the potential for effective change. Further, it can allow for an understanding of why their body is reacting in a certain way. This can help to facilitate self-compassion and understanding because behavioral responses make sense when put in the context of the particular neural state being activated.

Increased awareness of internal states is often not sufficient to allow for the soothing and management of intense affective experiences. Especially if there has been a history of traumatic experiences, the ability to self-regulate and prevent sliding into the danger zone is extremely challenging. Sensorimotor psychotherapy pioneer Pat Odgen and colleagues[17] refer to the *window of tolerance* as the extent to which a person can manage difficult affect without shifting into a DV/sympathetic shutdown or hyper-aroused panic state. For a person with regulation challenges, this window would be very small, thus their challenge zone separating comfort from danger is narrow (see Table 2). Self-regulation may not be possible, but co-regulation certainly can be. Co-regulation "involves the mutual regulation of physiological states between individuals."[18] This attunement is the first task of a mother (or other attachment figure) to an infant as she responds to her baby's cries and meets her baby's needs for soothing/food/sleep. Thus, following an understanding of the different neural states, helping to shift someone from the danger zone back to challenge or comfort zone can be possible.

If an individual is feeling agitated, experiencing an increased heart rate and racing thoughts, they can be reminded that this is their nervous system in the challenge zone. The social connection involved in naming and discussing this state can help to engage the VV circuit, keeping the hyperarousal at a manageable level. One example of how we do this involves orienting to the physical environment, much the same way a deer orients to its environment when it leaves a forested area and enters an open field. The deer will evaluate signs of safety, risk, and life threat to determine whether it should proceed from the edge. Scanning the environment can be a soothing experience, especially when one is invited to notice aspects they find beautiful, as it helps to send internal messages of safety to their nervous system. According to Porges, "Our cognitive evaluations of risk in the environment, including identifying potentially dangerous relationships, play a secondary role to our visceral reactions to people and places."[19] Thus, the step often missed is bringing awareness to the three internal senses, mentioned above, as security comes from feeling safe in the external environment and within our internal ability to cope in our environment.[20] This felt experience of safety is what is key to the co-regulation process.

Case Example
An 9-year-old girl was being seen for anxiety that was affecting her behavior in school; some activating factors included getting sick during travel (e.g., in cars, boats, planes). Since car rides heightened her anxi-

ety, she would often arrive to counseling in a hyper-aroused state. Her dysregulation was visible both in her words that expressed distress and in her body through repetitive movements in an attempt to self-soothe. She obviously was not in a state to be able to process any cognitive learning about coping skills at that time. (Attempting CBT interventions would be fruitless.) Fortunately, we met regularly in a beautiful public park with natural features including the ocean, creek, meadow, and trees all around. Thus, we learned to start sessions by walking to a grassy meadow by a pond nearby and lying down on a blanket (with her mom or dad present). The counselor started experimenting with playing the game I Spy, focusing first on colors then moving to textures (e.g., I spy something soft, spikey). Counselor, parent, and child would take turns asking questions, and the child could not help but become engaged in the game of guessing the right answer. Soon enough this girl would be happily playing I Spy, her nervous system returned to a VV state, and she was able to verbally express awareness of a shift in her internal sensations. By bringing attention to the senses in a natural setting, we were able to override the panic response and re-engage her prefrontal cortex in the process of therapy. This shift allowed us to move toward more insight-based conversations and work on skill building to manage her anxiety.

Expanding the Window of Tolerance
via Nature-based Play

How can a person assist another to expand their window of tolerance is a central question for helping professionals. One of the most effective methods we utilize is nature-based play. The engagement possible by being in a nature setting, health and development benefits associated with play in general, and the co-regulating effect of incorporating play into sessions all contribute to positive therapeutic and health outcomes.

As described above, *play* is the neural state of sympathetic arousal plus social engagement. It is important to note that play in the neurological sense does not include any solitary activities (such as video games, iPad apps, or even interacting independently with toys). Instead, play involves activation of the sympathetic nervous system (i.e., the game elicits excitement, laughter, curiosity, and focus) combined with maintained social connection, which serves to keep a person in a regulated state. Further, play includes movements and gestures similar to fight/flight behaviors that are followed by face-to-face interactions. This is evident in the play behavior of almost all mammals.[21]

Many children and youth who seek counseling and participate in our programs struggle to maintain social connection during play. Either they are disinterested and refuse to engage, or they become hyper-aroused and the play quickly shifts to aggression, fighting, and "having to win" or, subsequently, a feeling of defeat, collapse, and giving up if they are perceiving themselves as "losing." In both circumstances, they are not able to maintain a VV connection to help regulate their sympathetic arousal. Often these clients are described as having self-regulation challenges, along with a number of other common diagnoses such as ODD, attachment disruptions, ADHD, anxiety, autism spectrum. Sharon Stanley describes the neurobiology of play:

> During play, the ventral vagal circuit of social connection helps people stay in contact with each other yet explore the edges of fear through small doses of sympathetic arousal. If the arousal of the ventral vagal circuit of social engagement trumps the arousal of the sympathetic circuit, play is successful and participants can enjoy a bond of social engagement. If the ventral vagal arousal is lost for either participant, play can feel like bullying, harassment, or even the terror of life threat. When a child perceives his or her life is threatened in this kind of play, the neural state of "immobilization with fear" can take over and the child can collapse into patterns of blame, shame, helplessness, and powerlessness.[22]

Being in natural settings affords people a rich environment for both unstructured and structured play that can be tailored to their unique circumstances and promote the maintenance of a VV connection. By drawing on children's passions, such as hiding, seeking, sneaking, and exploring, we have found success in offering simple activities to engage our clients in play-based activities in nature. Because these are facilitated by an attuned helper, the child or youth is able to be supported to maintain social connection in situations that otherwise would have led to dysregulated states. Further, we can offer games of varying difficulty, depending on the goals to be achieved. If we are hoping to build a child's confidence, then awarding points for successfully navigating challenging terrain is an effective approach. The child can earn points for climbing obstacles and finding elements in the natural environment (scavenger hunt). The VV connection is maintained through coaching and reflecting back the youth's experience as they work through the challenges. If the goal is to help the child cultivate an inner stillness, then we include hiding games where being really quiet and camouflaged is required to succeed. We find that disguising mindfulness in nature through a game that demands stillness and observation for success is an effective approach to promote these skills in kids who would normally resist prescribed quiet time. Finally, if we are wanting to assist with the tolerance of discomfort, we may introduce a challenging game such as having to sneak quietly to retrieve an object without being heard. The child will have to work through their initial frustration that the game is not easy and navigate how to accomplish the task. Again, having face-to-face support, along with empathic connection and clear directions regarding the rhythm, pauses, and pace of the game and interaction, are key aspects in ensuring that the child is able to adequately process and maintain a prosocial stance and regulated neural state.

Case Example

A 14-year-old boy was struggling with strained family relations and had difficulty sustaining peer relationships. He had a long history of refusing to work with mental health professionals; those who did have a chance to assist him described the work as extremely challenging as he was so reluctant to engage. He was willing to work with me (Dave) because my outdoor approach sounded engaging and fun. He liked the idea of exploring the forests, making fires, and doing other adventure activities, such as using a knife to carve. We decided to meet in a nearby nature setting that was forested and on private land, which allowed us access to fire making and privacy. Early in our work, I noticed he was hard to read due to minimal affect and limited facial expressions. Further, he was reluctant to engage verbally, often claiming that he didn't trust people or like to share or interact with those he did not know well.

An activity he did enjoy immensely was playing tricks on people, such as scaring them or rough-housing in a way that often made them feel uncomfortable. Early on in our time together, a boundary was compromised with me that made it clear why these sorts of games were getting him into trouble. A game he really enjoyed playing with me was called jousting, in which we made eye contact and attempted to touch the other person with a branch (i.e., a safer version of a jousting lance). The game could be enhanced by having to balance on a log. Once a limb is touched, it is no longer a body part available to be used, and if the core of the body is touched, or you lose all four limbs, the game is over. What was immediately apparent was how quickly the game could turn from fun to discomfort for me and how my perception of him changed from a sense of safety to threat. I observed him becoming more agitated and using increasing amounts of force, despite my clear signs of unease. On one of our first occasions, he took a hard swipe at me and hit my face, causing me to cover my face and protect myself. I told him that I no longer wanted to play as I didn't feel safe and that we needed to take a break.

After this incident, we discussed his experience of wrestling with friends. He described how very few people are willing to do this with him and that the one time someone agreed, the "play" ended up in both of them getting upset and fighting. This particular client was struggling to understand why I was not enjoying myself during the game. Further, he was unable to maintain a VV connection and keep himself regulated. His interest in this game did provide an opportunity for us to build his skills at distinguishing activities that were playful (i.e., where we maintained social engagement) and others that were perceived as threatening. Further, I was able to draw on my own relationship with him, and the trust we had built, to express how I was experiencing the "play" as unpleasant, and to help him make connections with other situations in his life where people withdraw, despite his interest in maintaining friendship. A common thought he had shared with me is that he doesn't know why no one wants to be around him. Through the course of a number of sessions, with an agreement that I would continue playing only if I was feeling safe, we were able to continue exploring this game and provide a neural experience for him where he was able to expand his ability to maintain positive face-to-face interactions without shifting into a deregulated state. Finally, we were able to have these discussions and reparative experiences because he felt a sense of safety and interest in the different natural environment we were meeting in and he remained engaged in the nature-based activities that were being offered.

How Play Comes Alive in Nature

We have been asked before whether the games we offer need to be facilitated outside, and if not, what's the role of nature. Our answer is that because we are embedded and inextricably linked with nature and occupy animal bodies, engaging in practices that awaken and align with our mammalian nervous system will have the most profound impact. So, yes, some of our activities and counseling interventions can occur in the safe and predictable walls of an indoor space. However, if we are interested in moving beyond the establishment of comfort zones, then the wild or nearby nature spaces are exactly where we want to be. As the mounting evidence from environmental psychology suggests, our human co-evolution with natural spaces has had a profound impact on the humans we are today. We prefer and are designed to be in green environments more so than built ones.[23] As mentioned above, the sensory input in a natural environment is often calming to the nervous system, unlike the overstimulating input in highly manufactured environments. Thus, interventions that take place outdoors are enhanced and are able to come alive, much in the same way we see our young clients come alive when they chase each other in the forest or come across a deer skeleton on the ground. Interacting with the natural world, particularly through play involving seeking, sneaking, hiding, chasing, and exploring, gets people into their animal bodies and senses, allowing for experiences of vitality that are harder to come by in other settings.

Nature is filled with an abundance of flora and fauna that help engage people in the present moment and embodied exploration. These bring out curiosity in people and motivate a further connection with nature; some species are more rare, or have prominent characteristics; some display intriguing behaviors. Telling examples are trees that are perfect for climbing, eagles nesting or flying overhead, banana slugs crossing a trail, or the deer that are feeding and traveling through local parks and forests. Encounters with beings that can be climbed, tended, and taken in awe or wonder provide a powerful means to engage in the present moment and begin the process of acquainting them to their own nature, their own animal bodies, and specifically their mammalian nervous system.[24] Ultimately, this helps to link sensory experiences with emotions and thoughts and movement toward body-mind integration.

An important consideration when working from a somatic perspective with children, youth, and families, is that there may be a history of trauma (shock or developmental) that can create significant changes in nervous system functioning and responses to stressors. Somatic experience trainers Kathy Kain and Stephen Terrell,[25] experts in the physiology and treatment of developmental trauma, wrote an integrative guide to understanding and supporting circumstances where people may appear to be regulating but in fact are struggling with survival responses from past trauma. Ensuring that the context of a person's life is taken into consideration is vital, as is equipping oneself with the appropriate training to manage responses to trauma when working with vulnerable populations in the outdoors and from a somatic perspective.

This chapter has provided a basic understanding of the mammalian nervous system and how consideration for different neural states (in both ourselves and our clients) can inform and enhance nature-based practices. These ideas are further explored in the subsequent chapters.

6

Outdoor Risky Play
in Nature-based Therapy

Play is the highest form of research.

ALBERT EINSTEIN

Outdoor play, including its inherent risks, is, from an evolutionary perspective, a primary developmental experience for young
people—yet the opportunities for nature-based experiences are se-
verely restricted due to the highly urbanized, technological, distracted,
and risk-averse societies many of us live in. Researchers Mantler and
Logan remind us that

> ancestral experiences and evolutionary processes continue to
> influence the brain in ways that may escape conscious aware-
> ness by contemporary adults. It is becoming increasingly evi-
> dent that the 2.2 million years our genus has spent in natural
> environments are consequential to modern mental health.[1]

So, if our evolutionary blueprint still has much to teach us, we should
be open to the possibilities that some human functions, such as being
exposed to risk, may in fact be important. While most child injury prevention specialists, and others, would argue that this premise is seemingly dangerous and unnecessary, we (the authors) believe in risk as a
human experience, that it should be experienced in ways that provide
growing opportunities and stay within our ethic to do no harm. That

said, there is dignity, and a right, in being allowed to experience life fully, including its risks and possible setbacks. Author John Burroughs once stated he went into nature for his soul "to be soothed and healed, and to have [his] senses put in order." This commonly cited and Romantic notion of contact with nature for health, in our view, acknowledges that going to nature may in fact adjust or realign one's senses (feelings, thoughts, attitudes). This, to us, may happen through personal explorations and adventures, which might result in personal disruptions or discomfort. Being in nature, and participating in outdoor play, comes with risk, which, we argue in this chapter, is a necessary factor in child and youth development. Further, risk becomes a valuable means to engagement in nature-based therapy practice. We remind readers that risk is already present in the lives of many children and families due to social, economic, and other factors. Issues of marginalization and lack of safe and accessible outdoor environments prevent many children from free outdoor play, especially unsupervised in wilder spaces. We know we are speaking in general terms and that our offerings will not apply to all clients across contexts; this book, and the practices of nature-based therapy, are primarily directed toward those families who are experiencing issues that will benefit from a nature-based approach. Some children and families are already exposed to too much risk and deserve to be protected, and others are overprotected and deserve to experience risk. For our practice, we frame risk as a developmental need and specifically identify risks as being constructed during outdoor play in nearby nature. We advocate for practitioners and parents to begin dialog on "the right to risk" as equally important as a child's right to play. This chapter outlines some of the research and theory of outdoor risky play that support case examples throughout the book that utilize the approach.

A growing body of scientific evidence and supportive literature aims to shift thinking about protecting children from all harm (i.e., injury prevention focused on the elimination of all risk) to a position more open to risk exposure, with increasing understanding of risk's value in healthy child development. Risk has two sides: the potential for loss and the potential for gain. Modern Western society is highly risk averse and often forgets the positive gains that engaging with risk provides. While not easy to explain how we got here—for many children "here" is a hyper-protective state—the reality is that most of them are protected from many learning experiences more common to previous generations. Easy examples that those over thirty can remember include riding bicycles over home-made jumps (often without helmets), ranging farther from home at a young age, and that most outdoor play was unsupervised! Just reflect on how these opportunities provided lessons, even when things didn't go well, compared to children's experiences today. Research now suggests this change may be at a cost in child development: reduced capacities in creativity, judgment, confidence, and decision-making and increased phobias in later years.[2] From an evolutionary perspective, play, particularly in its rougher and riskier forms, can allow children to address anxieties and reduce reservation in certain contexts. This has been shown when children are allowed to complete risk-related activities repeatedly and when the challenging experiences become gradually more complex.[3] Outdoor play in general (not just risky play), often unsupervised, has also been shown to increase positive social relationships and creativity.[4] Our argument for outdoor risky play is bolstered in light of the evidence for a range of positive benefits in general: increased physical activity, social activity, vitality, positive affect, life satisfaction, and cognitive performance; improved heart rate variability; as well as reduced anxiety, depression, cortisol levels, sympathetic tone, systematic inflammation, and improved blood pressure.[5]

While the science and anecdotal evidence portraying positive outcomes from time in nature grows, the ever-increasing aversion to risk in our society exerts constraining forces upon teachers, human service workers, therapists, parents, and others who wish to engage with outdoor risky play. The struggle is when a practitioner experiences the tension between allowing healthy risk-taking by children and protecting themselves against claims of negligence. Social scientist and professor Ulrich Beck established a conceptual frame for what he called the *risk society*.[6] He claimed today's institutions (i.e., schools, government, etc.) and their subsequent philosophical belief systems, established during post-industrial society, marked a turning away from the guidance and wisdom embedded in nature and tradition. He suggested that the new risk society places higher value on technology and science, tending to ignore more culturally established belief systems, fate, seasonal realities, and common sense. It is concerned with control and systems of prediction to assess and manage diverse possible futures.[7] Science, technology, and the mechanistic worldview of Cartesian-Newtonian logic have become the central players in this transformation, leading to decision-making that operates at the conservative end of the risk spectrum.

Adding fuel to current levels of risk avoidance, today's incessant and pervasive hyper-media overexposes negative events and accelerates parent worry—for example, fear of strangers—creating hyper-parenting (i.e., trying to provide every advantage for your child) and helicopter parenting (i.e., trying to protect your child from any real or perceived danger). If one is susceptible to negative messages, most newscasts today could sink one into a depressive mood. The extent of change from a society of nature and tradition to one of scientific prediction of future risk has led to significant diminishment of childhood experiences like self-exploration, decision-making, and confidence-building through playing in nature. Opportunities to safely engage in outdoor risky play are all but gone, unless in situations we create. The days of children running wild around the neighborhoods until they are called in at dark is a thing of the past. We can be nostalgic about our experiences, if we had them, or we can be pragmatic about educating others and reversing yet another "extinction of experience." So, children have far less free play than previous generations, are spending only minutes outside playing each day, and when they do, often are on playgrounds designed by injury prevention specialists as opposed to child development specialists.[8]

Outdoor Risky Play

Risky play has been envisioned in six distinct forms, each providing a differing experience of risk and opportunity for child development. Norwegian early childhood education professor Ellen Beate Sandseter[9] has been at the forefront of this research and took the lead on developing the following categories of risky play, primarily in the context of early learning care and education settings. Consider examples for each type of risk from your childhood and that of your children or young clients. Imagine how and where each can be "experimented with":

- Heights (climbing, jumping)
- High speed (swinging, sliding, running)
- Dangerous tools (knives, axes, ropes)
- Dangerous elements (moving water, edges, fire)
- Rough and tumble (wrestling, play fighting, swordplay)
- Disappearing/getting lost (hiding, playing alone outdoors, exploring new areas)

Sandseter described children testing themselves with the ambiguous middle ground between feelings of *fear* and *excitement* during outdoor risky play, demonstrating a form of self-monitoring through engagement and avoidance of risk, which produces intense arousal and pleasure.[10] The *affordances* (theory described in chapter 2) of natural outdoor play spaces are closely tied to the intensity of the activities, along with the allowance of risk by nature-based therapy practitioners. Note that outdoor risky play is but one sub-category of *physical play*, which is described as active, exciting, and having elements of risk, and that we are not exploring here the full potential of play in general. Physical play itself is just one category in the broader typology of play. Although play has been thoroughly researched and articulated elsewhere for educational, developmental, and therapeutic ends, it often is overlooked and underappreciated in practice.

Taking a positive developmental approach to risk, and distinguishing *hazards* (potential for harm) from *risks* (potential for benefits too), allows us to design experiences and sessions that engage risk in outdoor play that does not unnecessarily place the client in harm's way. A child playing alongside a swollen and fast-flowing creek during spring runoff is exposed to a hazard, with little potential for a positive experience if he comes in contact with it. Conversely, a child competently climbs a tree to a height where she begins to experience fear; she has been exposed to risk in which she was challenged, and may be close to her threshold for risk, yet can develop risk-assessment and judgment in how to act and has also tested her physical capacity. It is the emotional place between fear and excitement that children have identified as

desirable in their risky play. Children in Sandseter's research, when trying to put words to these experiences, offered the descriptions "tickle
in my tummy" and "scaryfunny" that, in reflection, are quite insightful.

Kids are still playing outside at school, right? Sandseter and others[11]
have argued persuasively for the developmental benefits of less predictable and dynamic outdoor play spaces for children over the usual
artificially colored playscapes and flat playfields. Their basic argument
is that contrived government safety-approved playgrounds are not as
dynamic or diverse as natural settings and are designed to drastically
reduce hazards and risks, leaving much less opportunity to challenge
children's judgment, abilities, and curiosity. Trees, for example, afford
ample choices for branches, height, time off the ground, and a host of
play opportunities. Monkey bars, on the other hand, as safe as they
have been designed, clearly limit what children can do. The affordances
are radically different: equidistant spacing, stable height, identified
start and finish places, padded landing areas, etc. The manufactured
playscape pales in comparison to tree climbing from a self-directed,
creative, or exploratory perspective. In short, children develop more
skills and self-knowledge when they can engage with an environment, especially when the natural environment can provide nuanced
interaction to indicate success or failure. Think of crossing a stream
on stones spaced out at step length. How far apart are the stones? Are
they equal in distance, stable, wet or dry? What happens if I slip? Children prefer to use an artificial playscape in creative ways and not those
by design: climbing outside the structure rather than through it as
planned; collecting and sorting found objects under it; using it as an
obstacle in games of chase, tag, grounders, etc. Designers and builders
are not allowed to leave loose parts, a favorite of children. Surfaces
have to shed water and be soft and durable, so soil and sand are less
often found; again, playing in the dirt is another childhood favorite (although less so now as children are becoming far more sensitive to even
getting their hands and clothes dirty). Children and youth alike, and
many parents, enjoy building shelters in nature. This seems a natural
and evolutionary-influenced function to us (i.e., making a home in nature). Because the activity involves larger loose parts like branches and

fallen trees—not found in schoolyards, or even local parks—this type of activity requires being off-trail in a natural area.

Social, Psychological, and Physiological Benefits of Outdoor Play

"The biggest risk is keeping kids indoors." That was the title of the *Report Card on Physical Activity for Children and Youth in Canada* just a few years ago.[12] This annual report provides direction on children's health to Canadians through the lens of active play, physical literacy, and sedentary behavior, which are key factors related to numerous hypokinetic diseases currently on the rise, such as obesity and diabetes. That same year, two systematic reviews and a published position statement calling for increased access for all kids to play outdoors.[13] The authors, and there were many, promoted outdoor active play—along with its inherent risks—as an essential ingredient for healthy child development.[14] While child development is understood as more than just physical, others have also called for children to have increased contact with nature and free play for broader health benefits and potentially clinical applications.

Children and adolescents have had significantly reduced free play time over the past half-century in many nations while concurrently exhibiting a sharp rise in mental health pathology, which is not hard for today's parents to see.[15] This is an often-used play on adults' nostalgia: they only have to think back to their own childhood and compare it to their children's freedom to roam, play time unsupervised, and level of risk exposure. For me (Nevin), I try hard to allow my kids to roam and play as much as possible without direct parent supervision. I am privileged, however, to live on a quiet rural road away from traffic, city noise, and general busyness. Still, I consider my children's access to risky outdoor play more constrained than my own.

Benefits derived from contact with nature range from the restoration of attention, stress reduction, positive mood states, and emotional regulation to physiological health improvements from time spent in nature, as we outlined in chapter 3. Literature on connecting with nature accepts attention restoration theory without much critique and continues to suggest that nature is inherently stress-reducing and re-storative. We want to be clear that we contest this assumption because, for example, the risks of being lost, cold, or alone in nature are not likely be restorative experiences; likewise, wilderness environments may be associated with traumatic experiences in certain clients' personal, cultural, and generational histories. We do agree though, that under the right conditions and context, being in nature and accepting its inherent risks can be both restorative and meaningfully disruptive (i.e., burdensome, tiring, challenging) to one's mental, physical, and affective states. As Burroughs indeed suggested, we get our "senses put in order." Our recognition of the potential for both parasympathetic and sympathetic nervous system engagement allows us to design nature-based interventions and sessions which best address client needs.

Today, many practitioner-friendly and research-informed books de-scribe a range of outdoor therapeutic approaches; however, we haven't yet seen literature connecting therapeutic practice content with out-door risky play. Only recently the topic has gained some attention in the early childhood development field, and we welcome these efforts as they extend support for our work. We have found great resources pub-lished in the past few years that help define our understandings and practice of outdoor risky play in nature-based therapy. *Balanced and Barefoot*, written by pediatric occupational therapist Angela Hanscom, argues for unrestrained outdoor play, especially active engagement with nature, as critical for children's physical and cognitive develop-ment.[16] Her easily accessible writing is very hands-on for parents and educators, providing readers with plenty of activities and tips to try. Two recent academic textbooks have delivered the latest in research and practice on outdoor play. First, a 700-plus-page edited tome, *The SAGE Handbook of Outdoor Play and Learning*[17] describes theories, frameworks, and methodologies for research and critical reflections on outdoor play for children from leading international researchers and practitioners. The second, *Outdoor and Nature Play in Early Child-hood Education*,[18] will influence the education of child and youth edu-cators, at least in Canada. The authors have produced a comprehensive training book full of theoretical and practical applications, with case examples, images, and activities throughout. These publications are exciting for us to see, indicating that other fields and sectors are taking outdoor play seriously as an academic topic.

Facilitated activities outdoors range from sitting, walking, and exploring natural areas to more adventurous, and risk-related, play-based activities such as climbing, chasing, and sword play with branches. Professional and parental attitudes toward risk-taking are obviously influential on our work, and we take great care to ensure the safety of our clients. As we advocate for risky play as a central feature to our work, readers may raise additional concerns about this in therapeutic practice. What we can say is this: please read along and ask how risk sits with you. Do you see its benefits? Do you see limitations and challenges to this engagement in outdoor risky play? And what could you do in your context on this front? This chapter may prompt readers in the counseling, development, rehabilitation, and other therapy realms to consider how they *constrain* or *enable* outdoor risky play in their practices. If your contemplation of these questions has you interested in experimenting, then we may have done our job. We don't want children to get hurt through risky play. However, it pains us to think that many children miss out on potential developmental opportunities because they have not been allowed to experiment with risk—to test and expand their limits and to build confidence, regardless of ability, social, or economic contexts.

Nature and Play Therapy

Nature-based child-centered play therapy has recently been articulated in the literature and shares, in some ways, aspects of our approach, such as choosing a safe, accessible, and appealing natural venue for sessions; establishing boundaries; and utilizing natural materials for play and exploration. University of Florida researchers Jacqueline Swank and Sang Shin described this approach as a framework that brings traditional child-centered play therapy into a structured and private nature context.[19] They also stated that "nature is the playroom and natural materials are the therapeutic toys."[20] In contrast, our practice incorporates multiple approaches (i.e., play, adventure, family, narrative, somatic, and cognitive behavioral therapies) within diverse parks and natural spaces near our clients' community. Our practice is also philosophically centered on not perpetuating a human–nature dualism (i.e., nature as playroom, nature as toys). We try instead to connect our clients with nature in order to reunite them as part of nature rather than using nature as a resource to benefit from. This multifaceted therapeutic approach means we can adapt easily to logistical and clinical needs of clients and their families (accessible locations) and service a range of ages (~6 years old through adulthood). We have the opportunity to match outdoor locations to the goals and developmental level of each unique client and family. A young child may prefer a familiar park or beach to explore, while a teenager may prefer the challenge of a dense forest or rock scrambling to maintain their engagement in the therapeutic process. We can also match the inherent risk of the landscape and activity to their emotional and physical needs. It is often assumed that therapy demands containment and clear boundaries (such as in the case of trauma treatment); however, some presenting issues may be better serviced by encountering the unknown together (client and counselor), such as in the case of anxiety and emotion-regulation challenges.

Nature-based Therapy and Outdoor Risky Play

Children's highly constrained outdoor play, and specifically risky play, is effected by inflated public perceptions of risk, and subsequently enforced by the risk society. Also, any parent allowing their child to climb up the outside of a playscape in a public park may have seen, heard, or felt the uninvited scorn of other parents, even if they believe their child can competently complete the task. I (Nevin) had to answer to a group of older hikers on a local marine backpacking trail who were prepared to call the child protection authorities on me for allowing my then 6-year-old son to prepare and light a beach fire while I was cooking dinner on a portable campstove some 40 feet away. The reality of adventuring and playing outdoors is that children and youth, and sometimes parents too, may get hurt. Compared to accident and injury statistics of playing sports or being driven in a car, these activities are relatively harmless. In the case of my son, he was using his own knife, a 5th-birthday gift, which he had learned to use safely. He was asked to make the fire, a task he had completed before under supervision numerous times. I was not prepared for the negative reactions of the adults I encountered, most shocking as they appeared to be over 50 (i.e., I assumed they would be less risk averse). As my son looked to me for direction, I told our concerned visitors that all was well, and he carried on lighting the fire. The following three sections provide rationales for incorporating outdoor risky play in nature-based therapy: (1) to activate the anti-phobic response, (2) to assist in nervous system regulation and maintaining boundaries, and (3) to develop self-efficacy and foster resiliency.

So Why Risk?

In addressing childhood anxieties, the non-associative theory suggests that exposure to risk is developmentally related and that children need to be presented with opportunities to test and adapt to risk as they grow.[21] Anxiety around heights, for example, is developmentally appropriate at earlier ages, yet with exposure and practice, a child moves past the fear and can rationally determine how high to climb based on their competencies and self-knowledge. Given ample opportunities to experiment while tree climbing, a child can develop skills and knowledge about their own capacity, as well as the physical strength to manage various situations. If they were never allowed to climb trees, it stands to reason that they have not had the opportunity to overcome this fear.

It could be argued that our evolutionary capacities are not compatible with our current environments. Put simply, our indoor, electronic, and media-influenced lives have removed us from the daily challenges of outdoor living and travel for which we were evolutionarily designed (i.e., humans were designed to walk a distance of about a half marathon daily, acclimatize to daily and seasonal temperature change, and sleep when it gets dark and not stay up under artificial light). As most children grow and develop, the risks they face through challenging environments and experiences are significantly minimized today, and the fear of those risks that were appropriate earlier in life remain intact, thereby producing anxiety. While the evidence for this assertion is just being established, we know that inactive children become inactive adolescents and are much less likely to be active adults. If this truth stands, then it's not hard to accept that children need to address their fears and anxieties as they grow and develop, including those related to risky activity. Current levels of mental health issues (e.g., anxiety and depression) in adolescent populations mentioned earlier in the book should suggest that something is surely amiss in child development.

Real Risk, Co-regulation, and Respecting Boundaries and Limits

As outlined above, North American children spend much of their time indoors, and the likelihood of encountering authentic risk when outdoors is minimal due to the highly managed and constrained environments in which they now play (e.g., play spaces with cushioned surfaces, significantly lower swings). We argue that invaluable opportunities are being missed, such as navigating real risk, particularly with the support of an attentive adult. We advocate for children to have experiences of authentic risk to learn how to regulate their stress response and to develop respect for adhering to boundaries and understanding limits.

Real Risk

Opportunities to engage in risky play allow for the activation of our sympathetic nervous system. However, there is a clear beginning and end to the heightened experience due to it being offered in an intentional manner. Engaging in outdoor risky play brings forward the life-preserving faculties of our mammalian nervous system, which offer profound opportunities for self-growth and insight.[22] Throughout human evolution, these faculties were activated at key times when risk and the immediate demands of the natural elements were present. Modern life does not offer the same experiences as readily. Instead, a child's nervous system is constantly responding to abstract demands like maintaining peer relations, familial conflict, school expectations, news of environmental and social degradation, and other external stressors that can lead to chronic stress responses and subsequent mental and physical health ailments.

Navigating immediate perceived risk necessitates present-moment awareness and helps to shift people into the here and now, activating their senses and developing their skills to interact with the environment in a more nuanced way. Further, once the stressor has been successfully navigated, there is an opportunity to shift from sympathetic arousal to highly restorative and restful parasympathetic states. For example, when children are given the opportunity to cross a creek on wet and wobbly stones, there is often an apprehensive moment of pause just before embarking. They almost intuitively gather themselves and start interacting with their environment on a moment-to-moment basis. Knowing the consequences of slipping are real, they are no longer thinking about things in the past or future but instead are highly focused on the task at hand. Once within reach of the end, they often take a small leap to finish the traverse, followed by a smile and obvious vitality affects. The negotiation of embarking over the creek also involves the practice of risk-assessment, a very important life skill for children to develop. It is essential that we support clients in determining what activity lies within their *challenge zone* (see chapter 5), and is thus a reasonable risk to take, and equally what lies in their *danger zone* and sets them up for emotional or physical injury. Some questions they might ponder are how stable are the stones, how slippery are they, how deep is the water, is there a current, what will it be like if I fall. In contemplating these, they develop the capacity to pause before beginning and make an assessment of self and the environment.

Co-regulation

In the therapeutic context, risky play happens within a supportive and attuned relationship—as opposed to a child just taking risks on their own, or worse, among an influential peer group.[23] The major benefit of having a caring and attentive adult with whom to share the mutual exploration of nature and risk is the process of collaborative problem-solving and co-regulation throughout the activity. While allowing their child to climb a tree, parents often fall into the trap of focusing on "be careful" messages that may undermine the child's intuition or confidence and suggest the construct of "child as vulnerable" versus "child as resilient and capable of learning." From a neurobiological perspective, risky play activates the sympathetic branch of the autonomic nervous system (i.e., fight or flight) in combination with the social engagement system. Thus, risky play provides the opportunity to practice maintaining social connection while exploring the edges of "fear through small doses of sympathetic arousal."[24] Tree climbing in the context of a therapy session, for example, allows for the counselor to engage in a process of amplifying the present-moment experience of climbing the tree, helping to bring awareness to the child's emotions, cognitions, and decision-making processes and mirroring their process as they navigate the challenges the tree offers. The therapist may also join the child or family in the tree, navigating the risk together in a way that helps the child develop stronger awareness of choices, boundaries, trust, and positive self-talk.

Such risky play is profoundly relational and can assist in the development of social skills such as empathy and compassion.[25] Therapist, parents, and children become highly tuned into each other by necessity to ensure the safety and success of the activity. When facilitating outdoor risky play, knowing your clients and tracking their progress/ state is essential for success. Further, risky play, like other forms of play, involves the constant regulation of the limbic system by the neocortex.[26] Consider "talking down your fear" when trying to descend from a steep slope: one has to stay engaged in the present moment and access higher-order coping skills to prevent the body's alarm system from taking over and freezing. Child psychologist Daniel Siegel suggests to parents that when children are struggling and become flooded by emotion, it is best to first connect and then redirect. As counselors, we take the same approach when helping someone regulate themselves during a challenging moment. We acknowledge the tension, the fear, and uncertainty, and then attempt to cue their internal coping skills and highlight strengths. Engaging children in supported risky play allows for rich opportunities to practice and ultimately foster this "whole-brain approach" in our clients.

Respect for Boundaries and Limits

Helping clients to remain regulated and follow boundaries during risky play has proven to be a powerful experience in our practice, especially during activities such as fire-making, bushcraft tool use, and climbing. We have found that natural consequences associated with the risk are invaluable teachers. For example, we require that children learn and demonstrate safe knife practices before they are able to carve on their own. We call this the *sharps test*. It includes the skill of self-reflection by identifying if they are in a calm state prior to starting, learning how to use the tool responsibly, monitoring who is in their proximal space, and following these boundaries throughout the activity. Despite our attempts to prevent injury, inevitably there may be occurrences where the boundaries are pushed and small cuts result. The immediacy of the boundary transgression and the resulting consequence is a powerful teacher, clear and unambiguous feedback. The reality of the natural consequence supports future adherence to the boundary, not because they have been instructed to do so but because they know it's necessary in order to prevent injury. Further, when offering risky activities to clients, we clearly explain the limits regarding what is permissible to engage in during the activity. Clients know that they are being given the opportunity to participate in this exciting activity so long as they respect and adhere to these guidelines. The result is an increase in focused attention and a level of compliance that often surprises parents who are accustomed to witnessing their children in resistant and oppositional stances.

Case Example

A 10-year-old boy, Cody, was struggling with self-regulation and mounting conflict with his parents, especially when they enforced limits. As a result, many of his privileges had been taken away, and trust was seriously eroded. Cody was highly reticent about starting counseling, because it felt more like a punishment than an opportunity to help shift this negative pattern. After a couple of sessions to build trust and familiarity with the nature-based approach, and for the clinician to gauge his readiness for risky play, he was offered the chance to work with flint and steel (natural tools for creating sparks) to light a fire. Immediately, there was a level of engagement not seen before in the interactions. Further, to the surprise of his parents, he exhibited attentive listening and adherence to the boundaries laid out for the activity's success and safety. Cody was open to feedback, as the activity was challenging enough that without guidance he would not succeed. As he worked on this task, the counselor provided immediate reflections and observations, allowing Cody to regulate his mounting frustration as he attempted to create a spark to ignite the charcloth (pre-burned cotton material that a spark will ignite). Further, the experience aided the family in remembering that Cody was capable of being responsible and collaborative and following expectations. The fire was lit, and care was taken to ensure that everyone, including the environment, was not at risk from the flame. Cody left the session with a sense of excitement, relief from the bombardment of negativity he had been immersed in, and a successful experience of navigating boundaries and adhering to limits.

Risk and Developing Self-efficacy and Resiliency

Developing knowledge about hazards and the subsequent skills to navigate one's environment are key rationales for risky play in nature-based therapy. Being exposed to discomfort and challenging situations that can be overcome is essential to learning how to bounce back and have the confidence to do so. Nature is filled with examples of this resiliency (e.g., a tree that survives a windstorm often develops stronger root systems). Opportunities to learn and grow from our mistakes are becoming less available, as demonstrated by athletic events where medals are given to every participant and the tendency for parents to step in to solve their children's academic or social problems. "Helicopter parenting" may be perceived as creating more safety for our children and stronger attachment bonds, but it may also lead to heightened overall child anxiety and inability to cope with failure and mistakes on their own. Resiliency researcher and professor Michael Ungar has suggested that young children have been "bubble wrapped" and that their conditions for development in the risk-society are "too safe for their own good."[27] In nature-based therapy, we have the opportunity to work experientially with this concept by taking small risks, exposing kids to uncertainty or suspense, giving them chances to fail, and developing new approaches for success.

A favorite game for many of our clients is called Sneaker and may serve as an instructive example. It taps into the natural passions of children to hide and sneak in the forest, presenting a simple challenge with multiple opportunities for learning from mistakes, and ultimately building to success. One person acts as the prey animal and closes their eyes, while the other players act as predators who are trying to sneak up on the prey in short increments. If the predator is heard by the prey, then they have to move back to the start and sneak up again. This game can be played in treed areas or in rocky/hilly areas with varying levels of ground and bushes to hide behind. In this simple and exciting game, the risks involve traveling quickly over uneven and unpredictable terrain, and jumping behind natural barriers, with the potential to bump, slip, and trip along the way. The possibility of getting caught elicits excitement as well as that element of uncertainty or nervousness we aim to engage. Discomfort may occur from their hiding position or from the need to be quiet and still. (This hiding moment also provides the chance for kids to get up close with nature, smelling the bark, noticing the details of moss on the rock, etc.) Yet, even with this risk, uncertainty, and discomfort, the kids are generally keen and determined to reach their goal and catch the prey. Most often the children, and participating parents, are heard by the prey at some point and generally have to start over several times, providing the opportunity to work with feelings of disappointment and frustration. Ultimately, children learn to adjust their strategy to make a more successful approach, and when they finally tag that prey (could even be the therapist), they feel pride and success. A reflective conversation follows the game to explore the strategies learned, examine what worked or did not work, and amplify the qualities in the child that led to success (e.g., determination, focus, intention, planning, stillness, courage).

Case Example

An 11-year-old girl, Laura, was referred to us for severe anxiety leading to school avoidance, having already missed more than forty days of middle school. She had previously been successful academically and in extracurricular activities but was having social difficulties that were causing her stress. Office-based visits with a psychologist had not made any progress because Laura refused to speak to the clinician, sitting silent through several sessions. When meeting with one of us for the first time in a local forested park, she also initially refused to speak. After some introductions, and learning more about her current situation, we suggested playing Sneaker (described above). Laura immediately became more animated and expressed interest in playing the game alongside her father. They both got caught on their first few approaches, but ultimately Laura demonstrated great skill and persistence in making her sneaky approach on the prey (therapist). After experiencing her first success, she began to engage more openly, respond to questions, and was willing to discuss her struggle with anxiety. They played a few more times, and the prey became replaced with the concept of "school" that Laura now had to sneak up on. Through this game, we were able to amplify some of her strengths (courage, determination, and planning) and explore how she could apply them to the challenge of going into the classroom. After this session, Laura expressed willingness to attend further counseling and to begin exploring coping skills that would help her return to school. This form of outdoor risky play was able to build connection and pathways for communication that may have been unlikely to emerge in an office setting.

Conclusion

This chapter focused on outdoor risky play and distinct yet connected rationales for its clinical applications: self-regulation, setting and maintaining boundaries, and self-efficacy. While our propositions are primarily directed at practitioners and therapists with access to natural environments, we believe that a nature-based approach utilizing risk could be incorporated into early years, youth work, social work, education, and other helping and healing milieus.

We acknowledge that working in nature is not for every practitioner, nor is the concept and engagement with risk. We find the natural environment ideal for activities, sessions, and interventions that can easily be modified to increase risk in our clients' perceptions. The meaningful integration of environmental conditions and activity choices creates the milieu. Comfort with changing weather conditions, spending time in a forest, and getting dirty, wet, or cold are all a part of the work for us but may not be for all. We accept and adapt to the conditions that nature offers us. We encourage therapeutic practitioners desiring to use nature-based approaches to train in outdoor education and develop skills to facilitate experiential activities in nature. We must practice ethically and within the scope or mandate of our employment, competencies, and qualifications, especially in the context of risk; we do not support practice that otherwise ignores these necessary skills, abilities, and knowledge. Last, we stand by our conviction that play, and specifically outdoor risky play, holds significant and meaningful opportunities for many families to address issues and move toward healthier relationships and capacities.

7

Nature as Co-therapist

Nature itself is the best physician.

HIPPOCRATES

Nature-based therapy is located in a diverse range of ecotherapy practices, all involve partnering with nature for the joint purpose of healing both human and natural systems.[1] At first glance, these ideas may resemble traditional Indigenous healing practices where land and culture are considered sacred; while recognizing the danger in naming them as such, and to avoid acts of appropriation, we do strongly advocate for the reunion of humans with nature as an absolute necessity for all nations and peoples. We remind our readers that ecopsychology and related therapies have emerged as a counterculture response to Western conceptualizations of humans as separate and dominant over nature. Further, we are not immune to past and ongoing colonial processes of erasing and replacing alternate ways of knowing by our own dominant worldviews.[2]

Long-standing traditions of collaborative relationships with nature have been drawn on to promote health and wellness. For many Indigenous peoples, the land and their cultural practices together create the lifeways of their existence and health of their community. We recognize the incommensurability of speaking about nature as a separate entity that supports health and wellness with both ecopsychological and many Indigenous land-based worldviews. Discussions about partnering with nature can easily slide into the language of "using" nature for healing or personal gain. The extreme version of this slippery slope would be using nature as simply a pretty backdrop from which one's conventional therapy can take place. This chapter explores how practitioners can partner with nature in an impactful way, while maintaining the perspective of humans as subsystems of nature and inextricably connected, co-dependent, and co-arising.[3] We introduce a model of sharing nature with children and youth that was developed decades ago and is still widely used today, primarily in environmental education settings, along with therapeutic applications illuminated by case examples.

Following the release of Richard Louv's *The Last Child in the Woods*,[4] the conversation about children and nature took a momentous upturn. Louv's sloganeering with "Leave no child inside" and "nature-deficit disorder" became commonplace in the conversation aimed at counteracting an epidemic sweeping America: children suffering from a lack of contact with nature. A creative spin on the attention deficit diagnosis captivated parents, and many in youth-serving fields were talking about how to get kids outside and engaging in unstructured play, as they had done as kids. Developing a sense of enchantment toward the natural world and accepting one's inextricable place within the web of life is essential for the preservation and protection of life on this planet and also to partnering effectively with the natural world. However, among all the hyped frenzy of the need to get children outside, there is a danger of replicating ways of relating with nature that got us here in the first place: specifically, that nature is an external object, devoid of intrinsic worth, and existing for the sole purpose of benefiting humans. This perspective is pervasive, often subtly so: "We need to get our children in nature so they can be healthier" or well-intentioned medical professionals prescribing doses of nature to "treat" mental and physical health concerns. In both cases, nature is being valued for its instrumental use and is viewed as somehow able to be separated and packaged for human consumption and benefit. Florence William's recent book, *The Nature Fix*, exemplifies this not just by title but how she depicts the research and the researchers she interviews. Williams provides overviews of the type of effect nature has, as measured by each researcher, and then discusses the dose effect and how they relate to one another.[5]

A more holistic way of understanding human and nature relations is through a relational and ecological worldview where we hold a deep sense of connectedness and recognition that we are all entangled in the web of life, the dynamic living system of the Earth. From this perspective, nature is an extension of oneself, and tapping into our connection allows for insights and wisdom to emerge that otherwise would not be possible. For example, it is a stretch for most people from a Western background to give rocks or a tree a voice and to try to speak from their perspective. We have found that a considerable amount of unlearning must occur in order for people, therapists included, to comfortably be able and willing to take on the subject position of an earthly creature and let go of individualized egoic notions of the self in exchange for an understanding that a much larger ecological self is possible. We have found that providing clients opportunities to connect with their earthly selves, even if not initially recognized as such, is a powerful vehicle for shifts in consciousness toward an ecological worldview and ability to partner with nature in deeper and more complex ways.

Like other co-facilitation arrangements, the strength of the relationship between facilitators is a key part of an effective learning or therapeutic process. To what extent does a nature-based therapist see themselves as part of nature is a critical question that needs to be asked and addressed. To co-facilitate with nature, a therapist has first to establish a significant appreciation for, and relationship with, nature herself. Further, the extent to which clients see themselves as a part of nature is also important to factor in when considering how to partner with the natural world.

Nature operates at a different pace than the modern technological world. Constantly changing, her cycles occur simultaneously on different levels and at different speeds. Arriving at a wild space often brings with it a sense of relief and a homecoming as one is able to reconnect with that which is a part of them but also much larger than their "self." However, quite often children, youth, and families arrive at a session either with hesitation and concern about what the process is going to be like, especially early on in the therapeutic relationship, or distracted and disconnected from their body, nature, and the present moment. In the first situation, perhaps they were told they must attend, were dragged out of the house after spending many hours interacting with a screen, or were barely keeping themselves afloat with all the to-dos on their list. Attempting to connect with someone in a distracted and un-receptive state is incredibly challenging; connecting them with nature first is actually easier.

Nature is filled with dynamic living and organic systems. The rapid shifting of winds, crashing of waves, or cacophony of birdsong and in-sect noises in a forest or the slow unfolding of seasonal changes, geo-logical processes of erosion, or the carving and shaping of rivers are but a few examples of the different speeds of nature that are simul-taneously unfolding. Shifting into alignment and resonance with the language, speed, and felt sense of the more-than-human world is an essential component of partnering with nature as not doing so means you are not paying attention; nor are you in relation with one of your greatest allies. Being present to the messages of nature, allowing them to wash over you, seep into your cells, and shift and transform you, is the doorway to her medicine. How to assist people to tune in, become aware, share an experience, and amplify its benefits are critical tasks for a nature-based therapist.

The Flow Learning Model

Joseph Cornell, environmental educator, naturalist, and much-loved author of the *Sharing Nature with Children* books, articulates a simple and elegant approach to engage and connect with nature that he calls *flow learning*.[6] He recognizes the importance of meeting people where they are at and the often-challenging task of helping to shift people into a receptive and open state of mind (and body) optimal for connection. Through his years of work in education and training outdoor leaders, he began to realize a pattern was evident in the types and sequencing of nature connection activities he was offering across ages and popu-lations. These observations led to the four stages of his flow learning approach:

Stage 1: Awaken Enthusiasm
Focus: Invitation to connect and be present
Quality: Playfulness and alertness

Stage 2: Focus Attention
Focus: Sharpen awareness and receptivity of nature
Quality: Receptivity

Stage 3: Direct Experience
Focus: Let people experience for themselves
Quality: Absorption

Stage 4: Share Inspiration
Focus: Pass along meaningful stories of nature connection
Quality: Idealism

Note: For a detailed description of flow learning, and a great range of activities for each stage, see *Sharing Nature with Children II*.[7]

We have found these stages are effective in working with all ages and groups, although particularly good for ages 8 to 12. Developmentally, this group often needs support to shift into the present moment and away from external preoccupations, such as video games or rigid behavioral patterns. Further, kids this age are often less open to explore and discover than when they were younger (4 to 7) and often need some more coaxing to engage. Youth, 13 to 18, can be receptive to these stages, yet peer influence is a key factor to consider, as well as their drive for autonomy, which may create a reluctance to follow a particular plan or structure. The main point is that being present to nature makes all the difference, and this is not always an easy state to cultivate. In each of the flow learning stages, opportunities for nature to be a co-facilitator arise, and the assistance of a mindful facilitator can invite a fuller exploration, revealing more layers of potential growth and connection. The stages are a helpful framework, a map, but by no means are they the territory. Maps are helpful tools for direction, and in this case, the parts of the flow learning model can guide a nature-based experience, each offering insights into the transformative potential of nature-immersed counseling. The reality is that a nature-based counseling session is different than offering a series of nature connection activities in a recreational context, due to the therapeutic intent and agreed-upon goals initiated during consent to counseling. Therefore, it is important to understand the valuable potential each stage offers.

Rather than viewing them as a linear process, each nature-based counseling session cycles through these stages numerous times and ways; all aspects can be available at any given moment, but particular ones will be the focus, depending on the unique situation. What follows is an exploration into each of the four aspects of flow-learning from the perspective of a nature-based counselor. You may also consider how the flow-learning model informs your current work, and how you may utilize it relative to your clients' needs.

Awaken Enthusiasm: Reinfusing Aliveness

The word "enthusiasm" comes from the Greek *entheos*, which means the god within. The first opportunity for nature to assist with the therapeutic process is to reinfuse a sense of aliveness into a person's life. For people who are already nature connected, this may be facilitated by inviting a moment of silence and gratitude; for those less nature aware, playful activities that help them shift into the present moment are ideal. One-to-one counseling sessions could begin by inviting clients to notice things they find beautiful and interesting in their surroundings; this may allow them to slow down and orientate to the space and open up an avenue for expression of their appreciation for nature.

> Everything in nature
> invites us constantly
> to be what we are.
> GRETEL EHRLICH

Alternatively, other fun ways to awaken their enthusiasm can include visiting a nearby berry patch, climbing a tree, or finding a special spot in nature they feel drawn toward.

By awakening enthusiasm, you are inviting the child's body-heart-mind to arrive and adequately prepare to be receptive for the experiences to come in the therapeutic process. Cornell talks about drawing on children's passions, such as utilizing play to hook them into the experience. He explains how the quicker they are able to have a thought that "this is fun," the more likely they are to relax and open up to the experience. This isn't just the case with children. We have found adults too have their inner child just waiting to spring into action given the right conditions. Realistically, this most often occurs when a parent is accompanying their child; in individual sessions with an adult, feelings of awkwardness and concern about acting childish, are sometimes too hard to overcome.

The Coyote Mentoring Model from the Wilderness Awareness School[8] also talks about utilizing children's passions to foster engagement and describes the use of games involving hiding, seeking, sneaking, hunts, errands, adventures, and make-believe to light the fire of enthusiasm. The model also introduces the idea of "motivating species," which are flora and fauna one can climb, catch, easily observe, and harvest. It explains how these species tap into our ancestral drive to explore, gather, and hunt and are particularly powerful at shifting us into the present moment and captivating our attention. For example, a hawk flying nearby will more often than not cause a person to pause and admire the beauty and grace of its presence. Or a tree with branches spaced in just the right way, where you can comfortably climb and find a place to sit, is so hard to resist. Berry bushes, equally irresistible, allow for searching and harvesting a delicious reward to excite your taste buds. Utilizing play and drawing on children's passions is an effective approach at all stages of the flow learning process but particularly important to incorporate to some degree at the beginning of a session.

Having already discussed the therapeutic value of play in chapter 6, we are again emphasizing how nature affords us opportunities for rich, engaging play that is helpful not only in calming and regulating the nervous system but also in priming people for deeper interaction and connection with nature as the session unfolds. So often people arrive at sessions with their nervous systems on high alert. They are essentially in survival mode as they attempt to cope with the stressors of life; from a physiological perspective, they are in a highly specific neuropsychological state that is intended to keep them safe and mitigate danger. Literally, their perception of the world is altered through this lens of survival. By awakening enthusiasm and inviting the soothing embrace of both your own relationship and that of the natural world, you are inviting in a whole different way of being. Fostering social engagement puts the brakes on the sympathetic nervous system and allows for a different perception of the world to emerge, one that is more creative, flexible, and hopeful.

The Awakening Enthusiasm stage is also a critical time to establish the therapeutic frame, specifically, aiding the client to become aware that they are entering into a collaboration with the therapist and natural world to create a therapeutic space intended for the possibility of change and healing. This frame can be established in a number of ways, depending on the setting and participants. As Gretel Ehrlich so eloquently describes, once a person truly arrives in nature, present to their surroundings, they are then afforded an opportunity to be accepted for who they are and as they areand to be what they are.[9]

For sessions with children and their parents, after a brief welcome and orientation to the specific place and traditional lands, a check-in activity can be offered where the child and parent can interact with nature to help share their current inner space and hopefully encourage feelings of arriving and acceptance. For example, they can be given the option to select two trees and imagine a line reaching between them, one end representing ease and joy and the other end struggle. Having them decide which tree represents which end of the spectrum often leads to really interesting reflections and insights being drawn by the metaphors being presented (explored further below). The therapist would then invite the clients to move to the corresponding spot on the spectrum, based on their answer to a variation of the following questions:

- Right now, I am...
- Right now, my body feels...
- As you think of your week, how do you feel?
- Right now, how do you feel about your family?
  (Other topics could include school, work, friends, transitioning between parent's homes.)

Encouraging clients to reflect on their current experience of past events has been effective in assisting people to deepen their unfolding experience of the "here and now." The goal of this stage again is to raise aliveness and presence, so being too focused on cerebral accounts of past events, especially negative ones, can actually do a disservice to the client's ability to be receptive to the third entity, the dynamic living systems of the Earth, that is, nature as co-therapist.

Further, the therapist joining in and modeling skills of reflecting on their own experience is also a key aspect (e.g., possibly demonstrating an activity of appreciation for the features of the session location). It supports the normalization of sharing feelings as well as acceptance for whatever feelings are arising. Another playful check-in activity is called Faces. In this case, clients create three different faces on the ground, using natural objects in the surroundings. We suggest the faces represent happy, neutral, and sad and be arranged along a spectrum, with spaces between them, so all the nuanced feelings in between can be included. After the sculptures are finished, and admired, the client is asked to stand closest to the spot along the continuum that is relevant to how they are feeling in the moment. By being invited to move their bodies, interact with natural objects, and feel accepted for exactly who they are in the moment, clients will hopefully be more ready and willing to immerse themselves deeper into their experiences as the session progresses—or in future sessions if the activities take on a latent effect.

Focus Attention: Sharpen Awareness and Receptivity of Nature

Have you ever had an experience of being in nature, say going for a hike, and your attention has been completely enveloped by either thoughts of your life or conversations about topics that have nothing to do with your surroundings? It's similar to moments in your car where you may be switching to your favorite radio station and then you cannot quite recall how you got from point A to point B. A little frightening, but the key message is your attention was not focused on the environment and your body was on autopilot. To emphasize the frequency of this type of "doing-mode," we ask clients to join us in acting out what we call The City Shuffle. This often looks like people's eyes glued to their cell phones, a quick erratic gait, and zero interest in connecting with other people or their environment. Sound familiar? It sure looks funny as we bump into each other in this fun improv activity. With looming deadlines, frenzied mornings trying to get the kids off to school, and the fast-paced consumer society with its

> *If we live in awareness, it is easy to see miracles everywhere.*
> THICH NHAT HAHN

bombardment of advertising telling us we need the next best gadget, it's no surprise that this city shuffle is so often the norm.

Bringing awareness to this habitual way of moving in the world also creates an opportunity to practice another way of being, what Western mindfulness teacher and advocate Jon Kabat-Zinn calls the shift from "human-doing back to human-being."[10] After laughing about the hilarity of the dominant way we navigate our worlds, clients are then invited to imagine what it might be like to be an animal living in the forest and either hearing a predator or being one. Perhaps a rabbit, mid-snack, catches the sound of a red-tailed hawk flying nearby. Or maybe a more domestic example: their pet cat stalking a favorite stuffed mouse and preparing to pounce. The stillness and sharpening of their senses is palpable. They start moving with refined precision, as if they have tapped into the collective experience bank of their hunter-gatherer ancestors, who knew how to move in this way to ensure their survival. It's engaging and fun, familiar and foreign, all at the same time.

Cultivating the skills of selected awareness to one's outer landscape is a key component of nature-based therapy. This heightened awareness provides the necessary conditions from which all of the other work can unfold. Simply put, you need to be aware (e.g., all senses alert) and present (e.g., conscious in the here and now) in order to build meaningful relationships. This is true with friends, family, and nature. Further, as soon as people are invited to be present to their outer landscape, we have found that clients are more often than not grateful, and receptive, for this invitation. Perhaps it is because we have persevered as a species over hundreds of thousands of years of evolution by those ancestors who were aware of their surroundings and thus could keep themselves, and their families, safe and fed. Alternatively, it could be the fact that being mindful is healthy for our brains and for the management of stress. In this regard, we have found plenty of strong evidence and a broad range of benefits from mindfulness as a practice to encourage our clients to engage in it and develop this trait.[11] Whatever the reason, awareness is the key ingredient we are after.

Australian clinical psychologist George Burns shared his ecopsychotherapy approach in his 1998 book, *Nature-guided Therapy*.[12] He defined his approach as accurately describing the interconnection between mind-body and Earth. Early in his career, he recognized the profound impact positive experiences in nature had on his clients' lives and his own. He took particular interest in how sensory awareness of pleasing environments can lead to positive shifts, or what he calls a "desired positive affective state." He developed a sensual awareness inventory, which assists in identifying pleasant sensations across the five senses (touch, taste, smell, sight, hearing), and uses it to help design tasks that the clients can do on their own to bring about positive shifts in their lives. Interestingly, he found that almost all of the pleasurable sensations that clients listed in the inventory involved nature. One would think watching television, or the feeling of cool air blowing from a fan, would make the list, but surprisingly, they only rarely did. Burns explains how our senses

> are the vehicle for establishing the person-nature relationship, and can be accessed for developing therapeutic directives [,...] strategies that can shift us from an inner symptom focus to more pleasurable experiences: techniques that can facilitate our life-nourishing energies, assist us toward peak experiences, and promote a sense of health.[13]

The main technique he offers is called *sensate focusing*:

> a technique for helping the client tune into the sensations of pleasure, comfort, and well-being. It is a shifting of the focus from the unpleasant and the undesirable into the desirable. It is a redirection from an inner, ruminative, introspective focus to the pleasures that prevail in the natural environment and in one's relationship with nature.[14]

The basic premise is to move clients away from behavioral expectations and goal-oriented behavior and toward their own sensory experiences. By focusing on pleasurable sensations, the problem-solving, comparative, evaluative, and judgmental thoughts about doing it "right" slip into the background, while an acceptance for what is, and the sensual being that you are, assumes the foreground.

Activity to Focus Attention: The Nature Detective
As mentioned, helping to shift clients into the present moment is amplified by attending to the senses and how they are perceiving their world. The skill of focused attention can be developed, and then directed, to not only an examination of the outer landscape but also the child's inner world of thoughts, feelings, images, and sensations that are constantly streaming through them. An approach created to assist children to develop greater awareness of their inner and outer worlds is something we call the *Nature Detective series*. Essentially this is a nature scavenger hunt, which is scaffolded over the course of many sessions to meet the developmental level and therapeutic goals of the child. Again, accurately reading the client is key to the success of this practice, as some light up at the opportunity, while others see it as another undesired task they are being asked to do by an adult. This approach to increasing sensory awareness is often most effective in kids ages 6 to 11. Here is how a conversation introducing the nature detective series intervention might unfold:

Counselor: "What do you think is the most important skill we need to survive in the wilderness?"
Client: "Is it fire, or shelter building skills?"
Counselor: "Yes, those are very important, but there is something even more important. Any more guesses?"
Client: "Hmm, what about water, we can only live for three days without it."
Counselor: "Yes, again you are naming some essential things, but I've found the most important skill is awareness. Why do you think that is?"
Client: "Hmm, I'm too not sure."
Counselor: "Well, awareness of our surroundings and how we are doing is what allows us to know where the water is, how to set up a shelter in a safe spot, what animals may be around, and what food may be available. Does that make sense? Here's another question. What does a detective do?"
Client: "They solve problems?"
Counselor: "Exactly, they use their awareness skills to look for clues to

help them solve problems. My final questions: Do you like video games by chance, and are you good at them?"

Client: "Oh yeah, I do, and I am VERY good at them."

Counselor: "Wonderful, I thought so. That's perfect, because I have an activity for us to try. It's called Nature Detective. It's sort of like a video game in the sense that there are different levels and each level gets harder and requires you to learn skills. The detective part is that you will be using your awareness to find different things in the forest and solve problems. How does this sound. Is it something you'd like to try?"

Client: "Oh yeah. Let's try. Can my mom help me?"

Counselor: "Of course, working as team sounds like a great idea to me. Here is level one. Take your time to tap into the awareness skills we have already been practicing. Do you remember walking really slowly and opening all your senses to take in the forest? Well, you may need to use those techniques to solve some of the questions. Let's start."

The aim of Nature Detective is to engage the child so they will be willing to explore their outer landscapes and, through practice, start to transfer the skills of selective attention to their inner landscape as well. By framing awareness as the most important survival skill, any time the client demonstrates awareness of something that is unfolding in the present environment, such as noticing a mushroom peeking through the soil or a bird perched in a tree, the counselor can then acknowledge that behavior as "awareness" and positively reinforce it. Further, the counselor is now in a better position to model this behavior and have it received by the client as a desired skill. The video game analogy allows the child to relate the experience to something they may already have a positive association with, as well as ensure a shared understanding as to how the process may unfold with increasing difficulty, requiring skill development, and that the game can be mastered by getting to level 10. Rather than having a pre-established set of levels and questions, tailoring to the unique needs of the client as well as the environment is recommended. The first few levels focus primarily on the outer landscape and combine sensory exploration with learning about nature. Further, the tasks are easily accomplished, which builds confidence and helps to ensure engagement.

Sample tasks in lower levels:
- Find a leaf bigger than your hand
- Find a bird, a bug, a slug, mushroom etc.
- Listen quietly for three sounds
- Find a Douglas fir cone
- Find something prickly, soft, a certain color or texture
- Find a tree that fits you just right

As the client progresses through the levels, they are challenged with more difficult tasks, as well as being invited to explore their inner landscape at greater depths. Further, tasks that are very specific to the individual's goals can be incorporated.

Sample tasks of higher levels:
- Go on a feeling adventure: find things in nature that remind you of being sad, happy, scared, angry, worried, etc.
- Find a spot in nature that you really like and sit quietly for one minute
- Close your eyes and scan your inner landscape for thirty seconds
- What color are you (blue, green, yellow, red), and describe why
- Find an animal track that is not a dog; do you know what it is?
- Find a plant that can be used to make cordage

At the end of the ten levels, specifically with children, a certificate of accomplishment is a useful contribution to the client's file, which, according to narrative therapists, is an important element in helping clients shift from problem-saturated identities toward their preferred identity. More on this narrative therapy approach will be explored in the section on sharing stories. Tasks at each level may also incorporate and address therapeutic goals by adding related follow-up questions, such as asking your client to find an object that might represent a presenting problem.

Older youth may or may not show much interest in the seemingly childish activity as Nature Detective. Don't let that assumption stop you from trying though, as we have been surprised at how engaged some teens get with nature-based games—though you might just need to up the challenge level. The teen brain, different from the child's, operates generally at lower levels of dopamine although it spikes in intensity when teens are engaged physically and emotionally in an activity. The experience of boredom or passivity can be shifted to heightened levels of excitement if the activity is thrilling enough or has positive rewards, according to the teen.[15] Finding activities that focus attention for teens is doubly rewarding in that post-activity self-reflection and processing is then better facilitated. Tasks should be framed as fun and serious, challenging and rewarding, thereby meeting a number of needs for the teen brain and increasing engagement. Ask teens to trust their intuition, or to allow "heartfelt" decisions to be made, and then discuss later. Processing in the teen brain can lead to impulsive behavior, and if your tasks can trigger engagement, impulsive or not, reinforce this as a positive attribute. Teens seek novelty and often complain about being bored; that is the low dopamine stage. The need for challenge, unique experiences, and fun can result in negative or dangerous choices. Nature Detective and other activities can meet a number of these ideal needs for teens and engage the client-counselor relationship toward therapeutic ends as well. As child psychologist Daniel Siegel has pointed out, the teen brain responds to how you focus your attention; by engaging teen clients experientially and in what seems an entertaining way, you have increased your chances of relating to them in a more meaningful way as a therapist. An example of a Nature Detective tasks of higher levels with teens could be, "Find four trees that look like important people in your life and write what you need to say to them but haven't yet."

Direct Experience: Deep Discovery

If we surrendered to earth's intelligence we could rise up rooted, like trees.

RAINER MARIA RILKE

Cultivating a presence of mind infused with awe and wonder at the brilliance of nature is the most desired state of being in this work; attention to self, others, and the environment is heightened. Realistically, clients will begin therapy with many things on their mind and with different degrees of receptivity to nature (ecological identity). As Joseph Cornell highlighted, including the stages of awakening enthusiasm and focusing the senses can help shift a person into a receptive state where they can absorb their experiences with nature in a deeper and more impactful way. The psychological, physical, social, and spiritual benefits of direct contact with nature have been detailed above and in numerous other texts. Thus, the focus here will be on how practitioners can partner with nature to enrich the direct experience of children and youth toward therapeutic aims. Specifically, we will explore inquisitive wandering, creating a culture of awareness and appreciation for stillness, engaging with the elements, and the metaphorical possibilities of nature.

Child-centered and Child-led Inquisitive Wandering

As described above, people have their own pre-existing relationship with nature prior to commencing nature-based therapy. For many, their connection is what has drawn them to the approach in the first place; however, for others, they have exhausted their options with conventional office-based approaches, and their parents are drawn to try something new. The fact that the approach is experiential, which means the client is actively participating in the experiences versus talking about them, is a key attribute. If the client is hesitant to engage, simply offering pleasurable experiences outside is the first step. Thus, the sessions may appear to be primarily addressing the awakening enthusiasm stage. However, as time progresses, and the client has positive experiences to draw on, there is often a curiosity sparked, which allows for a honing of the senses and a deepening of their inquisitiveness regarding learning about the natural world. The practice of child-led inquisitive wandering is something that cannot be overdone with a client. Each wander, or journey of discovery without a predetermined destination, builds off the last experience, extending and strengthening the practice. Being child-centered means attending to the gifts, interests, and proclivities of the individual child and allowing them to lead the way. As Rachel Carson so eloquently stated, "If a child is to keep alive his inborn sense of wonder... he needs the companionship of at least one adult who can share it, rediscovering with him the joy, excitement, and mystery of the world we live in."[16] Thus, the practitioner's job is to companion the child as they discover, to wait as they make decisions, and to encourage as they try new things. Further, being a mirror for their feelings, thoughts, and behaviors allows for the client to experience being fully seen, as well as helps them to gain emotional literacy and validation for and understanding of their inner world.

The approach of supporting children in nature can be considered a form a mentorship, whereby the adult takes great interest in the child's individual journey and assists them to push edges, make discoveries, and ultimately grow as a nature-connected person. A great deal has already been written on the topic of nature connection and mentoring. One model we draw upon is the Coyote Mentoring model, as many of their collected writing, activities and insights are applicable to the aims and settings of nature-based therapy.[17]

"I don't want to hike" or "Hiking is boring" or "I want to stay home" are common responses to the invitation by many well-intended parents who are trying to help unplug their children from screens and get them outside. Coyote Mentoring teaches how to tap into children's passions by fostering engagement through offering quests and adventures versus "hikes." Incorporating games into the wander is a useful way to break past the common resistance to be there, as it turns up the fun factor in a major way. For example, on a recent wander with a 6-year-old boy, we created a goal of reaching 1,500 points. To earn points, he had to accomplish challenges like crossing fallen logs (100 pts), jumping between boulders (150 pts), spotting common or rare animals (50–500 pts), or quietly walking the trail for a period of time. He was immediately pulled into the experience and eager to earn points and explore the forest. Another common strategy is to frame the experience as a special adventure where the child is entering a world of magic and we need to work together to save the day. Entering through a "portal" and following the child's imagination is a powerful way to foster engagement, perhaps shifting into animals and moving through the forest as their favorite creature or becoming the guardians of the forest and sneaking around in order to stay hidden from the humans. Finally, being a mentor means modeling the types of behaviors, skills, and enthusiasm you want to evoke in the child. This is greatly enhanced by exaggerating, in an authentic way, your own awe and wonder for nature: if you are looking at a track, get right down on your hands and knees;

if you are amazed by the magnificence of a new mushroom, vocalize your amazement and make your passion known. Your own genuine enthusiasm is contagious and helps to ignite the curiosity and genuine wonder of the child.

A Culture of Awareness and Appreciation for Stillness

The incorporation of mindfulness strategies has become ubiquitous with health and mental well-being. The ability to slow down and notice what is unfolding with acceptance and a non-judgmental stance has been shown to rewire the brain from its deeply habituated state of scanning for danger, problem solving, and constant rumination. As a result, mindful states put the brake on stress and the corresponding survival cocktail of adrenaline and cortisol. Nature offers a magnificent forum to cultivate a mindful presence. The more a person deeply observes, the more they discover. However, in order to observe, the observer must be still. As prominent Canadian nature artist Robert Bateman stated,

> Stillness is a blessing too often absent from the lives of today's children. After a moment of stillness to tune your attention outward, quiet the inner commotion, and drink in the world through wide-open senses, you come back to yourself subtly refreshed and changed.[18]

In this particular articulation of nature-based therapy, mindfulness is taught as an opportunity to train oneself to hold attention on particular stimuli either unfolding in their outer environment or internal world. Another term for this is *tracking*: an ability to keenly observe the nuances of the environment holding a sense of curiosity and a "not knowing mind" with regard to needing to figure things out. Delaying the response of "naming" something has been discussed by other nature authors as a way to enhance one's connection versus immediately identifying what it is according to scientific categories. Further cultivating an appreciation for stillness and how it provides the foundation for awareness is also key. There are many ways that both the culture of awareness and appreciation for stillness are cultivated with children, youth, and their families. Starting with the outer landscape, we introduce awareness as a critical practice for thriving in the natural world.

Through activities such as the Nature Detective and wandering shared above, awareness can be modeled and reinforced. For example, on a fall wander in the Pacific Northwest, there will undoubtedly be a world of fungi to discover. Spotting them and taking the time to revel at their beauty and magnificent design is sure to captivate even the more distractible minds.

Another effective avenue for cultivating awareness and stillness is to disguise them in games that require these skills to be successful. For example, a well-known game among nature educators is Camouflage, where people hide in a natural space as close as they can to the "spotter" and have to remain hidden, still, and alert, until they are given a signal indicating what to do next (e.g., to switch spots). A common practice by facilitators may be to stretch out the time between signals to give the participants a little extra time of stillness. Additionally, the signal "appreciation," has now become a part of the game for us, where after hearing that signal, participants are to notice things in their immediate surroundings that they find beautiful and offer gratitude. It is truly amazing to see the level of engagement that occurs and how children who typically cannot remain still for more than a few seconds drop into the game and exude stillness and awareness of their surroundings.

Disguising opportunities to be still and aware is an effective strategy to cultivate these skills. However, giving people an opportunity to connect with nature on their own, in a place they have selected, has repeatedly proven to be one of the best ways to foster deep nature connection. A common activity we offer, especially in group therapy programming, is called Place Bonding or Sit Spots. This practice has the potential to radically transform a person's life by providing them with a chance to be alone with their earthly selves and develop a sense of belonging in the world. Clients are invited to follow their internal compass and find an inviting place to sit on their own nearby (a rock, log, under a tree, etc). In a group context, youth are directed to spread out, so that no one else is in their direct line of vision or close enough to talk to. Once in their spot, the kids are asked to not move around, to stay in silence, and to observe different aspects of their spot. (We cue them to notice sounds, colors, textures, bugs, etc.) Ideally, clients would be able to repeatedly return to the same spot over the course of therapy to observe seasonal changes and deepen their bonding with a particular place. While considered an essential routine for building nature connection in many nature-based programs, Sit Spot should be offered with intention, and only when clients are receptive to the idea; it can be easily overused and hence underappreciated and less effective. Slowly increasing the length of time spent at the Sit Spot helps to build capacity for appreciating extended time alone—undistracted—a skill that is seldom gained by children in today's fast-paced culture. Framing the Sit Spot as a special opportunity, and introducing it with stories of your own animal encounters or numinous observations when being quiet and still, can help to instill the sense of magic into the experience. Another essential ingredient to amplifying the Sit Spot experience is to make space for listening to each person's stories afterward—even if it is the most simple observation. For some youth, offering a journal to bring to their spot can help increase comfort and willingness to try the activity and can provide a space for drawing, poetry, and reflections.

Adult clients should also be encouraged to develop a Sit Spot practice. One adult, who felt guilty and irresponsible for taking time for herself to be seated in nature (outside of sessions), reflected on how she at first was flooded with thoughts of her son's struggles with ADHD and his tumultuous life at school. She eventually began recognizing the value of her practice in calming her and improving her patience with her son at home. Her goals and the goals for her son were being met indirectly through Sit Spots as she invited him for walks into a local park to sit together. She was not firm and did not hold him accountable to his sitting as she realized how valuable the unstructured and less-supervised time her son was now having in nature was. She said he was actually making attempts to be less noisy for her benefit while he climbed trees and ran around.

Outdoor Living (Survival) Skill Development and Engaging with Elements

A key component of our approach to nature connection with children and youth is developing their survival skills. While we accept the term *survival skills* for its ease in recognition, we prefer *outdoor living skills*. This narrative shift conveys that these skills are not developed to save themselves when lost in the wilderness. We prefer to teach these skills so that our clients can thrive, not just survive, outdoors. Common activities include starting fires with friction, making tools out of natural materials, or making shelter from sticks and natural debris. We also see a sense of self-confidence and capability that exudes from the participants in doing these activities, as they interact with their environment, problem solve, and ultimately take care of some of their basic needs themselves. The experiences of utilizing natural materials to genuinely meet a need may also engender feelings of gratitude for the help that was provided. According to the authors of *Coyote's Guide to Connecting with Nature*, outdoor living skills,

> are valuable, ultimately, not because we need them for daily living, although they may indeed save someone's life, but for the way they help us to develop connection to place and teach us to relate to nature in the oldest, most fundamental way. We learn the most when we have an intense need to learn, and nothing creates need like survival.[19]

Becoming proficient with basic skills for outdoor living, such as fire making, shelter building, and foraging, can increase one's sense of self-sufficiency. The list below provides some idea of the outdoor living skills we incorporate into counseling sessions. Having to think about environmental conditions and make decisions about your personal welfare increases confidence and capacity to care for self and others. When one considers some of the common mental health challenges facing youth today—low self-esteem, external locus of control, isolation, and lack of belonging—it immediately becomes clear how incorporating these skills into sessions can be profoundly beneficial. It is in the intentionality of the therapist and matching of activities with the client's goals and skills that will determine their effectiveness.

- Identifying and preparing edible and medicinal plants
- Navigation (stars, compass, geocaching)
- Fire making (flint & steel, friction fire)
- Cooking over a fire/stove
- Shelter (tarp, natural shelter)
- Camouflage techniques (animal observing, sneaking games)

A telling example of how cultivating survival skills can be incorporated into a counseling session occurred with a 15-year-old boy whom I (David) was supporting following the separation of his parents. Living with his mother and her new boyfriend, he felt his life was totally out of his control. He was currently not speaking or spending time with his father, as they had a recent falling-out. He despised his mom's decision to have her partner move in. Further, his home life was filled with arguments over screen time, chores, and school performance, which would escalate to the point that, despite his attempt to get space in his room, he would be pursued until he'd flee the house and go for a walk around his neighborhood to cool down. It was clear that he needed support navigating this tumultuous time and, in particular, working with his mom to strengthen their relationship and communication skills and establish healthy patterns for navigating conflict. However, he was reluctant to attend counseling as he'd had negative experiences in the past. When I offered to focus on learning survival skills, he immediately lit up and agreed to meet with me just once to get his mom off his back. He had already been doing lots of research online on shelter building, wild edibles, and fire making. In our first session, we decided to collect some trailing blackberry leaves and grand fir branch tips to make tea. He shared how he wanted to learn more about survival so he could escape if things got too bad at home. I suggested we meet regularly and work together on building his skills. We started with learning how to use a knife for carving and splitting wood, followed by learning to make natural cordage, and finally building a shelter in a local forest that he could visit on an ongoing basis. He expressed that having the shelter made him feel secure, knowing that if he had to leave, he'd be okay as he had a safe place to go. Further, knowing that he could take care of himself raised his self-confidence and lowered his reactivity to his peers and teachers, which had been an issue. During the course of our work together, we were able to discuss his growing connection with the natural world and how he felt that nature was the one thing in his life that was not judging him but rather a place where he could feel accepted and safe from criticism. I continued to meet with him, and as he matured and his life stabilized, he no longer felt the need to maintain the shelter. It was left to deteriorate with time, yet it carried with it an important story of a particularly challenging time in his life and the support that nature provided. In a session, years later, we came across the shelter, now flattened by the wind and rain of many Pacific Northwest winters. In the middle of moss- and grass-covered debris, we noticed a small Garry oak sapling reaching for the sun with its delicate needles. He immediately opened his pack and took out his water bottle and fed the new growth some water. No words were exchanged, but a shared silence captured the power of the moment, which was teeming with symbolism. From the debris of his former life, he too was bearing new leaves and branches, reaching for the sun, seemingly transformed.

It is important to point out that communicating with clients and their parents about the potential risks of learning outdoor living skills and the subsequent possibility of injury is essential to ensuring that no unintentional harm is caused. For example, if choosing to focus on edible plants as an avenue for connecting with the potential of plants for food and medicine, it is essential that the counselor have sufficient training in edible wilds and that this knowledge is shared in a way that honors the plants as well as encourages safe and respectful harvesting practices when the client is not in session.

Metaphorical Possibilities of Nature

Direct experiences in nature are filled with opportunities for meaning-making with clients regarding how they understand themselves and their lives. Imagery and, in particular, the rich symbolism that nature offers is readily available to tap into for therapeutic and developmental purposes. The utilization of metaphors, the transfer of meaning from one thing to another, for learning, reflection, deepening understanding, and shifting perspectives has long been present in different counseling modalities. The use of client-generated, counselor-generated, and co-constructed metaphors have proven to be useful in nature-based counseling with children, youth, and families. Two possible ways in which nature can serve as a metaphor are as a *mirror*, where clients' inner experiences or life journey are reflected back to them, or alternatively as an *exemplar* or *mentor* image offering insights and wisdom about the big lessons we all need to learn about our life and existence (e.g., living and dying, change, letting go, resilience, and healing). Further, exploring what UCLA clinical professor Allan Schore collectively refers to as *affective embodied experiences* (sensations, movements, gestures, reflections on lived experience) can amplify and deepen the healing potential of these experiences versus just talking about them and keeping them on a strictly cognitive level.[20]

Example of Nature as Mirror

On a wilderness experience course I (Dave) was on, we were asked to blindfold ourselves and walk along a trail, led by a rope that meandered through the forest. I had done similar activities many times, yet this situation was a bit different. First, I was going through a particularly tough time in my personal life and was feeling more vulnerable and unstable than usual. Second, I was not in a facilitator role, as I had signed up to give myself an opportunity to "practice what I preach" and create intentional time to deepen my own connection with nature and her healing capacities. This combined to create the following somewhat surprising and welcomed situation. The instructions were to pick up the rope and navigate the "trail" on our own until we reached the end. The activity was framed with the metaphor (i.e., facilitator-generated) of the rope representing a cord that connects all of us to the web of life. This relationship is for me at times strong and vibrant and, at other times, distant and seemingly out of reach. While donning the blindfold, I immediately felt a sense of vulnerability given the heightened turmoil of my inner world. My bare feet were in contact with the soil, and the distinct textures of the ground were immediately apparent, as if the volume on a muted television was suddenly able to be heard. After a moment of breathing and taking in all the new sensory information, I felt a blanket of comfort wrap around me as the mental chatter was finally quieting down. I began to walk, gripping the rope tightly. The trail was flat at first and then had a step down through salal bushes and ferns. I heard a fellow participant in front of me stumbling and struggling to navigate the coming section. A tension built up and ran through my chest, and I braced. I thought, How do I also brace myself and tighten up when I am facing a challenge in my life? I tested the rope for support and pressed my feet into the ground to better anchor myself, repeating, I need to trust in my path, stay connected to the rope, and walk slowly. As I made my way through the forest, there were times my focus was highly tuned to sounds and sensations around me: brushing past branches and leaves and hearing birds chirping nearby. At other times, it was as if I were on autopilot, with my mind in a different place, occupied by racing thoughts regarding things that either had happened in the past or may happen in the future. In these moments, I would tend to trip, stumble, be abrasive with the plants and trees versus really acknowledging their presence and needs. At other times, I would slow down and really take in the forest, moments the famous psychologist Fritz Perls called losing your mind and coming to your senses. This grounding allowed for a heightening of my relationship with nature, and I had an overwhelming sense of being gently guided to stay on the right track. This deeper sensation of connection was comparable to being greeted and supported by a group of friends in a time of need.

After approximately thirty minutes of navigating the undulating trail, I was met with the words "Welcome, you have arrived." Where had I arrived? A moment of silence ensued, suggesting I hadn't arrived at a specific place. Instead—and this is where the metaphoric potential of this type of activity is explored—I had arrived at the potential to truly know that my life is deeply connected to the web of life in its own unique and brilliant way. This metaphor could have been further developed to include that my path could be filled with times of flow, struggle, fear, and comfort. Most importantly, though, I experienced a cellular knowing that I was not alone. Even though it may have felt at times that I was on my own, when I opened up to my senses, the Earth and all her beings waited to greet me. *Alone* was, in those moments, transformed to *all-one*. The felt experience of being on the trail and knowing, in an embodied way, that the Earth and her beings are there to guide me was reaffirming to me. Truthfully, I was surprised by the depth of meaning I took from this activity. When I had signed up a number of months prior, I thought I would get a few new tricks and tools for my tool belt. The combination of being in a vulnerable and thus more receptive state, and actually giving myself the opportunity to connect with nature in a meaningful way (practitioner's ongoing connection), allowed for the power of the experience to resonate in a more profound way. Further, these insights were not superimposed but rather emerged from a combination of paying attention to the embodied cues and having the support of the facilitator's curiosity and questions to amplify them, allowing for an organized and coherent reflection to emerge from the metaphor offered.

Transformative experiences, such as the one described above, are readily available for children, youth, and families engaging in nature-based work. It is important to recognize that Dave, in the example of the forest trail, has been working on his relationship with nature for years, and that our clients may need far more support and involvement in these facilitated experiences. Some may need to start with eyes closed versus blindfolded, or maybe with socks or shoes on versus barefoot. You need to really know where your clients are at and engage in ways that are positive, meaningful, and rich with sensory opportunities and unique yet challenging enough to be enriching experiences. The process of inviting a person to notice and observe the natural world, encountering their subjective experience of being in the world, and then reflecting on how these observations mirror aspects of their own life is a powerful tool. A key element that makes this possible is how nature does not have any predetermined meaning. A tree losing its leaves is not good or bad; it just is. Meaning is constructed through an interaction of the person's life experiences with the images of nature being presented. Further, the fact that these images are external can facilitate a sense of safety that otherwise may not be possible if one were looking directly at their inner experiences. In addition, the opportunity for a different perspective is enhanced due to the differing vantage point at which the inner experience is being viewed.

Drawing upon nature as mirror is an exciting tool that the nature-based counselor can draw on to support the growth and development of clients, as well as the healing of past adverse experiences. For the practitioner to be effective, it is critical that they refrain from imposing their own projections onto the client's experience. The counselor should encourage the client to be aware of the tendency for cognitive processes to jump to meaning before really allowing a bodily felt sense of the experience, from which meaning also arises. This cautionary note is similar to one offered by Sharon Stanley in her Somatic Transformation work with trauma. She asserts that the most therapeutic images are the ones that come from attending to the affective embodied experiences being generated in a safe relational container versus ones generated by top-down cognitive processes. She calls for a bottom-up approach, which entails tuning into the lower brain stem (sensations) and mid-brain (feelings) first and allowing reflection and meaning making to follow.

The opportunities for application of nature as mirror for children and youth are rich, although the depth at which the metaphors are explored needs to match the developmental and cognitive abilities of the child; otherwise the practitioner could fall into the trap of imposing meaning and leaving the child behind. However, in our experience, the practitioner does need to take a more central role in inviting curiosity and exploration, as the utilization and generation of metaphor may be a new skill or more difficult to access because of developmental constrictions. Metaphor can help young clients explain the unexplainable, can be embodied visceral expressions of lived experiences that have been hard to find words for, and may even occur nonverbally, when a child can show and feel through a lived-body experience something that needs no verbal processing, if even at all possible.[21] It is important to remember that meaning-giving and metaphors do not, and cannot, be invented; they present themselves and emerge from the interplay between client, therapist, activity or experience, and nature. There are, however, some clients for whom metaphor simply does not make sense and serves to confuse rather than assist in communication.

The following is a case example of how nature as mirror can be used to assist children and youth to explore their own different neural states of hypo-arousal, regulated, and hyperarousal. Such explorations can increase awareness and naming of internal processes, ultimately to help self-regulate or seek out co-regulation when necessary.

Case Example

An 11-year-old boy was living with his grandparents and had very little contact with his biological family (i.e., none with his dad, minimal with mom; uncles and aunts were peripherally involved). He was referred to counseling to assist with extreme dysregulation (i.e., excessive fear, anxiety, anger, or sadness), both at home and in school. In particular, according to his grandparents and teachers, even the smallest event could send him into a heightened state, often with no warning or pre-dictability. Following a blowup, he would have little recollection of what happened and would want to reconnect and be reassured. This would sometimes be challenging for the grandparents, teachers, and even fellow students because they were still struggling with their own reactions to the intensity of the experience. When asked about what is going on inside him, he replied that he doesn't know and does not remember what it felt like aside from being really mad.

One of the therapeutic goals was to assist him in deepening his understanding of himself and both his emotions and sensations that accompanied the different neural states of being regulated (calm, safe, ready to learn, socially connected) and states of hyperarousal (anger, rage, reactivity). Enhancing his emotional literacy and awareness of his body by just talking did not appear to lead to any helpful insights or shifts in behavior. The intention was to invite him to go on an ad-venture to find places/things in nature that reminded him of these two states (regulated and hyperarousal) so he could learn more about his inner world in an embodied and engaged way. First, he was invited to find things in nature that reminded him of some basic feelings, such as happy, sad, mad, frustrated, excited. During this task, he would run around eager to see what was around that he could share. Happy was a giant maple leaf that he found on the ground that was bigger than his whole face. Mad was a thicket of Himalayan blackberries with their big thorns and creeping vines. Sad was a rotting and splintering branch on the ground. The question about why he chose these specific things was asked with genuine curiosity and no expectation for an answer. For Happy, he said the maple leaf reminds him of his mom, and how he loves her; for Mad, he said the prickles reminded him of how he hurts people when he is angry; and for Sad, at first he was not sure. I (Dave) asked him to describe what he saw. He said he saw a dead, rotting branch that was being eaten by bugs. Staying with just the description also allowed him to arrive at the conclusion that the branch is not with its tree anymore, and it never will be again. The counselor's intention is to remain curious, validate the child's experience, and focus on the process of exploring and discovering rather than trying to arrive at de-finitive answers.

Following the exploration of these feelings, the client was invited to see if he could find something in nature that reminded him of the experience of calmness and safety. (Remember the green zone from chapter 5.) It was offered via a question: Can you find a place that you really like and feels safe and good? He was encouraged to try out different spots and notice what he was feeling and how it differed between the spots. Eventually, he settled in a big cluster of maple trees and was asked what it feels like to know this is the spot. He said it just feels right. He was encouraged to climb right inside the middle, which he eagerly did. He was then invited to see if there was a movement or position he could take that really captured this current feeling of safety. He decided to lean back on one of the trunks and rest his head, allowing his arms to fall. He also let out a big sigh and closed his eyes. I asked if it felt like he was being supported by the trunk, upon which he said yes. It feels really good to be held and supported doesn't it, I reflected. After encouraging him to really soak in this feeling, I inquired into what he was noticing in his body. I offered him some possibilities, such as lightness-heaviness, warm-cold, and tight-loose. He was able to choose the ones that fit him, and I offered encouragement for the awareness he was demonstrating. I then asked him if he could remember feeling this way at a time in his life. He immediately named being with his grandmother and surrounded by some of his biological family. I asked if the trunks around him might represent his family members and the one he was lying on his mom. He smiled and started naming which of his family members the different trunks represented. His breathing was calm, his eyes were bright, and he appeared to be feeling regulated and safe. After taking some time for him to really soak in this experience, I asked if he could close his eyes and try to visualize this moment so he could return to it during the week until we would meet again. I then asked him if he would be willing to find something in nature that reminded him of anger and the times he felt really, really, mad. It did not take long for him to find a big stick. Again, I invited him to see if there was a movement that he wanted to try that captured how it felt. He started hitting the stick on the ground. Offering encouragement, I kept inviting him to explore this and see if he could try to amplify the anger he feels at home and at school to this moment just a bit more.

The invitation was well received, and he started playfully hitting and jumping, and saying things that had happened in past experiences such as "No, that's not fair. I don't want to get off my game" and "Go away: No it's mine." I provided encouragement and reflected back the words he was saying, "Yes, it's not fair" and "Yeah, you're really, really mad; that was yours." Eventually, I started to see him slow down and eventually stop. "That was so fun," he said. We processed this experience in a similar manner, bringing awareness to his feelings and sensations, what he noticed had changed, and followed by reflecting on times he felt that way in his life.

These two incidents provided an experiential and engaging way to explore his inner world and the vast difference in neural states that he was undergoing. He was able to explore these states in the company of an attentive adult who was reflecting back his experience and encouraging him. The natural world provided a vast array of possible reflections for him to choose from, and the collaborative exploration of these spaces/actions facilitated a deepening of his self-understanding, as well as enhanced his comfort in discussing this topic, due to having something externalized to focus on. He still had a long journey ahead in terms of tending to the relational trauma and other attachment injuries that were likely contributing to his high reactivity and difficulty self-regulating. However, we did now have a rich and embodied image of his experience of both anger and safety/belonging, and this could be used by his supports to assist in developing his ability to notice and name what might be going on and what he may be needing during these tough moments.

Nature as Mentor

Metaphors seem to have the most impact when generated and experienced in an embodied manner versus simply laid on top of experience.[22] Further, the process of selecting metaphors begins with slowing down and a willingness to observe and track both outer and inner landscapes. It is possible to intentionally look at how nature navigates similar struggles to the ones showing up in the clients' lives, or to allow space to just observe and then ask questions. One could be, What do you think nature has to teach, given what you have observed and your current situation? It is evident when a metaphor is landing because the meaning making appears effortless, and a sense of vitality and vulnerability may be present. Conversely, it can feel forced, and the counselor may be doing more of the work to maintain engagement: a clear sign to let it go. When a metaphor has landed, follow-up questions can be asked to amplify the experience, and clients can be invited to continuously notice how the image/knowledge is residing in their body, through particular movements, gestures, sensations, sounds, and feelings. The metaphor can be brought back in subsequent sessions, as well as drawn on by the client in times of need. The following is an example of the process of nature as mentor with a 17-year-old client who was feeling insecure in his romantic relationship and struggling with jealousy and disturbing ruminations. The session took place in a nearby forest, and the client was standing with his back against a large Douglas fir tree. After a few minutes of inviting him to settle his nervous system through orientating to the forest and simple grounding exercises, such as noticing sounds, his breath, and body and feeling the pull of gravity connecting him to the ground, the following conversation occurred:

Counselor: I'd like to invite you to really feel the support of the tree on your back. Would you be willing to see what it's like to offer the weight on you back to the tree?

Client: Yes, sure. Just lean back? It feels nice; it feels solid.

Counselor: Ah, it's feeling nice and solid. What else do you notice?

Client: I am feeling pressure on my back and warmth going down my shoulders and chest.

Counselor: Ah, warmth and pressure on your back, down your shoulders and chest. Stay with those sensations and just notice how they shift and move.

Client: There is a softening of my shoulders, and my face is feeling tight.

Counselor: Notice the softening and also the tightness. Is there a way you might be able to offer your jaw to gravity and release even a little bit of the tightness there?

Client [Wiggles jaw back and forth and takes a deep breath]: I am noticing it soften.

Counselor: And the tree supporting you. What do you notice from that?

Client: It still feels solid. It's holding me up, and I can relax into it. I just got the image of the tree's roots hugging the earth and wrapping around rocks, anchoring itself to the ground while my body presses against the trunk. That feels really good. It feels strong, and I am starting to feel my legs feel strong.

Counselor: Excellent noticing. What would it be like to press your own feet into the ground and remain connected with the tree on your back?

Client [Sighs, takes a breath]: I am noticing sensations of warmth and solidness in my legs. My stomach I can't quite feel, but I can notice my shoulders and arms are light. They are like the branches on the tree.

Counselor: The branches of you are feeling light. Your legs are feeling solid. [The client places his hands on his belly.] Now what's happening in your belly?

Client: I am starting to feel my breath move into this part of my body. It's feeling like it's softening, and I am noticing it's like the hard wood of the tree. A container of strength.

Counselor: Wow, a container of strength. So, you have your roots anchoring you to the ground, the hard wood of your stomach and trunk, and then your branches light and swaying. See if you can stay with those feelings/sensations of strength and rootedness. Really let them be here with you in this moment.

Client [A number of breaths pass by.]: I feel like I am strong and rooted and that my mind is clear for once. I feel a sense of safety and trust that I can weather storms when they come. Just like the tree, I have a strong root system and core, and these qualities will help me bend and be flexible yet strong when the big winds of insecurity roll through.

Counselor: Wow, that is a powerful and profound insight. Is your sense that this is an image that can be helpful for you in your life? Do you think it can hold some of the pain you are experiencing?

Client: Yes, definitely. I can feel a sense of inner strength that I have not felt in a long time.

Counselor: Inner strength. Yes, take your time to really feel the qualities of this inner strength. This rooted and strong inner sense. [Time passes and the client opens his eyes.] Is there a way you'd like to thank the tree for its support in this process?

The session went on with the practice of giving gratitude to the tree for the support and guidance provided and for the ways its rootedness helped this particular person to explore and embody their own sense of rootedness and resilience.[23] In this case, the metaphor emerged primarily from the client (with some counselor scripting) and after some time grounding with the support of the tree being felt. Importantly, the metaphor was generated from the client taking time to notice his sensations of being in relationship with the natural world. If it had not emerged, the counselor may have chosen to pose a question to see if something was waiting to emerge, such as, "When you lean back on the tree and feel its strength and support, is there anything you think the tree can teach you about how it remains strong and grounded?" The important point is that metaphors need to emerge and not be forced.

Another possibility for nature as mentor is looking to the natural world for insights regarding particular struggles being faced by the client or by humans/societies in general. Engaging in a conversation and being open to hearing answers can be an uncomfortable experience, as most people in the West are not used to communication with the more-than-human world in this manner. If the client is not open to this type of dialogue, simply bringing forth an example of a natural process and engaging in conversation can be generative. A common example is how everything in nature is constantly cycling. As Rachel Carson describes, "There is something infinitely healing in the repeated refrains of nature—the assurance that dawn comes after night, and spring after winter." This idea can be introduced by naming some of the different cycles that occur in nature. After naming tangible examples, such as the shape of our eyes, flowers, effects of wind and water, the example of the monthly full moon, seasonal cycles, and even the life-and-death cycle can be discussed. Simply naming the ways that weather shifts and changes, and relating it to different emotional states, can be a relieving insight to someone who feels their current mood will never end or that something is wrong with them for having a particularly tough period in their life.

The cyclical processes found in nature can also offer guidance in exploring the natural relationship cycle, introduced to us by Sol Marie Doran, a somatic counselor with extensive training in nature connection work. The basic concept is that relationships cycle between connection, rupture, and repair, and that each cycle is an opportunity to examine our own relational patterns and enhance our connection to both self and other. This is particularly helpful when trying to engage youth and families in learning healthy repair processes, as it shifts the notion that times of connection are good and rupture is bad to knowing that all stages are important and that families need to learn about the potential of each of these possibilities. This has proven to be a powerful concept to normalize times of struggle and provide hope that things will shift. It can also provide a rationale for overcoming the urge to avoid the repair process and promote openness to learn these important skills.

In a recent session, an 8-year-old girl and her parents arrived following a really challenging night at home. It ended up escalating into the child throwing things at her parents and a night of rupture, frustration, and emotional pain. Eventually, everyone did go to sleep, but it was from utter exhaustion as no repair had been made. Our session began in the morning with a check-in about how their week had been, and it quickly became evident that they were in the rupture phase and needing help shifting. They were invited to name the cycles they could observe on the beach, as well as in the sky. As described above, the conversation progressed to natural cycles, and I (Dave) was able to introduce the concept that relationships also undergo cycles (i.e., rupture, connection, repair). I then had them find objects on the beach that represented each of the three stages. Rocks, sticks, and barnacles were chosen for the rupture stage, feathers and flowers for connection, and grass for repair. We discussed why they chose the different objects and what qualities they had that could teach about the different stages (e.g., barnacles had hard shells to protect themselves; the feathers and flowers were beautiful but fragile; and the grass was flexible and could change shape). We then explored which stage they thought they were in and what ideas they had for shifting from repair back to connection. Each family member offered their ideas, which included how they needed to apologize for the hurtful action, learn from the experience, and clean up the mess at home. They were also invited to come up with an action they could all do to mark this intended transition. The daughter proposed throwing rocks into the ocean all at the same time. The example of their relationship as a natural cycle provided both comfort and guidance that the family needed to hold space for the important stage of repair.

The potential for nature to serve as a mentor for life's challenges is endless and desperately needed in these times of rampant disconnection and degradation of planetary and social systems. The process needs to be genuine and grounded in authentic connection with the more-than-human natural world versus something being forced or told by someone in a position of authority. Inviting embodied ways of knowing is a key way to integrate these insights in a deeper and more impactful way. Further, drawing on patterns found in nature can allow for the normalization of difficult experiences, as well as provide a reference upon which to understand the not-so-pleasant yet critically important dimensions of life. As with all mentorship relationships, being open, humble, and most of all grateful for the gifts of the more-than-human natural world are keys to the successful engagement with nature as mentor.

Sharing Inspiration: Passing Along
Meaningful Stories of Nature Connection

The reverence for all things and their stories is a critical part of Cornell's flow learning approach and is the final component of the four aspects being explored. Simply being in nature is not enough for nature-based therapy. We need to create spaces for sharing, being heard, and being present with those who may not articulate their experiences verbally (i.e., when we speak of stories or narratives, we include other ways of sharing stories, such as through art, movement, eye contact, silence, and other forms of expression). Sharing of stories, in whatever form they come, is necessary in order to realize the full potential of our relationship with nature. Furthermore, in this time of ecological crisis, it is as critical as ever to be open to allowing the world to speak through us. Giving voice to the diverse and rich array of creatures, beings, and ecosystems who share this one small and beautiful planet is critical for bringing forth a life sustaining world. In doing so, we cannot help but be transformed in the process: an enlarging of our self to include all the beings who coinhabit Earth. An ecopsyche, where "eco" (*oikois*, Greek for home) and "psyche" (Latin for breath, life, soul) combine as a self inextricably linked to our earthly home.

Breathe or put life or spirit into the human body; impart reason to a human soul.

MIDDLE ENGLISH
DEFINITION OF "INSPIRE"

Recognition for the importance of story in therapeutic practices is a central component of narrative therapy and well aligned with nature-based therapy. A narrative perspective purports a relational view of human experience and an understanding of multiple realities versus one concrete truth. At first glance, personal narratives can appear to be solely a subjective and individualized process. However, the language available to tell the stories of our lives is highly reliant on the culture and power relations in which we are embedded. The work of narrative therapists such as Michael White and David Epston[24] have articulated numerous ways in which relational processes are involved in the authoring of people's identities. In turn, they have created therapeutic interventions, such as the externalization of problems, attendance to alternate stories, and the establishment of communities of concern, to assist people in resisting dominant self-narratives and facilitating the re-authoring of preferred stories of oneself.

Sharing stories of nature is an ancient practice found across land-based societies from time immemorial. Both telling these stories and having them heard assists in personal and collective re-authoring processes and bolstering the possibility for alternate stories to emerge in at least three ways. Specifically, (1) stories of connection help to narrate oneself as belonging to the web of life, versus being isolated and alone; (2) personal stories of growth and development are able to be witnessed by a caring community who assist in destabilizing problem-saturated narratives of ourselves, allowing for positive accounts; and (3) telling the stories of our connection with nature shifts us out of dominant ethnocentric and individualized notions of reality and opens possibilities for other cultural stories and myths to be possible.

Mirroring: Opportunities for
Personal Stories and Strengths to Be Witnessed

Few human emotions bring with them the depth of pain of loneliness. Believing there is no one present to hear your stories, your sadness, and your joys can make living almost unbearable. The chronic condition of loneliness appears to be an unfortunate by-product of capitalist societies' endeavor for endless growth, accumulation of wealth, and control over nature. A *New York Times* article in early 2018 covered the appointment of a Minister of Loneliness in the United Kingdom following a report that more than nine million people in the country were claiming to often or always feel lonely—despite the "hyperconnectedness" of the global web of social media.[25] The article explains how chronic loneliness is worse for one's health than smoking fifteen cigarettes a day and brings with it a host of risk factors, including cardiovascular disease, dementia, depression, and anxiety in elderly populations. No one is immune from this predicament. Age is irrelevant; loneliness doesn't differentiate. Sharing stories of connection with nature has the potential to shift this harmful narrative of being alone and instead promote the realization that one can never be truly alone when coinhabiting a planet teeming with life.

On a recent group program, participants were invited to find a spot to sit with nature (Sit Spots as described above). They were encouraged to open their senses and observe what was unfolding in their particular spot. Further, they were encouraged to cultivate a *not-knowing stance*, which means that rather than being quick to name the things they were seeing, instead appreciating how things were expressing themselves. How were the trees being trees? How were the birds being birds? How were the rocks being rocks? After thirty minutes of sitting, we gathered to share our stories. One of the participants, a 15-year-old, had the following story to share:

> As I sat in my spot, I really noticed my mind racing. It was reminding me how I hate bugs, and I kept thinking about ways I could get out of the discomfort I was experiencing. There was a shift though, I remembered the saying, "I am nature. Nature and I are one." This allowed for a shift, and I became curious about

the bugs and who they were and how they lived. Their wings and bodies are so delicate. What a hard existence trying to survive with wind, rain, and predators constantly trying to eat them. I began to see their vital importance in the web of life and how they are a part of the ecosystem. I ended up watching them in awe and gratitude for the remainder of my time, and when we were called back, it felt like an instant had passed. I had a feeling that I wasn't alone in my own struggles. That I too shared the struggle for survival with these critters that I originally didn't want to look at.

Providing a space to have people's experiences heard is where trans-formative potential lies. Cherokee, Tlingit, and Filipino artist Gene Tagaban has been revealing stories from his life and culture for decades with the hope that people will come to realize that they too are story-tellers, encouraging everyone that their lives are worth relating. Cre-ating space for people's stories to be shared, no matter how seemingly mundane, is a powerful practice that counteracts self-narratives that "I don't matter," "My life is not important," and "I don't have anything to share." Further, the act of hearing one's own stories over time can allow for larger themes to become evident. Here is where the role of an atten-tive listener becomes key as problem-saturated portrayals may hinder a person's ability to notice the larger story they are creating and a part of.

Tara Brach, American psychologist and Buddhist teacher, reminds us of the negativity bias we all have a predisposition for, a tendency to emphasize negative events over the positive ones will often lead to-ward negative self-accounts if not held in check.[26] Having our stories mirrored back to us by attentive heartfelt listeners has the potential to counteract this by emphasizing themes of strength, growth, whole-ness, resilience, and other accounts of our personal narrative that are important to acknowledge when understanding ourselves in a positive light. Effective mirroring is both a technique and an art. From a narra-tive therapy perspective, it is a powerful practice that has the potential to help people shift toward life-affirming accounts of themselves. In nature-based therapy, we advocate for the importance of having a clear mirror to reflect our clients' stories and to assist in locating these within their life narrative and the larger stories and myths of society and culture. This requires both being present and knowing these myths so you can offer the possibility that the person is living out a larger story.

The Need for Alternate Myths:
Shifting Dominant Cultural Narratives

In his 1991 book, *The Cry for Myth*, American existentialist Rollo May argues for the need people have for myths to anchor them in their lives and make sense in a senseless world.[27] He describes myths as "the beams in a house: not exposed to outside view, they are the structure which holds the house together so people can live in it."[28] In his view, myths serve the function of making sense of our existence. He shows how the modern era is a world devoid of meaningful myths, and as a result, people are vulnerable to anxiety and existential crisis. This dominant view certainly is not one shared by Indigenous cultures around the world, and there has been a growing movement of Western cosmologists, such as Brian Swimme[29] and Thomas Berry,[30] who have been offering an alternate story of our universe, maybe closer to a unique human origin story—one that holds everything in it as sacred.

Spending time in nature and forming deep bonds with beings and places has the potential to radically shift the ways one understands themselves and the world we inhabit. Through time on the land, a deep sense of kinship can form with the places and beings interacted with. For many, this embodied knowing of all things being connected, animated, and sacred creates a dissonance with the dominant narratives of the Western world (i.e., growth, consumption, technology, etc.). Here, myths of our cosmos can anchor people in an alternate way of viewing themselves and the universe. If shared by a community of like-minded people, the potential for shifting these dominant narratives becomes even greater. Recounting one's own stories of an animate world in conjunction with larger cultural stories and myths can create enough support for an alternate way of viewing reality, that even when the group departs back to their day-to-day lives, the old beams of rugged individualism have been replaced with a life-affirming view of the cosmos.

Nature as Medium for Ritual and Celebration

Being in nature invites relationship, and in relationships we can communicate and share our thoughts, feelings, and responses to the world. We occasionally do not have words for our experiences, so we turn to nature for metaphor, insights, and meaning (as described above). We can also find ways to honor or celebrate successes; passages; grieving; developmental milestones; and the opening or closing of sessions, groups, or events with symbolism or acts of remembering, honoring, or intensifying the experience. One common ritual in the related literatures of adventure therapy and outdoor education is rites of passage. Young people on outdoor programs, away from home, having challenging experiences, and then returning home are described in the literature as having a rite of passage. We caution practitioners from following this path without a critical perspective, as it is not free of issues.

The term *rite of passage* was coined by French ethnographer Arnold Van Gennep and was conceptualized as a three-phase structure of rites: one of separation, one of transition (initiation), and one of return.[31] He understood rite of passage as the rituals that humans go through as they navigate the challenges of their lives and progress to a following stage (e.g., transition to adolescence, marriage, birth, death, overcoming crisis). Recognition for cultural variation exists, but his main idea was that these practices are seen worldwide throughout history. Van Gennep significantly influenced the work of American mythologist Joseph Campbell, in particular his articulation and belief in a universal story form that he calls the *hero's journey*.[32] He arrived at this particular metaphor after comparing numerous myths and cultural stories from around the world. This archetypal story has had a profound impact on popular culture, including major Hollywood movies (think *Star Wars* or *Harry Potter*), and its impact on the outdoor industry is no exception. However, recent anthropological studies have debunked the assumptions of researchers who were willing to state that this hero's journey can be considered a culturally universal experience.[33] Further, the important dissertation of Druscilla French, novelist and cultural mythologist, highlights how the supposed universal hero's journey actually contains subtly dogmatic views of how one attains personal transformation, based largely on Campbell's own underlying assumptions about life.[34] Another strong and obvious critique has been the use of appropriated rituals, ceremonies, and materials from Indigenous peoples and other cultural groups (e.g., sweat lodges, medicine wheels, smudging, adopting totem names) without the proper permission.

That said, we are strong advocates for the intentional and meaningfully appropriate use of ritual and ceremony. We do not, however, subscribe to any practice that is not culturally relevant and conceptualized at the client-counselor level (or a ritual idea brought to us from the family). Julian Norris,[35] outdoor educator and leadership professor at the University of Calgary, suggests that practitioners engage in developing ceremony or marking passages with "ritual sensibility" and cautions to be wary of justifying your actions with "shaky theory"—in short, to ensure practice is ethical. Some suggestions from Norris in developing rituals sensibly include the following:

- Be authentic and connected: Ask questions; follow your client's lead; draw only from cultures you are from or are permitted to engage with. His litmus test is whether or not you would be OK discussing your planned rituals with an elder from that cultural group and if they would be supportive or not.
- Think about ritual as "marking" or celebrating development or change versus thinking that ritual creates or is responsible for transitions (i.e., that the ritual itself is transformational).
- Articulating the change model and engaging at your level of training. Rituals should not be undertaken without clear understanding between client(s) and counselor as to their meaning, structure, and process. Counselors should also not engage in ritual that is beyond their scope of practice, training, and knowledge base (e.g., use of fasting or hard physical ordeals of some rituals portrayed in outdoor programs as rites of passage).

Case Example

Nature provides such diverse prospects for symbolism and meaning that ritual can take many forms, and the possibility to develop a ritual practice is fairly easy for counselors and clients alike. A simple example illustrates one such cocreated ritual. Geoff, a 15-year-old boy, was on a month-long court-ordered wilderness expedition. During the second week of the program, I (Nevin) had a number of conversations with him about his family and school life. He identified a number of crises and issues he had to deal with when he got home. Through one-to-one sessions, and some heartfelt sharing with his peers, this young man chose to address, and then leave behind, some emotional burdens. In discussions while hiking in the mountains, Geoff identified rocks as the symbolic representations of the issues he faced in his life. Choosing to work metaphorically, the youth chose one rock, and after discussing what to do with the rock, I suggested the youth name the issue (family conflict that he felt guilt and responsibility for) and carry the rock as a reminder of it. Geoff saw the potential and meaning of the activity and agreed to the burden of having this rock (about the size of a tennis ball) in his pack. A few days later, we were hiking up onto a higher ridge, where a full view of the valley ahead was possible. After several discussions regarding the symbolic meaning of the rock (family issues and burden), I asked Geoff if he felt he needed to take the rock home. His response was that the time to reflect on carrying this particular burden had allowed him to gain clarity that his family dynamics needed to change and that he could only play his part in that process. He was able to see that his burden, which he was carrying both emotionally and physically, was not his to hold. When we reached the summit and could see the expansive valley—which was a few days of hard effort— this youth shared with the group his process and then left the rock on the small summit cairn. This was a simple gesture, with a small effort on both the part of the client and counselor. It was not preplanned or a routine happening within this program. It involved being open to nature being a co-therapist to assist with one young man's burdens. There was no need to borrow or appropriate cultural practices. It involved no mysticism or magic and may (or may not have) become a lasting memory or touchstone for this youth. Equally important is that we as counselors don't overmanage or invest in the rituals, which may not be fully endorsed or made sense of by our clients. In the case of Geoff and the rock, I offered invitations and co-constructed a meaningful ritual (of "carrying" and "leaving behind" metaphorically and literally). Utilizing ritual sensibility, we ensured the youth was feeling connected to the practice and leading the process versus having a particular meaning and structure imposed on his experience.

There is great potential for ritual to deepen experiences by illuminating meaningful moments with symbolic acts. A recent study in the *Journal of Personality and Social Psychology* found that, in the aftermath of loss, engaging in rituals can minimize negative feelings by supporting the restoration of control, the very thing that has been undermined by the loss itself.[36] Further, it has been pointed out that, in positive situations, such as having a meal, graduating, or shifting roles, rituals can in fact heighten experiences as they bring more presence and attention to the process and with this comes increased satisfaction. Undoubtedly, incorporating rituals and symbolic gestures during nature-based therapy can add tremendous value to a client's experience and help to deepen their connection with the natural world, as well as support them in their lives.

Conclusion

In this chapter, we have explored the numerous ways that a nature-based counselor can partner with nature to bring about enhanced connection with self, community, and one's place in the web of life. Joseph Cornell's flow learning model provided four gateways through which we explored nature as co-facilitator. Drawing on the work of many talented and creative nature connection facilitators, philosophers, and therapists, this chapter aimed to illuminate some of the processes of doing nature-based counseling with children, youth, and their families. It is by no means complete, yet hopefully it will serve to inspire creativity and awareness of the limitless potential of turning to our greatest teacher, the natural world.

8

Nature-based Therapy for Families

Family is one of nature's masterpieces.

GEORGE SANTAYANA

I (Katy) have two young boys, ages 5 and 7; they are loud, rambunc-tious, curious, physical, and full of pulsating energy. Typically, when we are inside the house, they fight over toys, they call each other names, they hit each other, they struggle to entertain themselves, and their voices are much louder than the space can handle. I can easily feel irri-tated and overwhelmed at these times, exacerbated by the never-ending demands of chores I need to focus on. I find myself getting caught in cycles of negative feedback and mediation, nagging, saying no much more often than I would like, and raising my voice in a way I didn't ex-pect in my imagined parenthood. Does this sound familiar to anyone? Now take the very same two boys, and the very same mother, and put them on a forest trail. The kids' voices are absorbed into the layers of wood and leaves; they can be loud and wild, and I can breathe deeply. Their pulsating energy is released as they run, hide, and climb—explor-ing every intriguing stump, hole, and mushroom they find. They don't hurt each other; they are kinder; they follow each other and laugh; and there is nothing to fight over, except the odd super awesome stick... luckily there's always more to discover around the corner. My older son is in his pure element here, appreciating all the beauty around him, and feeling confident in his body as he discovers the undulation of the land. Take these same two kids to the beach, and they dig in the sand

and jump in waves, find crabs, precious rocks and wild seaweed—and they are happy for hours. They are never "bored," and they don't ask for screen time. This mother is delighted by the ocean, peaceful and capable of handling anything. The difference between my indoor family and my outdoor family experience is striking; it is the reason I take my kids into nature as much as possible. Nature is where we bond; it is where our nervous systems are regulated by the surrounding rhythms, where my children can step fully into their physical selves in a healthy and appropriate way—where we are all fed and loved by our collective "mother."

Drawing from my experiences, I know that the well-being of myself personally, and my family as a whole, depends on a balance of work and play, of relaxing time at home and physical adventures that allow my children to be their wild selves. I have a sense that if chores, work, screens, and overwhelm dominate the family experience, then the lasting effect of stress on the whole family system can be damaging. The most common diagnoses in children entering into our practice are anxiety, ADHD, and general emotional dysregulation (often creating challenges at home and school). Families are seeking help for managing these issues in children as young as 5 years old—an age when they should ideally still be living out their days shielded from the darkness in the world, worry free, and full of imagination and play. We propose that it can be helpful, if not essential, to the mental health practitioner to both view and address these problems within the wider systemic lens of family, society, and ecological relations.

The Original Attachment Wound

In family therapy, the presenting symptoms and relational conflict we address can often be traced back to early childhood attachment wounds that continue to impact healthy family functioning. Significant stresses such as early separation from birth parents (i.e., losses such as death, divorce, and adoption), parental mental illness, family violence, and neglect can all impact a family's early days. It has long been established that damage to the secure parent-infant attachment can have lasting effects on the child's developing brain and socio-emotional capacities.[1] The importance of that formative bond, which communicates to a baby that they are safe, seen, and nurtured, allows the child to begin confidently exploring and knowing her environment. The reciprocal and responsive gaze and the sharing of smiles set forth the neural connections in the right hemisphere for empathy and caring. When disruptions to this early attunement pattern occur, it causes confusion, fear, and uncertainty. Needs are not always met, cries go unanswered, smiles unrequited—and the child may learn to not always trust her environment or rely on her caregivers; her sense of bonding and belonging to her world is shaky. We should clarify here that our notion of family is not one of modern Western society's "nuclear family" and may be composed in numerous combinations of significant others. Santanya's idea of family being a "masterpiece of nature" still rings true for us, regardless of composition, in that it has the capacity to support, encourage, and stick with us through our difficult times.

We can find parallels in this process to our human relationship with the original parent, our Mother Earth. Our attachment and attunement with the cycles of Earth (diurnal patterns of day and night, moon phases, seasonal changes), which at one time in human history may have been deep and unwavering, are now in a state of "dis-ease." In Western society, with our dualistic Cartesian roots, we are often taught from the youngest age that we are not part of the living Earth but simply using it for our benefit and satisfaction. That initial feeling of complete belonging and oneness with the world is severed early on in our culture, leaving us with an insecure attachment where humans are habitually acting from fear, trying to extract resources for our needs, rather than knowing that reciprocity with our Earth mother begets caring and sustenance. As Anita Barrows so eloquently articulates, "It is indeed the illusion of bodily separateness that is the genuine sorrow, that accounts for our loneliness, and isolates us and leads us to exploit and violate one another, the world we live in, and, ultimately, ourselves."[2]

Thus, it is the great potential to discover one's essential belonging to the Earth that is the unique and beneficial healing power of nature-based approaches. And when working with family systems through this lens, we have the inimitable opportunity to work on both levels simultaneously: healing the parent-child attachment wounds as well as the family's human-Earth attachment wounds. When we step away from isolating the child in his pain and address his struggles within the larger family and community system, of which he is inextricably linked, we are honoring the true nature of ecosystems—just as we could never restore an ailing apple tree without considering the nutrients of the soil, the climate, the insect community, and neighboring species. And while considering the importance of family systems is now a more widely accepted therapeutic practice, extending our assessment of the presenting problems to the child's and family's relationship with the natural world is less common. We have already described the multitude of ways that nature can be woven into the healing process with children and youth, and we have found that when families can experience this process together, the impact and lasting results can be even greater.

One existing model of bringing families together outdoors for therapeutic intent can be found in wilderness therapy as outdoor family therapy "intensives."[3] These brief and powerful encounters can provide insight and momentum for the family trying to adapt to their changing youth but are also limited by the duration, cost, and distance of service provision, all affecting the transference of meaningful change to the home context. Our experience with these "add-on" models of family therapy encouraged us to develop an approach to serve local families as a whole when we can. This nature-based model of practice differs from an adjunct (or add-on to therapy) approach in that we aim to bring families together and into connection with nature on a regular basis, within their own communities, and adaptable to their work and school schedules. By meeting with families outdoors weekly or bi-weekly, we can continually integrate learning into their daily lives, provide support for extended periods of time, and work with all ages of kids in developmentally appropriate ways. In this approach, it is not just the child who may gain self-awareness and a new sense of connection in the world; it becomes a shared experience of success and transformation between parents and children. As the saying goes, "Families who play together, stay together," and the essence of nature-based therapy is to give families the opportunity to play and explore the natural world in shared appreciation. Louise Chawla,[4] from the Children, Youth and Environments Center at the University of Colorado, has repeatedly asserted that one of the most significant factors that predicts future pro-environmental behavior is when children have had positive experiences outdoors with a caring adult. She suggests that when adults share special places with children, they are equally showing their deep care for the child and nature.

This chapter introduces you to the potential benefits of bringing families into nature to share together in the therapeutic process. We will discuss why this approach may be a good choice for your practice and describe some key elements we have found useful for setting up successful nature-based family therapy sessions.

Why Take Family Therapy Outdoors?

As with most traditional therapeutic services, family therapy is ordinarily provided within the confines of an office setting. The room likely has couches, and maybe some toys and art supplies, and the general expectation is that family members are mostly sitting in the room for an hour of therapy. The benefits of the containment and focus provided by this space are certainly evident—but there are the occasions where a room and chairs can be limiting and may even serve to amplify the large energy that family dynamics are bound to produce. Many therapists have experienced that moment of intimidation when entering a family session, carrying the responsibility for a positive outcome, and hoping that all family members will be willing to participate, both young and old. It is likely that those family members, and especially the kids, are entering with even more trepidation for the experience than you, carrying with them all the uncertainties of being asked to be vulnerable in front of a "professional helper." The experiential approach of nature-based therapy is effective at breaking down many of the barriers at the outset of family therapy, especially from the kids' perspective. Children and youth, who may normally be resistant to engaging in therapy, might be enticed by the idea that they will be playing at a beach or visiting a favorite park with their family. Depending on the child, the chance to move their bodies, play, and expel energy during a session can be more developmentally appropriate than being asked to sit attentively on a couch for sixty minutes to talk about feelings and problems. Because the very nature of being outside brings the client to be mobile, physical, engage multiple senses, and interact with the external environment, it becomes more possible to encourage clients to make mind-body connections and to show up authentically. Children, youth, and even adults who have limited verbal expression or capacity for introspection can find ways to participate and contribute to the process, whereas, in an office setting with the whole family, the child or parent may feel put on the spot and freeze up. As family members encourage one another through a group challenge, or find themselves laughing while playing hide-and-seek in the woods, they inadvertently let down their protective defenses, and corrective experiences are made possible. As discussed previously in chapters 5 and 6, the state of play is a pathway to healing in the nervous system, as well as a tool to bring our bodies and minds into the present moment and out of negative thinking patterns and emotions.

Additionally, for many of the kids in our practice, their struggles tend to show up in the context of formal settings of authority where the expectation for sitting and listening is a priority (e.g., school). Therefore, to begin a therapeutic relationship where they are expected to do the very same action that puts them in a state of shame and dysregulation does not necessarily set them up for success. By meeting kids in environments where they feel safe (and ideally close to home) and are more likely to thrive, and giving parents a chance to witness them in that state, we can set the stage for a bonding and healing experience between parent and child.

For example, 7-year-old Ralph had been referred to us for treatment of anxiety, as well as behavior problems presenting at school. He had also been frequently getting into conflict with family members due to his tendency to invade personal boundaries and his constant desire for attention. This little guy was always on the move, eager to explore, and full of knowledge and curiosity for the natural world. Ralph was not very interested in trying counseling and had rejected an earlier attempt with an office-based counselor after the first two sessions. His parents knew that he thrived most outdoors and chose one of his favorite beaches for the first session, a place they knew he would be comfortable. The first few sessions were led by Ralph's fascination for the intertidal zone, and the counselor encouraged his parents to share in his excitement as they explored together, guided by missions that inspired the senses. (See chapter 7 for the *Nature Detective* initiative.) Through his relationship with the crabs and sea anemones, we were able to safely explore vulnerable topics such as boundaries, emotional expression with his parents, and bullying at school. By taking Ralph into a space where his strengths and heart shone, his family was able to more easily enter into sensitive topics that would typically end in arguments. Both mom and dad had experiences of connecting with Ralph in new ways and came out of therapy understanding him better. By participating in the nature-based therapy process together, the family could also develop a shared language for taking charge of anxiety at home, and in school.

You might wonder which ages of kids or family combinations are the best fit for nature-based family work. We do find that, when working with younger children (~ages 6 to 11), situating the majority of nature-based therapy within the family context is effective and developmentally appropriate. The younger the kids, the more likely we would conduct sessions with at least one parent, and in some cases, when content appropriate, with siblings as well. Young children tend to have less insight and language to express their emotional worlds, and part of our work is to find ways to help them develop that expression. Sharing those moments of awareness with the parent present, and coaching the parent to validate that child's feelings, can mean that transference of the new skill, language, or understanding back to the home is more attainable. In family therapy, we are working toward open, honest, and clear communication among family members; and having family members present in counseling together really fosters the practice of this communication. If a problem that is continually showing up at home is getting in the way of healthy family functioning (e.g., getting ready for school without a fight), we can practice problem-solving through fun interactive means in an outdoor activity and then move to problem-solving new practical solutions for home. At its essence, however, including the parents in the nature-based therapy process is about fostering healthy attachment. We are modeling how to play, follow the child's lead, and mirror their emotional states, as well as encouraging moments of positive connection between parent and child. The more connected the child feels to their parents, the more available they are to enter into difficult conversations. The parent's presence also demonstrates commitment and a willingness to be vulnerable too, especially through play. As much as the parent gets to learn more about their child's inner world during nature-based therapy, so too the child gets the chance to discover more about the parent's thoughts and feelings. They might witness their parent being nervous about a blindfolded sensory activity or watch them getting uncomfortably dirty when hiding in a bush for a game that the child loves; these moments can lead to beautiful conversations about courage, discomfort, honesty, and boundaries. The process of counseling can be a very scary prospect, as it asks us to be vulnerable and expose our shadow sides to a person outside of our close circle. When parents join their children in this process, it demonstrates to the child that they alone are not the problem and that the family is in this growth process together.

With older children (ages 12 and up), we might suggest family sessions at the outset, in order to establish safety, expectations, and open communication, before shifting to individual sessions once the youth is more comfortable with the therapist and the location(s). We certainly have to be aware that meeting a child/youth in an outdoor setting is very different from when a parent brings their child to an office and then waits for them outside in the hall. We have to ensure that the youth feels a sense of safety and ease within the chosen setting and that they can build trust with the therapist in this context. Of course, this changes on a case-by-case basis, depending on the presenting needs for counseling. For example, a youth who experiences high anxiety may request to have a parent present for longer and then slowly move toward one-to-one sessions when they are ready. A different youth may not want their parent present at all in the beginning, especially when the youth's concerns are centered in family dynamics issues and trust has been eroded. In this case, we may begin the counseling process one-to-one with the youth and then invite the parents to join in sessions once the youth feels they have built the confidence and self-awareness to engage in difficult conversations with them. In that scenario, the nature-based setting can become a neutral setting, one outside of the home and offices, where adults often wield power. When the nature setting has become a powerful resource for that youth, then the opportunity for them to demonstrate their connection, knowledge, and skills within the nature context can be very empowering.

A Guide to the Nature-based Therapy Family Session

There are myriad issues relevant to family process that can be addressed by nature-based therapy for families, including emotional expression, accountability, conflict resolution, boundaries, self-regulation, shifting family roles, grief and loss, self-esteem, trust, routines, managing anxiety and depression, and school stress. Once the family has identified those issues important to them, the therapist can plan for activities that will elicit experiences relating to those themes and that are appropriate to the family's emotional and physical needs. There is no simple prescription in nature-based therapy informing the therapist of the perfect intervention for each family issue. With a slight alteration in framing, any one activity can be adjusted to highlight several different topics, and for any one topic, there are countless variations of activities that may be suitable. The ability to be creative, spontaneous, and flexible is a strength required of a nature-based therapist, as the therapist must be constantly adapting to the presenting state of family members, the environment, the weather, and the arising needs. As working with multiple family members normally requires increased containment and directives, in therapy, we find it helpful to approach family sessions with a vision and plan and then be ready and willing to completely alter that plan based on what comes up. As we know, plans are only maps, not the territory.

The next section offers a progression one might follow when setting up a family session for success in nature, based loosely on these four stages:

- Family check-in
- Games
- Focused therapeutic activity
- Closing and debriefing

This is just a general guide and obviously not prescriptive to every single family or session. Because we are always first and foremost client-centered, we would consider our client's ecological assessment and therapy goals and always be willing to follow what arises in the moment. Each stage will be explored with case examples from our practice.

Family Check-in

We make the intention to begin each family session with some form of check-in that gives each individual a voice and a chance for the family members and the therapist to get a sense of everyone's present emotional and physical state. This awareness will help to guide the subsequent direction of the session and may elicit a current problem or a present dynamic that the therapist had been unaware of. Of course, being nature-based, we don't simply ask "How is everyone doing?" Instead we partner with the natural world to provide a variety of languages of expression for the children and parents to draw upon. Bringing in metaphor is a favorite tool for eliciting awareness of the client's present state, and two forms are common. One is to request them to relate their internal state to a natural process (e.g., What weather system would you be today? What animal do you feel like right now?). A second form is to draw from the direct environment for inspiration, asking the family members to each find a tree, pick up a leaf, or discover any plant, rock, or part of the surrounding that could express their current state. This method is especially helpful when a child is hesitant to speak, and they can simply pick up, or point, to a natural being around them. It is amazing the insight that can be drawn from such a simple activity, and often the client even discovers something new about themselves in the process.

Case Example

Jen, 12 years old, and her single father were attending family therapy for the treatment of Jen's severe social anxiety. Her nervousness in social situations extended to school, public interactions, family gatherings, and crowded events. Her anxiety got in the way of her confidence to speak with anyone beyond her closest friends and family—and likewise she was very quiet in therapy as well. We often met at a local lake, a setting that was a resource in Jen's life, exploring the lakeshore and trails together as a window to conversation—though Jen often tried to turn to her father to provide answers for her. For our check-in one day, Katy suggested that we each find an object on or near the trail that represented how we were feeling that day. After a few minutes of exploring, Jen picked up a knotted brown clump of plant roots and expressed that this is how it feels to be inside of her mind. When asked for further descriptors, Jen shared about the confusion and frustration that she felt on a constant basis. This visual, and its opening to further explanation, was more than she had been able to previously share about her internal state—both with the counselor and her father. This was an understanding of her interior experience that I might not have learned about if Katy expected her to express herself in words alone. Sometimes the check-in alone can hold enough significant content and energy that it can morph into a full session.

Games

We almost always turn to interactive and playful games as the next step in a family session. Even those "too cool" 13- and 14-year-olds can't resist a good hiding or sneaking game that gives them a chance to show off their speed, strength, or sneaking skills. The pleasure that shows on a child's face when the parents are asked to play with them is palpable: diving into the dirt together, hiding behind trees and giggling, or chasing their dad around a field. This is the moment where we are working on healing attachment, where family play elicits our ventral vagal neural network, the mirror neurons fire, and that feeling of being loved and attuned tightens the family threads. Jennifer Kolari, child and family therapist and author of *Connected Parenting*,[5] presents a convincing case for the importance of rough-and-tumble play with your child, no matter how old, especially when the bond is thin from cyclical negative interactions. She often assigns parents to the task of instigating adrenaline play (e.g., chasing games, pillow fights) and baby play (e.g., tickling, horsey rides) as pathways to increased connection with their kids. As prolific developmental psychologist Gordon Neufeld and physician Gabor Maté write in their classic parenting book, *Hold On to Your Kids*,[6] the move toward peer orientation versus parent orientation is one of the most threatening trends to a child's emotional health. What better way to bring a child back into your fold than by laughing and playing together? Just imagine the feeling in your own heart when you have a good laugh with your child (or remember laughing with your parent), when you let go of inhibitions and exhaustion and just get silly. It's the stuff that children crave but that we too often let slide due to the constant demands and exhaustion of schedules, chores, work—all the things that lead us to impatience, demands, and disengagement. Along with family bonding, the early introduction of games serves further purposes. Play helps to disarm resistance in the child, opening them to the process and strengthening their connection with the counselor and nature as allies—building comfort, trust, and familiarity. It can also help to release any jitters or nervousness, allowing the child to move energy through their bodies so that they can be more receptive to focused learning or sharing afterward.

We aim to pick games that can highlight the strengths of the child and set them up for success rather than struggle or failure. That does not mean it can't be challenging but that we can scaffold the game in a way that they will eventually succeed, ideally in collaboration with the parent(s). In this way, we are building the family members' self-esteem, emphasizing strengths, and fostering connective experiences. Integrated into the chosen games, we can apply our framing, debriefing, and metaphoric skills to add layers of meaning that relate to the family's experience.

Some kids also come to therapy with a knack for creating new games, and you can simply follow their lead (though sometimes you need to adjust the rules and boundaries to ensure safety and inclusion). It can be inspiring to watch a kid being so excited to come to therapy because he has been thinking all week about the game he wants to play (often some version of tag, dodgeball, and hide-and-seek). With families, this often ends up being a process of modeling to the parent how to follow the kid's interest, engage fully in play, and be flexible. I (Katy) have worked with several parents who are very uncomfortable in this state—they have not engaged in physical play with their child in a long time—and thus it becomes a chance for the kids to witness their parents stepping out of their comfort zone to connect with their children. Many learning opportunities for problem solving and conflict resolution inevitably emerge during games, as boundaries are crossed and rules are broken, fairness is navigated, and the capacity to handle "losing" builds resilience. Last, these engaging games also carry with them the possibilities for therapeutic relationship development and engagement of the therapist with the client and family system.

Case Example

A very simple and fun way to introduce nature-based play that works well in a forested trail setting is Ambush and Flash Flood. This game can be introduced at the outset of a session and then returned to periodically to help blend focused attention and frustration with movement and release. It involves inviting the clients to call out the words "Ambush" or "Flash Flood" at any time along the trail, and then participants have to respond accordingly. "Ambush" means that everyone gets ten seconds to run up the trail and hide within a couple of meters of the trail. The caller then walks by, trying to spot the hiders; if the hiders are not seen, they can jump out and yell "Ambush" to surprise the seeker. When "Flash Flood" is called out, everyone has to jump onto something a few feet off the ground. Ten-year-old Robbie and his mother, Jan, had been referred to nature-based therapy because Robbie was having ongoing negative interactions with teachers and the principal at school and had been diagnosed with ADHD and anxiety. He had low awareness of his impact on other people and a difficult time verbalizing his internal struggles with anxiety to his mother. Robbie was open to the idea of meeting with the counselor but not exactly eager to jump into discussing problems, but he certainly loved exploring outdoors. Jan was often caught in a pattern of correcting and redirecting Robbie, concerned with his manners and his ability to listen to adults and follow instructions. To help her become more relaxed and move into connection (rather than correction) with Robbie, the counselor introduced Ambush and Flash Flood. Robbie was eager at the opportunity to play this game and loved calling out the words along the trail for the pleasure of seeing his mother and counselor jump up on logs and hide behind trees along with him. Laughter inevitably ensues from this game, releasing the sense of pressure and tension involved in the formality of counseling. This game helped to build rapport with the counselor and also let Robbie witness his mother in a playful state, even being surprised by her skills at jumping and hiding. The spontaneity of this game meant that the therapist, Robbie, or his mother could be the leader at any point, thus shifting out of a power dynamic where the therapist is always in control. Eventually the trail took us to a creek, where we stopped to find rocks that could help Robbie represent the various "problems" that were getting in the way of his success at school. After releasing his energy, and being in his joyful place, Robbie was then willing to open up and name some of the things he was struggling with.

Focused Therapeutic Activity

This next stage varies widely and is completely responsive to the identified therapeutic goals, emerging issues/concerns, and present emotional state of the family. Depending on their needs, we might move toward some form of psycho-education (e.g., to work on emotion-regulation, coping with anxiety), family initiatives (for addressing trust, communication, problem solving, etc.), or sensory awareness activities (to develop attention, mindfulness, stress-reduction, nature connection, and family bonding).

Psycho-education: We find that having the family together when learning these skills and concepts is valuable, as it provides a shared language that they can continue applying outside of the therapy session. Of course, while occasionally some paper and markers are helpful (especially for the art-oriented clients), we still provide psycho-education within an experiential framework, so as to integrate the information on both the mind and body levels. The Zones of Development (i.e., comfort, challenge, danger as described in chapter 5) is a concept we introduce to almost every family we work with. This model provides a framework for the therapeutic process of growth, for bringing awareness to the areas in their lives where they succeed/struggle, and for encouraging openness among family members. We also find it quite valuable to teach families about the fight/flight/freeze functions of the nervous system (also described in chapter 5). Most clients come to us for help with emotion regulation, and we find that providing both parents and kids with a shared knowledge of our basic mammalian survival responses can greatly assist in developing self-awareness and empathy. To help clients tune into their unique emotional/physical sensations as they relate to the various states of stress response, we often encourage kids and parents to map out the fight/flight/freeze on a body drawing, using colors and shapes to identify where and how their body responds to fear, anger, sadness, joy, etc. For some kids, however, even the task of drawing can be difficult to focus on, and our creativity as nature-based practitioners is called into action, as illustrated by the following case.

Case Example

Riley, a 9-year-old boy diagnosed with ADHD, had a body constantly in motion, just vibrating with energy, and a lack of awareness for other people's personal space. He was getting into increasing conflicts with his father as well as repeated incidents with peers in school, which were drawing attention and concern. Riley also had a giant heart, was sensitive and caring, and held a deep appreciation for nature and its multitude of creatures. The therapist was inspired by his talent for embodying various animals and introduced the fight/flight/freeze response by asking him to act out different animals (bunny, deer, lion, wolf, hedgehog, turtle, snake). The therapist enacted the animals with him (matching and mirroring him), and then his dad was asked to enter into the scene as the predator, or challenger, of that animal (in a playful manner). Riley and the therapist would then respond to that threat in the same way that each specific animal would typically respond. For example, a rabbit happily nibbling on grasses would suddenly bolt and hide behind a rock when a coyote appears. The scenes were easily amplified by the natural landscape in which we played (a treed meadow with rocky outcroppings). In this manner, Riley was able to experience the various states of arousal somatically (rather than just on a cognitive level) and could easily relate to the different animals upon reflection; he realized that he sometimes reacted like a lion and other times like a rabbit. Riley and his parents were able to identify which animals they most often turned into under stress, as well as which animals they see in one another. This approach brings in a lightness to the heavy topics of anger, fear, and shutdown and provides a pathway for developing awareness and conversations about how these states show up in family dynamics and at school.

Family initiatives: There are some excellent resources that list a variety of interactive, experiential initiatives that can be undertaken with families in the outdoors to reach a variety of therapeutic goals.[7] Such activities often utilize various transportable props (ropes, balls, cups, etc.) that can be brought along in the therapist's backpack or objects found in nature (sticks, rocks, etc.), which we prefer. Team initiatives can be beneficial when you notice that youth need more of a challenge when trying to help a family gain insight on communication and teamwork dynamics, and to bring members together in a united purpose. When introducing initiatives into the session, it is essential to appropriately *frame* the task so that instructions and expectations are very clear (or you will produce unhelpful frustration) and so the family can view the activity through the lens of their personal experience and goals. By introducing effective stories and metaphors, you cue the clients to begin reflecting on their process from the outset of the initiative. Likewise, skilled *debriefing* of the initiative will help to prompt the clients to reflect upon what happened (or is happening) in an activity, bringing awareness to their own roles, behaviors, thoughts, and feelings and ascertaining how they can transfer the learning back home. While the therapist may have preconceived notions of the insight a certain intervention may elicit, it is essential that the therapist stay open to processing the experience as it manifests uniquely for each client. Inspired by Gestalt therapy, and developed to strengthen learning experiences, school teacher Terry Borton's reflective model produced the popular debriefing questions of *what, so what, now what?*[8] The question "what?" asks clients to make nonjudgmental observations of their behaviors, relationships, and feelings in the activity, in essence, objectively describing what happened. "So what?" invites clients to reflect on the impact and consequences of those actions, in essence, how they or others may have been effected by what happened. "Now what?" asks clients to use the information gained from the activity and the two previous questions/responses to make choices about what to keep the same, leave behind, or do differently next time; this is where family members may make new requests or commitments to one another in the service of working toward their goals for family therapy.

Case Example

Two siblings, ages 10 (a boy with a chronic illness) and 12 (a girl), and their parents were attending family therapy for coping with the loss of grandparents and sibling conflict. At the second session, I (Katy) introduced a ball initiative called Seek and Defend with the intention of learning more about the family, building their cohesion, and engaging the youth. Balls (tennis or whiffle balls work well) for the game were chosen by the family to represent the *values* of laughter, honesty, and respect. In this game, the therapist represents an obstacle that gets in the way of those family values (which the family, in this case, named as fighting). The therapist's job is to hide all of the balls and then try to tag the family members while they search for and retrieve the "value" balls and safely transport them back to their home base. As the family ran around the forested area searching for the hidden balls behind bushes and rocks, they were full of laughter and squeals. The therapist worked hard to chase them all, tagging each member a couple of times, so they had to "recharge" at home base. As the "teams" were four against one, the family had the advantage and were able to work together to finally retrieve and protect all of their values. They discovered more success getting the balls back to home base if they threw them to each other, rather than trying to run with them individually the whole way. Upon debriefing the game, the parents were able to identify with the stress of being chased (i.e., feeling it in their bodies), the children reflected on the importance of working together and being creative to achieve goals, and they all expressed feelings of excitement and joy in playing together. The family acknowledged that they rarely made the time to be silly together and craved the opportunity to be on the same team working toward a common goal.

Sensory awareness activities: We have already described in detail the ways that sensory awareness practices are a key element of the nature-based therapy approach (in chapter 7), but it is worth reinforcing the value of this practice as it pertains to family systems therapy. When we can offer the parent and child the opportunity to deepen their attunement to the outer landscape while in relationship, then we are simultaneously moving toward healing attachment between generations and between each person's relationship to nature. Teaching a child the ability to observe and witness the Earth's multitude of gifts is that much richer, and hopefully more enduring, if their caring adult can see through the same eyes. And when families are given the opportunity to slow down enough to share in a sense of wonder, gratitude, and respect together, then a culture of appreciation is formed. In the human-serving sense, we are hoping to strengthen the family's capacity to seek out contact with nature as a resource in their lives; to navigate stress, loss, and change; and to experience healing. In the Earth-serving sense, we are hoping to develop humans who will care deeply and act compassionately in service of the environment. Sensory awareness can be introduced in varying intensities according to the developmental level of the child, from Joseph Cornell's "camera" activity, where parent and child take turns surprising each other by pointing out beautiful close-ups of nature, to silent blindfolded walks, where each person has a turn diving deep into their sensory experience of the landscape, while at the same time developing trust in their guiding family member. It is important to scaffold the sensory experiences for families, allowing the therapist to assess the person's level of comfort with opening up to the senses, with sensory deprivation (blindfolded activities), and ability to focus and attend to sensations. We would not want to enter into a blindfolded sensory game on the very first day of counseling before trust with the therapist has been built and expectations for moving clients beyond their comfort zone has been established.

Case Example

The Hug-a-tree activity is a beautiful opportunity for stepping deeply into one's senses at the same time as working on elements of trust, communication, and connection among family members. For example, a newly blended family of four (two single parents and their children) had been attending nature-based therapy sessions for a few months to work on easing relationship tensions and developing cohesion as a family. The children (girls, aged 9 and 13) were working on accepting and trusting their stepparents, while the parents were working on valuing each child uniquely and figuring out how to co-parent. The Hug-a-tree activity was offered as a way to emphasize the progress they had made as a family and to continue building trust. Each parent was partnered with their stepchild and instructed to lead them blindfolded to a tree; the specific tree was to be chosen by the parent, based on valued qualities that reminded them of their stepchild. The child was asked to get to know the details of the tree so intimately with her senses that she would be able to find that tree again with the blindfold removed. In order to set up the activity safely, the child was asked to express clearly to the parent how she wanted to be led, and they were to make a plan for communication before moving into silence for the game. Many rich conversations emerged from this activity, along with precious moments of bonding. The children were able to sink into a bodily feeling of trusting their stepparents while they were being led to the tree, a sentiment the 13-year-old had been hesitant to acknowledge previously. This aspect also led to awareness about the importance of clearly asking for what you need and respecting boundaries. The girls were excited about being able to eventually find their tree again, proud of using the sensory skills they had been developing over the course of therapy. Lastly, the opportunity for the unique trees to act as mirrors for expressing appreciation for one another had a strong impact. The trees represented assets such as strength, resilience, creativity, beauty, humor, and friendship. After the parents pointed out the special qualities they had noticed, the children were also able to see themselves in the chosen trees, and the feeling of joy in being witnessed for their strengths was palpable. Furthermore, whenever the family later returned to this same grove of trees, the kids often visited "their tree," enhancing their connection to place.

Closing and Debriefing

As in most counseling sessions, an intentional closing to the time spent together is important in acknowledging the transition out of the therapeutic space, strengthening concepts learned, and recognizing the current state of each family member as they leave. It is also very easy to lose track of time when exploring outdoors together, so a key skill of the nature-based therapist is staying attuned to the amount of time spent moving through the environment and ensuring that you return to a designated starting spot (e.g., a trailhead) in order to close the session at the agreed-upon time. Sometimes kids want to keep exploring, or have a hard time stopping a fun game, so part of our job as the therapist is to maintain clear boundaries around ending. The "check-out" process can be fairly simple, with the main goal being to provide a voice for each family member to relay the impact the session had for them. More detailed questions might be, What are you taking away from today? What today was like a rose? What was like a thorn? What was a highlight of our time together? But if you do run short on time, or have children or clients less inclined to process verbally, you might turn to brief options for closing expressions and feedback. Some ideas include return to your check-in activities and repeat (e.g., a quick weather metaphor, which is great if you started out the same way and thus get a sense of changing "internal" weather systems); ask them to rate themselves on a scale of 1 to 5 (giving the option to show the rating on fingers is even less intimidating); or do a one-word checkout that asks them to sum up their feeling state in one simple word.

The steps outlined above are simply a guide, an offering of the rich variety of ways you can step into your own creativity as a nature-based therapist to explore family dynamics in partnership with earthly elements. We invite you to challenge your own fears and uncertainties of breaking with conventional office-based practices and to discover the myriad opportunities for enhancing family well-being outside of the office walls. This practice can be adapted to all sorts of helping professions that find themselves with the daunting task of assisting families to heal and move toward improved functioning and happiness.

9

Multi-family Nature-based Therapy

A thing is right when it tends to preserve the integrity,
stability, and beauty of the biotic community.

ALDO LEOPOLD

We know that involving families in an ongoing and integral basis throughout counseling, instead of as an occasional add-on to youth and child mental health services, is a powerful avenue to achieving meaningful change in the lives of families, when appropriate. We acknowledge that circumstances can prevent family engagement, or at times working individually can be more effective and productive. That said, we always work toward some level of family involvement.

What if we were to bring multiple families together as a treatment model? If a service provider's philosophy acknowledges that one person's struggle contributes to, and responds to, larger systemic dynamics in the family and community, then this understanding should be reflected in the treatment structure. Many programs express a desire to acknowledge the family role and the influence of the local environmental factors but do not, or cannot, work from a family-centered perspective where the whole family, rather than the youth, is viewed as the client. As a result, the involvement with families is often not intensive enough to address the complex and deep-seated patterns that serve to keep families in a state of stress. Beyond the family structure, and from a broader system-theory perspective, lies the community. If we hear the wisdom in Aldo Leopold's quote above, we must recognize those actions that protect the larger communities, beyond the individual, beyond the family, and into community and, ultimately, the community of all living things. In this chapter, we share a model to move from individual and family-based responses to multi-family nature-based therapy. We do this by describing how the Family Roots program in Victoria, British Columbia, came to be.

Adventure programming (e.g., adventure therapy approaches as shared in chapter 2) often utilizes the power of group experience and processing to create and highlight personal growth; so too, nature-based therapy for families can benefit from the group format and the experiential and adventurous activities.[1] In this approach, multiple families of various compositions and key issues (e.g., single parents, grief and loss, family conflict, addictions, chronic illness/injury) are brought together for an immersive and facilitated nature experience. Family members find a community of support and empathy through shared group experiences, along with the knowledge that they are not alone in their struggle and their courage. The potential for the multi-family therapy model to decrease isolation and self-judgment, build resilience, and establish lasting resources for family well-being is extensive[2] yet not explored widely enough among mental health services, especially not with an outdoor approach. Frequently, strained social services are stuck trying to fix and put out fires through a problem-focused lens that leaves families feeling judged, labeled, and isolated in their pain. We have heard this story often from parents frustrated with long wait-lists, brief isolated solutions, and contextual barriers that prevent them from providing their kids with the opportunities they need to thrive.

Sprouting the Family Roots Program

Our interest in bringing the benefits of nature-based therapy and adventure opportunities to families with barriers led to the birth of the Family Roots Program, a multi-family adventure therapy program based in Victoria. For the past ten years, we have had the immense privilege of witnessing the transformative journeys of over fifty brave families who have participated. This unique program emerged out of the benefits of collaboration and community support. At the time of its inception, we all had been heavily influenced by family approaches to adventure and nature-based therapies. Katy had been inspired by observing family-intensive weekends during wilderness therapy treatment for teens with addictions, and she completed her master's thesis (2008) on outdoor family therapy. She was most fascinated by the rich learning moments that were uncovered through the brief family encounters during the three-month residential treatment; however, she saw limitations to these short intensives where the families only began to scratch the surface, unearthing negative interactional patterns, and did not have enough time to practice new ways of relating. Nevin completed his doctoral studies (2007) in wilderness therapy, specifically assessing the impact of family involvement in the treatment process. His research was driven by previous frustrations in working with youth outside of their family systems in youth justice wilderness rehabilitation programs. For him, seeing individual-level growth and development in youth quickly diminish following their return to family and community—which did not understand, recognize, or honor the learning—was difficult to re-live year after year. Dave also completed his master's thesis (2011) in the family realm when he worked in an adventure program serving families where one parent had an acquired brain injury. While all three of us had years of guiding and outdoor leadership experience with groups, primarily with youth (and some adjunct family work), we were all taken by the power of family engagement in therapy, especially with multiple families. In short, we strongly advocate for family involvement in therapy, and in the case of Family Roots, the added benefits of multiple families working/walking together has proven immensely powerful as it represents a community-level intervention.

Before describing the model, we feel it's worth sharing a bit of the backstory to the program. We do so because it is important to acknowledge that its success was due in a large part to the collaboration of multiple organizations, people, and resources, and that no one organization would have been as successful going at it alone. That said, we advocate for you, too, to explore partnership opportunities in your communities for program development.

In the beginning of Family Roots, Katy was working with the Sooke Family Resource Society (SFRS), providing counseling and family development support to families coping with cases of neglect and abuse. Thus, she sought to develop a model that would locate healing within the family system for the duration of treatment and put the onus of change and growth on all members. Knowing that the social services agency where she worked did not have the resources to run a complex outdoor program on their own, she reached out to other community organizations who were already engaged in the business of providing rich nature-based experiences to people with barriers: the Boys and Girls Club of Victoria (BGC), where Nevin was a former program supervisor, and Power To Be Adventure Therapy Society (PTB) where Dave was working at the time.

Through sharing the resources of counseling and family therapy skills, outdoor site and facilitation, risk management and group adventure expertise, and a researcher with experience grant writing, an innovative program was born in a very short period of time. All three organizations believed in the value of connecting people with nature, had the experience of running effective and safe group programs, and had the passion for creating accessible opportunities for families. PTB, a non-profit whose mission is to empower people living with a barrier to explore their limitless abilities through adventures in nature, continues to champion the Family Roots program through its generous funding and program delivery. It was through the conception of the Family Roots program that two of us, David and Katy, first met and laid the groundwork for developing our approach to nature-based therapy, and their clinical practice Human Nature Counseling and Consulting.

The Family Roots model brings five to seven families together once per month, over a period of six months, to share in adventure, play, nature-connection, and learning to enhance healthy family functioning. Unlike nature-based therapy described in other chapters, the Family Roots program was not designed for just short sessions but rather includes short family sessions (which may be sixty to ninety minutes), full days, as well as overnight and multi-day experiences (weekend-long). With the help of PTB's resources, families have the opportunity to kayak, canoe, hike, camp, swim, and try ropes courses within a supportive and safe environment. It is an approach that focuses on strengths, acceptance, and connection to change the stories of families, as one father so powerfully shared with the group at the end of his family's six-month involvement: "When we first signed up, I thought there must really be something wrong with my family to need help, but now I realize that every family struggles, and we were just brave enough to do something about it."

From our years of experience facilitating the Family Roots program, we have distilled the core components—the *BALANCE model*—that we believe leads to the successful outcomes of a multi-family nature-based approach. By offering these insights here, we hope to inspire more agencies serving youth and families to develop holistic experiential programming that builds connection with family, community, and the land. The components are listed and then described separately below.

The **BALANCE** model for family systems change:

- Bonding
- Alternate story
- Long-term support
- Awareness of family change process
- Nurturing holistic health
- Challenging homeostasis through adventure
- Education and skill development

Bonding

This component is all about connection—at all levels of the system: self, parent-child, community, Earth relations, and sometimes even spirit. Through extended immersions in nature (a full day or longer), therapeutic rapport can be built that allows all family members to sink into increasingly connected and open spaces to allow for healing: defenses begin to drop and vulnerability is safe to express. This kind of familiarity is harder to develop in the brief therapy hour, and when we drop the agenda of "expert–client" to paddle alongside, share food, and sing songs by a campfire with our clients, then we can know them in a more holistic and authentic way. The importance of *play* in healing attachment wounds, once again, cannot be understated[3]—and the opportunity for *all* family members to engage in fun, energetic, interactive games, where they must let go of effortful appearances, is a key ingredient to each daily schedule. Here the group component is an aid to letting down defenses: facilitators model a willingness to be silly; parents inspire other parents; and kids watch other kids move out of their comfort zone and laugh together—laughter is essential. The community that is built among the families, whose pretenses of "perfect family life" can be left behind, is a protective factor for incidents of depression, anxiety, and overwhelm so often felt in the isolated homes of closed-door neighborhoods. One single mother, whose teenage son had been living full-time with his father, shed tears when she sank into the realization that this perfectly constructed opportunity to bond with her son on a monthly basis was soon coming to an end. She was inspired to figure out how to continue bringing her children together, removed from electronic and peer distraction, to share in connective experiences. The genuine friendships she made with other mothers in this group also continued to sustain her long after the program.

Bringing multiple families together to learn, grow, and challenge themselves in community has the benefit of enhancing the possibilities for friendships and mentorship. Kids learn that they can have safe relationships with multiple adults, get to know other kids in similar situations, and feel the care of the team of helpers. This program is normally facilitated by three staff plus a team of up to five volunteers and practicum students. The variety of leaders involved means that each participant can usually find someone with whom to build strong therapeutic rapport. We often hear feedback from parents about how touched they are that the volunteers give up their precious weekends to support their families—the impact of being held and respected within an accepting community cannot be understated. As one alumni parent wrote to us, three years after her participation in Family Roots, "We all learned so much...You know it is an amazing feeling being loved, supported, and knowing we are not alone, all the love without conditions."

Alternate Story

The opportunity for families to redefine their story, with a focus on strengths rather than struggle, is a cornerstone of this program. The use of story is woven throughout the programming, whether through a continuous narrative that is told each month, collective nature-art making, or writing a family song that is shared around the campfire. These processes allow the families to reflect on the journey they are taking together and to amplify the resources, strengths, and experiences of lived success they encounter. Within the safe context of the group, nature, and adventure experience, family members can begin viewing one another in a new light and in new roles—outside of the labels applied to them by societal systems. Time and time again, we hear parents expressing deep gratitude to finally have entered a safe space where their child is being accepted and honored for his gifts rather than feeling shame and embarrassment for the "wrong" way he is behaving and trying to control his behavior. Within the nature context, their children have adequate space and resources for self-regulation, and they can participate in engaging activities that allow their skills and abilities to shine (e.g., canoeing, kayaking, ropes course, hiding games, hiking). The transfer of learning and insight from the specific activities experienced during therapy to other contexts is often facilitated by the use of metaphors. The concept of metaphoric connections is introduced by the therapist and serves to link the interventions, and the skills and strengths used to complete them, to the changes the clients are trying to make in their lives. Metaphors, inspired by nature and most impactful if generated by the clients, also allow families to view their own process and history from a new perspective and with acceptance for the natural cycles of life: birth, death, change, storms, competition, and reciprocity. For example, in an activity called the Nature Sculpture, family members are asked to slowly walk about a forested area to search for two natural objects they can pick up: one they are drawn to and one they are repelled by. Family members then regroup and are asked to present each object and why they chose it, describing its physical qualities and oddities. The therapist then helps them to draw connections between the qualities of the object and aspects of themselves that embody the same nuances, thus bringing awareness to the assets they bring to the family as well as their prickly parts. The family is then instructed to build a sculpture representing their whole family by placing their nature objects in relationship to one another. By doing so, the family is able to gain a visual representation of their experience of family dynamics, and similar or divergent perspectives may be elicited and discussed. Further metaphors about their family story can be drawn from where the family places objects (e.g., are they close or far apart, is the sculpture colorful, soft, breakable). The more-than-human natural world provides the therapist with myriad metaphors from which to draw parallels to the family's unique processes and personality.

Long-term Support

In the development of the Family Roots program, we believed that consistent, longer-term involvement with the family system was essential for meaningful change to occur. Within the multi-family format, this allows for the natural development of group processes to emerge, as family members slowly build trust and familiarity and, eventually, mutual connection and understanding. Community is built through large-group activities, in addition to smaller-group processes (kids-only and parents-only groups) and unstructured time for mingling. We also focus on shorter-duration excursions (one to two days) and more accessible locations that allow families to easily commit to the whole program, working around work/school schedules and travel cost barriers. We are thus able to serve families with children as young as 7 years, although the ideal range for children is 8 to 14 for this program. Ultimately, Family Roots is a mental health promotion model where we address risk factors early on in the child and family's life, improving self-esteem, self-regulation skills, open and non-violent communication, access to external resources, and healthy attachment bonds, which lay the foundation for less risk-taking in adolescence. We have also built in a referral model that requires interested participants to become members of a local social service agency that they can continue to access for support and counseling after the program is finished. Having been an important presence during key transition periods and turning points in the families' lives, we often hear from participants months and years after the program. Sometimes they are reaching out for further help, but other times it is to share a success or to help other people in their lives get connected with resources.

Awareness of Family Change Process

It has been well-established that client motivation for seeking change is one of the top factors that contributes to successful mental health treatment.[4] It makes sense then that whole-family system change would require that each family member is motivated. Therefore, an intake process that focuses on the "family" as the client seeking support, rather than an "identified patient" with a tag-along family, makes the difference in maintaining low attrition rates and consistent program buy-in. An intake interview with every family member present is essential for determining the interest and commitment of each person, especially considering the intensity of the outdoor and group context and the results of an ecological assessment. We have encountered situations where one of the two parents is wavering in their motivation or where a youth is resistant from the outset; those instances have always ended in less-than-ideal participation and outcomes. We describe to the family in detail what they should expect out of the program—physically, emotionally, and logistically; and full consent from all family members is both essential and ethical. Experiential and nature-based activities that bring focus to themes of family identity, values, goals, communication, negotiating rules, strengths, and resources are woven throughout the program.

Through intentional processing and debriefing of experiences, clients are influenced by the input of other families to consider new perspectives or adopt different approaches to a problem. Transfer of learning back to the home environment is aided by pairing the immersive adventure weekends with monthly or bi-monthly separate family check-ins. These family therapy sessions assist in the integration of new skills and also allow the family members to address more private or specific concerns, trauma, and emerging needs. When we can know clients both in the wilderness environment as well as seated within their daily existence, that helps the therapist to get a clearer view of the processes that contribute to ongoing obstacles for healthy family and individual functioning. The true power of nature-based therapies is in the opportunity for clients to both talk and walk their changes. Because the family is in the field together, they can directly observe growth moments in action and thus hold one another accountable in the moment, and hopefully also when back in their home environment. A reflection from a parent of two expresses this best:

> Within a few hours [of the program starting], we were all laughing and playing with our families and each other. One of the themes that first weekend was to get out of your comfort zone and into your challenge zone! We did that by scaling the outdoor climbing wall, and I was really proud of my daughter for pushing herself and conquering her fear. The support of people that we barely knew made all the difference. We left that first day really realizing how much we needed to make that more of a priority in our lives, and at the end of the first weekend together, we left with something even more important, HOPE; for our family, as a whole, and for each of us individually.

Nurturing Holistic Health

Holistic is a buzz word these days, but its essence is wholeness—that means not separating the mind, the body, and the spirit, not prioritizing the cognitive over the emotional self; it means treating a person (or a planet) as a whole and interconnected systemic being, with each component important to overall health. Thus, in this model of family systems healing, we attempt to address multiple aspects of healthy living. We provide healthy meals and snacks throughout the day, and junk food is not to be brought by clients. By providing the food, we also decrease the stress on parents in preparing for the weekend; for parents, having a break from the stress of food provision is often on their list of favorite aspects of Family Roots. The focus on physical activity sets templates for active living, including visiting multiple accessible outdoor locations that the family can continue to go on their own time. Integrating nature-connective practices into the program routines, such as Sit Spot and sensory awareness exercises (examples in chapter 7) gives all family members the opportunity to tune into the rhythms and sounds of nature, slowing their nervous system and providing space for reflection. These practices also open the window for parents to tap into their spiritual selves (nonspecific to religious beliefs), as they are removed from the stress of everyday life. A favorite activity we offer on the camping trip is called the Drum Stalk. In this activity, participants have the chance to trust their bodily intuition and step into an enchanting dance with the Earth by walking blindfolded in the night forest toward the beat of a drum, their only guide. Many parents have expressed deep gratitude for having this facilitated opportunity to explore their relations with self/nature which often holds a spiritual essence for them.

Our participants are often single parents who rarely get time to themselves, and certainly are not afforded the intentional space to sink deeply into their senses and the present moment. Which brings us to the other essential ingredient in health promotion: connective interactions uninterrupted by the impediment of screens. The smartphone and tablet (along with TV and video games) have become a detractor in many family relationships: face-to-face conversations interrupted by beeps and messages, family activities usurped by video game addiction. We are all culprits of the downturned-eye syndrome: missing the smile on our kids face, the cool scooter trick they want to show us, or the simple story they are trying to share because of the constant allure to check that smartphone. And vice versa, the parent–child bond is facing big competition with the peer-focused demands of constant social networking online. At Family Roots, phones are to be used only for emergency purposes during the program, and other electronics are not allowed. Even one full day without screen time can be a big challenge and complete rarity for many modern families; the immersive nature-based therapy approach allows families to practice taking an intentional break from the web-connected world.

Challenging Homeostasis Through Adventure

In nature-based therapy, a common tool to spark the seeds of change is to unbalance the family homeostasis (the patterns and roles they are stuck within), allowing room for new possibilities of relating. Changing the status quo involves family members having the courage to step out of their *comfort zone* and into their *challenge zone*, where new experiences and uncertain outcomes exist. We do not engage this process until we know the family has achieved a grounding in nature-based practices and family reconnection (i.e., regulation, communication skills). To enter into "adventure" too quickly is not advised; it takes a sensitivity on the therapist's part to assess family preparedness. Adventure, challenge, and shifting homeostasis present risk to family safety; by helping to increase safety within the families, we invite their courage to then take risks. The adventure therapy field has been challenged on this front, yet the language and practices presented in text, and often in practice, suggest moving to risk too soon with groups and individuals. The initial challenge could be as simple as spending the whole day active outside or participating in an unfamiliar large group; for many people, that is intimidating enough to know they are engaging with a new experience. This positive experience of stress, coined "eustress" by Richard Lazarus in 1974,[5] serves to unbalance the family's homeostasis and thus open possibilities for new ways of interacting with one another and the world. The task is to induce enough subtle stress that clients step out of their comfort zone yet to not push them so far that they enter a state of distress,[6] which might prompt increased family dysfunction and possible therapy termination. The idea that a certain degree of stress can be a motivator for learning and change was first theorized in 1908 and was called the Yerkes-Dodson law.[7] In this theory, arousal prompts adaptation (developing healthy behaviors), but when arousal becomes too high, performance decreases. When clients have to navigate discomfort elicited by these new environments, physical challenges or emotional interactions, their latent strengths, resiliencies, and problem-solving skills become activated and reinforced. For example, kayaking and canoeing are great nature-based activities for families to explore. In Family Roots, paddling partners are chosen based on the family dyads that need increased connection and practice in navigating conflict. Because the family may not have prior paddling skills, each member is automatically placed under a slightly stressful situation where they must learn the new skill of paddling and collaborate in order to be successful in arriving at the destination. A wide range of feelings—from frustration, nervousness, and impatience to excitement, appreciation, peace, and joy—may be elicited. Some may love paddling, and others may find it frustrating, and the typical roles may be reversed, where a child is competent and has to guide their parent in the task.

The stress of the new environment and task thus promotes the discovery of some new abilities, necessitates enhanced cooperation and communication in order to move the boat along, and likely elicits moments of connection and laughter along the way.[8] On several occasions, we have witnessed parents absolutely fall in love with sea kayaking who normally do not have the time or resources to try new activities and interests for themselves. They discover a sense of self-efficacy, flow, and peace in that paddling rhythm, and then they seek out further opportunities to pursue this interest in their lives. Being able to share in that journey with a client, to walk them through the initial nervousness of a new experience and see them through to success, is widely different than suggesting a client take up a new sport or physical practice from one's office chair and hoping that they follow through.

Education and Skill Development

Intentionally incorporating practical tools (e.g., communication skills, activities for self-care) and psycho-education at the appropriate times for families, relevant to mental health and family functioning, is but practice that separates nature-based family therapy from just a nature camp. Depending on the therapeutic goals that families name when entering the program, themes are integrated into the nature and adventure programming to facilitate learning and growth. Relevant topics such as non-violent communication, conflict resolution, emotional competency, managing stress, and self-care are woven into the program curriculum through experiential approaches (never lecture style). The best description of this dynamic comes from the participants themselves, as one father of two said reflecting on the Family Roots program:

> In a busy world of work and school, Family Roots gave us a chance for some well-supported together time, for the kids and parents to do some emotional and other learning mixed with fun team tasks like the rock climbing, voyager canoeing, hikes, games campfires—the list goes on. All intermixed with thought-provoking activities and opportunities to talk freely and rise to the challenge of speaking up—possible here because of the type of support that the staff and volunteers fostered, and (as a

consequence) the fellow participants were comfortable to embrace as well. It was effective therapy without the kids realizing that's what it was.

In a society where mental health issues are often stigmatized, diagnoses such as ADHD and childhood anxiety are on the rise, and families live increasingly separate existences (even kids playing together in the streets is becoming a rarity), the need for family-centered services that enhance community building and foster reconnection along many systemic levels is paramount. We need to become more creative in our approaches to reaching out to struggling families and generate opportunities for both kids and parents to witness one another in their strengths and beauty, rather than focusing on what is wrong or needs to be fixed. We are witnessing more mainstream efforts to engage families in nature and well-being initiatives across North America.

A Brief Exploration of Earlier
Multi-Family Outdoor and Experiential Therapy

The Family Challenge program, as described by Clapp and Rudolf (in Gass, 1993),[9] was influential and led to the development of other family-based adventure therapy interventions across North America. One multi-family experiential therapy (MFET) program was developed by Omni Youth Services in Buffalo Grove, Illinois. It is delivered over a number of weeks, including weeknights and weekend mornings and occasionally an overnight camping/adventure trip. Three therapists work with four to six families (up to a maximum of twenty individuals) with multiple configurations (e.g., single parent, adopted, differing numbers of children/youth). The model was developed through the blending of a family enrichment program and adventure-based theory and practices; the opportunity for enrichment and therapy exist depending on level and style of interventions they engaged in. In wanting to better understand the process and practices at Omni, during his doctoral studies Nevin interviewed John Conway, a colleague and Omni MFET therapist. John mentioned the need to stay focused on the group as a whole (all families) when conducting activities, the family when working with individual families, and lastly the individuals of each family when necessary and time permitting. He described his concern of therapists slipping into family or even individual therapy when the intentions are multi-family, at the community level. This indicates that a high level of intention exists within the program staff to use time and resources effectively. When asked to expand on a few areas related to the concept of *change* in multi-family approaches, John shared the following:

Nevin: How can MFET assist clients with change?

John: Clients change on multiple levels. There is change on the individual level, family level, and even community/system level, as a result of multiple families co-creating change together. Each family has goals made up of individual family members' goals and then integrated together, so change at the family level necessitates some movement on the individual level. Because of the high degree of feedback that is encouraged from each family (even across families), there is systemic or community change that I believe breaks down the walls that many families in treatment build around themselves, leading to further isolation and a vicious "deficit-based" cycle.

Nevin: Can you describe why you believe MFET works?

John: Multi-family allows for a greater degree of peer-review and feedback, a greater degree of "normalizing," and confrontation/support cycles that aid in the overall integration toward change. Each family tends to embrace the "homework-like" feature, again allowing for further integration and insight development. Community building is a strength for any family structure and is an integral part of the family challenge program, given that many of the games involve multiple families. Intergenerational issues are dealt with on a whole new level, with supports and feedback cycles in place. Post-activity debriefing allows for a constant reworking of family goals and insight.[10]

An Evaluation of the Family Roots Program

While we will quickly admit the need for further research and evaluation of the Family Roots model, we wanted to share some of the findings from an evaluation completed after the first year of programming.[11] Fourteen individuals from four families participated in three separate days and two weekend-long sessions (similar to the MFET model of Omni mentioned above). With the support of the staff team of four, and over 100 volunteer hours, there were eighty-five hours of client service delivered, with sixty-five of those being outdoor experiential and adventure therapy and counseling sessions. Programming included games, initiatives, adventure activities (canoeing, kayaking, wall-climbing, hiking, and nature-connection activities), psychoeducational sessions, as well as individual family sessions on days in between the multi-family adventure days.

The evaluation consisted of pre–post measures utilizing the family environment scale (a measure of the social climate of family) and a customized survey with open- and closed-ended questions to gather the voices of the participants. The family measure showed improvements (not statistically significant but meaningful) in *family cohesion* and *family system maintenance* (indicating improvements in organization and control of family dynamics). Considering the relatively short duration of the intervention, we were pleased to see measurable change. The qualitative responses from participants suggested notable improvements in the home environment, such as reduced family arguments and increased family evening time together, both being strong indicators of positive family functioning and cohesion. While still happily engaged in delivering the Family Roots program, we can only offer here our conviction in its value, while we also own the responsibility to state that it requires further research to validate its effectiveness. We can offer plenty of the anecdotal support by ending with a quote from a past participant:

> FRP really enabled my son to express himself and open up and gave me the support I needed as parent. To have an outside third-party—and many different third-parties'—perspectives really helped to find alternate ways of handling conflicts and issues.

Conclusion

We hope the mental health profession can learn from and adopt ideas from this intuitive approach to enhancing family well-being. The potential exists to provide more opportunities for families with barriers to join in a community of care regardless of presenting issues or family composition (be it a history of trauma, loss, mental illness, poverty, immigration, separation, etc.). We know that bringing multiple organizations and professionals together can be trying and does not always lead to successful programs and services. We do know that we have worked through growing pains, with changing faces at organizations and allotted budgets, and yet have maintained a wonderful program for families that we know couldn't have been conducted by one person or even an organization alone. (This we learned during our first evaluation.) We have observed that bringing families together to explore the natural world in community fosters empathy, bonding, regulation, inspiration, peace, self-esteem, acceptance, self-awareness, and growth. This approach removes both clinician and client from the power dynamics and stigma of entering a social services office building for treatment and into a space where we can all be witnessed for our humaneness and our interdependence on the living systems of the Earth.

10

Group Applications
in Nature-based Therapy

*There is evidence that certain clients may obtain
greater benefit from group therapy than from other approaches,
particularly clients dealing with stigma or social isolation
and those seeking new coping skills.*

IRVIN YALOM

Nature-based therapy is inherently a systemic and transpersonal approach as it addresses the ways individuals are embedded and influenced by their surrounding systems on multiple levels: the internal mind-body experience, family systems, societal influences, environmental and spiritual elements. As such, nature-based practice also lends itself beautifully to the application of group work—in ways that almost seem unavoidable. Chapter 9 described how multi-family group therapy was the initial source and inspiration for the development of our (Dave and Katy) nature-based therapy practice. It was through the evolution of the Family Roots program that we first saw the need to provide a wider array of nature-based services to support mental health in our community. We observed that, within the nature-based context, children who carried with them labels of ADHD, ODD, anger, anxiety, and other externalizing issues were, maybe for the first time, thriving and developing new concepts of self-worth, acceptance, and belonging. By letting go of our dependence on the reliability of offices and worksheets, and entering into the richly varied context of the natural world, we are able to offer children and youth a nurturing context that has the potential to build resources in their life.

Nature-based groups provide a multitude of opportunities to address the developmental needs of children, including play, imagination, exploring bodily senses, problem solving, exercise, creativity, belonging, connection to the natural rhythms of the Earth, opportunities for mindfulness and self-reflection, and building resiliency. One of Katy's mentors, Katie Asmus, a faculty member at Naropa University in Boulder, Colorado, and founder of Namasté Healing Arts, strongly believes in the therapeutic potential of nature-based groups. Coming from a somatic perspective, she regularly observes how bringing groups out into the natural environment profoundly impacts clients' nervous systems in positive ways, allowing them to resource and connect more easily. A person might be nervous about meeting a new group of people, but their body is simultaneously responding to the positive influence of sunlight, birdsong, and swaying leaves. Likewise, offering groups outdoors gives children the opportunity to engage with and express their energy in ways that both soothe and stimulate their nervous system.

While a large portion of our counseling practice involves providing individualized services to children and families, we have been consistently called upon to create group-based opportunities for nurturing well-being. These two types of services are not mutually exclusive, rather they complement one another by filling in the gaps where each falls short.[1] Some children and youth refuse to engage in the intense focus of one-to-one counseling but are willing to participate in a group program, motivated by the possibility of friends, fun, and outdoor activity. Other children, who do thrive in individualized counseling, may need the exposure to groups in order to transfer their learning to wider social situations or to counteract prior negative social experiences.[2] Group therapy may be the only option for some families, due to cost barriers or scheduling issues, which is why we began offering after-school programs and school-based groups which reduce some accessibility issues by bringing the group opportunities directly to the children who need it.[3] Of course, for some the group context is not the right fit; issues such as physical aggression, debilitating anxiety, developmental challenges beyond the scope of the program, or a lack of motivation can inhibit positive participation. As with all types of group work, effective screening and intake is essential for composing a successful group, and some children do need individual counseling in order to create enough safety for successful participation in a group context.[4]

Over the years of offering group programs to our community and responding to requests based on the specific needs that parents, teachers, and school counselors were expressing, we have designed three different types of programs that we have found to be a particularly good fit with the nature-based therapy approach. In reflecting on the applications of nature-based practice to group work, we will draw on examples and learning from these group programs:

- New Roots: Therapy group for youth who struggle with managing anxiety and worry. This program is delivered in nearby parks after school for two hours per week and combines nature connection practices with play, experiential learning, mindfulness, cognitive strategies, and narrative therapy.
- Coyote Tracks: Full-day or full-week immersive programs for children struggling with ADHD, regulation, and social skills. This program incorporates wilderness living skills and deep nature connection practices. Coyote Tracks provides a safe and supported space to practice social-emotional learning, while also building self-esteem and confidence through igniting their passions among a supportive group of peers and trusted adults.
- School-based programming: Nearby park and wild spaces are utilized for small groups of children and youth during school hours to build self-regulation and social skills (elementary school) or mental health promotion and stress management (middle and high school). These programs are tailored to the needs of the specific schools and are enhanced because the barriers to participation are low. Children who may benefit are selected by school counselors, and the programs are designed to help the students build internal and external resources within the school setting.

In addition to exploring these programs, this chapter aims to elucidate how nature-based therapy addresses and enhances many of the therapeutic factors of group work as articulated by Irvin Yalom, professor emeritus of psychiatry at Stanford University and influential thinker on the process of group psychotherapy. It is our belief that many of these curative factors of groups are enhanced by partnering with the more-than-human natural world, particularly in the context of supporting children and youth.

Yalom's Therapeutic Factors of Groups

Irvin Yalom has made significant contributions to group psychotherapy through decades of research, writing, and practice. Of particular interest here are his therapeutic factors or, in his words, the elements making change possible, which are an "enormously complex process that occurs through an intricate interplay of human experiences."[5]

Yalom's therapeutic factors of groups are

- Instillation of hope
- Universality
- Imparting information
- Altruism
- Corrective recapitulation of the primary family group
- Development of socializing techniques
- Imitative behavior
- Interpersonal learning
- Group cohesiveness
- Catharsis
- Existential factors

Yalom explains that the boundaries between these elements are blurred and highly interdependent, together touching on the levels of cognition, behavior, emotions, and preconditions for change. He also readily admits that they are provisional guidelines, just one of many maps attempting to explain what accounts for therapeutic change in groups. Despite these limitations, we find them to be helpful in illuminating the potential for healing and change offered through nature-based group work for children and youth. We will attempt to make this clear by exploring eight of the factors that resonate most with nature-based practice. If it's not obvious yet, we are fans of Yalom's work.

Installation of Hope

The first of Yalom's therapeutic factors of groups is the installation of hope. He explains how the maintenance and protection of hope is essential to any successful therapeutic experience and emphasizes how the expectation that the process will be helpful is a powerful intervention in its own right. Referencing the growing body of research on the placebo effect, he asserts that both a client's and therapist's belief that the intervention will be healing do in fact matter and influence the impacts. As explored earlier, there is a surge of research and excitement regarding the healing potential of connection with nature. This enthusiasm, combined with the fact that nature-based therapy groups are not yet common, can bolster a sense of hope for children, youth, and families to engage in something very much needed, yet hard to come by, in the context of their lives.

Parents who register for our programs often foster a belief that participating in a group experience will help their child and family. Many of our young clients have a history of unsuccessful experiences in groups, whether in the school system or extra-curricular programs. It can be deeply painful for parents who are used to watching their children get in trouble, being kicked out of activities, or avoiding group situations all together; a feeling of helplessness can set in. Thus, when parents contact us to register their children in a nature-based program, they are usually reaching out with hope that this approach will be different, and often this is because they have noticed that their kids tend to thrive when outside. While hope within the children themselves often starts quite cautiously, maybe with hope for friendships and fun, it tends to build through the experiences of the program. As feelings of safety (knowing that not only physical but emotional safety is prioritized), acceptance (knowing their unique feelings and personality will be validated), and a sense of belonging (to both the group and the natural world) are established, then hope for change can build. We have witnessed parents picking up their children from our Coyote Tracks group with tears of relief for seeing a smile on their child's face at the end of the day. Hope in therapy is essentially about believing that things can and will change, that whatever pain exists currently will not always be there. By attuning to the natural cycles of the Earth, we can witness change in its inevitability; as change is the only guaranteed thing in life. The sun will rise and set, the leaves will turn colors and fall, the fiddleheads will eventually uncoil. Supporting children and youth to directly witness these cycles can help them to trust that growth and transformation are possible in their lives too.

Universality

The realization that we are not alone in our struggles is at the core of the universality factor. Yalom describes how in groups, especially during the early stages, learning how one is not unique in their circumstance can allow for powerful feelings of relief. We believe that a crucial element of group work is its capacity to reduce the isolation and stigma that so often accompanies mental health struggles. For some children, just the idea of requiring counseling to address problems can sometimes emphasize their self-judgment and the belief that they are "broken" or "bad." In this case, group work can become a bridge to introduce the child or youth to the development of self-awareness and self-reflection, while also serving to reduce isolation and shame. Sharing commonalities within a group counters the assumptions of "I'm all alone," "I'm different," and "Nobody gets me." Anxiety can be an especially isolating experience that, by its very nature, leads people to avoid social situations and withdraw from resources that could be helpful. For some youth who find solace in nature (sometimes more so than in people), a nature-based program may be a less intimidating environment to enter than an office-based group. Many children in our programs also experience universality in their shared love for nature: in their desire to admire the slugs, romp through the forest, and listen to the birds. Meeting like-minded children who are sensitive to the world and its creatures can be very comforting. Similarly, they discover a context where the big energy of their bodies can be accepted: where their need to move, run, climb, and sneak is encouraged and supported. (These impulses are often restricted in mainstream institutions for a large portion of children's days, leading to frustration and low self-esteem.) The Coyote Tracks and school-based programs give children a chance to connect with their wild selves, the parts that are all too often criticized in other contexts, and from that place of validation, they begin to build awareness and choice regarding how they want to be in the world.

Imparting Information

Offering psycho-education and practical coping tools is an important part of the group therapy component; however, finding developmentally appropriate ways to do so can be a challenge with children and youth. How do you maintain interest in the process while also making sure that tools are learned that can apply in everyday life? Instead of didactic methods of teaching, nature-based groups provide a rich possibility for imparting learning in an experiential and dynamic way that engages the mind and bodies of children. For example, for years we have been running nature-based after-school programs for middle school students who are experiencing anxiety. They come after a long day of trying to focus in school, and possibly a long day of nervous system overload if their anxiety is triggered by the school experience itself. The ability to function successfully at school can be affected by sensory sensitivities, social anxiety, test anxiety, learning disabilities, ADHD, bullying, trauma-related hyper-vigilance, and other issues. The last thing these kids need after school is to sit in another room at desks with the expectation of being able to continue exerting their prefrontal cortex (which may have been turned off all day while their brain stem was in charge trying to keep them safe).

The intention of nature-based groups is to help kids to regulate their nervous systems so that the prefrontal cortex can indeed come back online and to develop higher-order coping strategies that stick. Therefore, we meet youth where they are at, create safety, and give opportunities to move energy through their bodies (often running and hiding forest games). We offer resourcing through community building, sensory awareness, and mindfulness; and *then we* offer psycho-education to help them understand how they can take charge of anxiety. Topics are introduced in experiential and creative ways to keep youth engaged and open. For example, to help youth externalize their "worry," we often ask them to find a rock that can represent the heaviness of their worry, and then invite them to name the rock and write words on it (in pencil or chalk) that describe their anxiety symptoms—at the end of the program, this rock can be tossed into the water to symbolize letting go of that worry. To introduce the concept of "thinking traps" (negative thought patterns that often show up with anxiety and depression), we play the game Unnature Trail (drawn from Joseph Cornell's work), which involves hiding various objects representing each trap along a trail. For example, a globe to represent "global thinking," a danger sign to represent "overestimating danger," and a crystal ball to represent "fortune-telling." The youth then have to walk silently along the trail and use their keen observation skills to try to spot each "unnatural" object, counting how many they can find. Once all the objects are found, the youth are then more curious to learn about them and can work together to match the objects to the corresponding "thinking traps"; after this activity, we find that youth are more willing to acknowledge and name which cognitive traps they often get caught in. Even teaching mindfulness tools can be easier out in nature as the rich sensory experience offered by the landscape can provide alternative avenues for developing "presence" and focus that are immediate and powerful. There also is the imparting of information between participants. This can be knowledge and stories about the natural world and the sharing of skills or about specific strategies they have learned to help themselves cope with a particular challenge. Irvin Yalom suggests that this type of participant sharing can serve a particular purpose, as it can demonstrate and promote mutual interest and caring among group members.

Altruism

In this therapeutic factor, Yalom discusses how group therapy gives members the chance to have a positive influence on each other, to discover that they can be important and of value to someone else. Opportunities to experience this positive impact on others abound within the nature-based therapy context due to its experiential and highly interactive attributes. Games, team-building initiatives, and practical outdoor skills (e.g., fire making, whittling, fort building) provide many openings for children to help and mentor one another in spontaneous ways. In our Coyote Tracks program, which takes place over the course of several full days throughout the school year, we include a wide range of ages (from 9 to 14). As youth return to the program, they build knowledge of the routines and expectations and of the skills being offered in nature connection. A growth process emerges where the older or more experienced youth can mentor the younger ones: helping them with skills, teaching them games, and reaching out to those who appear hesitant or nervous. These youth, who in their own lives may feel judged by peers or family, have the chance to step out of that typical "bad kid" role to try on a new identity of being caring and helpful to others. This opportunity opens the window to forming new positive self-concepts and reparative experiences.

Through positive interactions with younger participants, the youth mentors can feel safe, accepted, and valued. For example, a participant in Coyote Tracks may be encouraged to engage a younger person who has been staying on the outside of the group by asking him to help with a task (say, gathering kindling for the fire or plants for tea). The youth then feels value in helping the younger child feel useful and included, and at the same time, the youth gets practice asking others for help in a non-threatening way. In our school-based programs, we have witnessed many sweet and spontaneous moments shared between peers, even within the short context of a sixty- or ninety-minute nature-based group session. A poignant moment came with Don, a 9-year-old from a very unstable home environment, who had various learning and behavioral challenges that led to him rarely making it through a full day in class. One day he was witnessed acting out of self-motivation to help another boy, James, who had fallen and slipped on a rock during a running game. They walked back to the group together with Don's arm under James, helping to hold him up as he limped. The smile on Don's face was priceless and communicated a sense of pride both for being able to help James and for knowing a child was willing to *let* him help. Don was used to being the disruptive one, rejected by other children, and not in the helping role. The school staff who witnessed this interaction were able to acknowledge the uniqueness of this moment and offer positive affirmation.

Another possible place for altruism is in relations toward future groups, community initiatives, and nature herself. In all of our programs, there have been opportunities to engage youth with meaningful ways to care for the land and build relationships. In our New Roots program, each group participates in an invasive species pull to help the local park combat the spread of English ivy. This opportunity offers the youth a chance to give back to the land in which they have been playing, and simultaneously provides tangible metaphors for pulling out the invasive thoughts in our minds. We then glean the ivy leaves and turn them into cordage for weaving material. Each group prepares the ivy for the subsequent group to use, thus connecting the groups to one another across the year.

Development of Socializing Techniques

We have noticed that children who need support with emotion regulation and social skills often respond well to the personalized attention of individual counseling. However, since the therapist is able to immediately respond to the child's needs, the challenges faced by the child within larger, unpredictable social situations often don't arise during one-to-one sessions and thus can be harder to practice. Children may display turn-taking and flexibility during individual counseling but still face immense struggle out on the school playground; transferring skills from one context to another can be tricky. Therefore, there is great value in offering group opportunities for children to practice newly learned skills, yet still within a safe and supported context. Group therapy can be a bridge from the safety of controlled environments to the great unknown and unpredictability of social life. Nature-based programs, whether ninety minutes, six hours, or multiple days, can offer rich opportunities for building social resilience and the capacity to navigate conflict in a healthy and productive way. Playing fun nature games (that involve boundaries and rules while also being exciting and motivating) sets the stage for kids to practice self-regulation in response to the unpredictable outcomes that emerge. Inevitably, through the course of a game, issues around fairness, personal space, rule interpretation, accountability, competitiveness, flexibility, conflict, and empathy emerge. This gives the counselors the opportunity to work with children in the moment to (1) recognize when a rupture in relationship has arisen; (2) pause the game to address concerns; (3) bring awareness to each person's feelings and needs; (4) work on repairing the connection, or negotiating the rules; and (5) try again, or move to other activities once everyone is present and calm again. Whereas on the playground, with little support available for intervention, a game of tag may turn into a screaming match, shoving, exclusion, hurt feelings, and withdrawal. We work with many children who recapitulate the same boundary crossing and interpersonal failure at school over and over again. In the small and safe group, these powerful moments do not get left unattended, and the chance to see a conflict through to resolution can build new templates for social success and self-regulation—experiential learning at its best.

The other beauty of the nature-based context is that when a highly activated child needs to take some space to calm their nervous system before engaging in conflict resolution, they can easily get distance from the group without being fully "separated." Instead of getting sent out to the hall or a "calm down room" (which can be a shame-inducing event), the child is able stay within the visual field of the group while sitting on a rock, leaning against a favorite tree, or swinging on a branch. The calming sensorial stimulation of nature gives them immediate tools for downgrading their arousal level, be it listening to the singing of the birds, feeling moss under their fingers, or watching the efforts of a busy squirrel.[6] While resourcing themselves, the child can simultaneously observe the continued activities of the group and be drawn naturally back into participation.

Imitative Behavior

Yalom speaks to the therapeutic benefit of group participants being able to observe the changes in other group members, imitate the communication patterns of the therapist, and try on new behaviors within the group. The process of youth being influenced by the example of others to stretch their challenge zones is a powerful force in nature-based groups as well. We find that youth are often looking for cues for acceptable behavior and level of disclosure and will choose their degree of sharing based on what others in the group are doing. As therapists, we also influence these norms by modeling reflection ourselves and by developing routines that give youth opportunity to practice a skill repeatedly. For example, we always begin sessions with a personal check-in where each participant is asked to express their current emotional and physical state. As described earlier, we offer a variety of creative ways for youth to express themselves and often include nature-based metaphors. As group facilitators, we also lead by example to model reflection, honesty, and sharing. If one of us is feeling tired and foggy, then we will be honest about that experience so that the group knows it's okay to not feel 100 percent well. If a youth decides to pass on sharing, then often others follow suit, as it becomes acceptable to not always actively participate. A great way to avoid this progression is by sharing our own check-in first before asking who else is ready to check-in; the volunteer then sets the template for sharing. As nature-based therapists, the way we model sincere engagement with the program activities and the participants is paramount to influencing the youth to positively participate and connect with one another. As facilitators, we are constantly being observed by the youth and modeling integrity, honesty, openness, gratitude, emotional awareness, regulated nervous systems, flexibility, empathy, clear boundaries, and positive leadership. When we set up games such as Fox Tails (a version of tag using bandanas), it is essential that we are playing along with the kids and not just setting up the rules and watching them play. Playing *with* children builds rapport, trust, and feelings of joy and happiness through firing off those powerful mirror neurons,[7] the visuospatial neurons that respond the same when observing an action and performing the same action yourself. It is proposed that if I see you laugh, then the motor neurons for laughing may also fire in my own brain; this relational mirror neuron process is reasoned to help in explaining aspects of empathy. We literally build the client's capacity for feeling joy by *doing* joy with them, rather than just talking with the youth about ideas for joyful activities they might pursue to combat depressive symptoms. Likewise, when a counselor dives into a bush for a hiding game, that gives encouragement and permission for the child to do the same, to get close-up with nature and physically uncomfortable yet excited, even if for only a few minutes.

In our school-based programs, we rely on imitation to help foster leadership skills and confidence in the children. In the early stages of the program, we choose and lead nature connection games that we think the kids will like, thus modeling boundary setting, clear communication skills, and flexibility. Then, each week we give one child a chance to be the game leader, and we mentor them to effectively teach and facilitate their chosen game for their peers. In this process, the first child imitates our example, and then subsequent child leaders learn from one another, slowly building capacity and self-efficacy among the group.

In our Coyote Tracks program, there are plenty of opportunities for imitation and mentoring among children, as the older or experienced youth gain leadership roles over time. For example, we may ask a senior group member to help introduce the guidelines for a particular activity, such as archery (using simple forest-made bows and arrows). If we ask them to be the facilitator, then they learn the responsibility of holding boundaries and "fairness" for others, and often the younger ones respect the older kids' judgment. This can be valuable learning, as in their own lives the youth mentor might be angry about their parents' rules/boundaries and have a hard time following through on responsibility. The more we give children the chance to try on novel behaviors, the more they can learn what is possible and witness themselves as capable.

An additional way that imitation shows up in nature-based groups is in the important task of learning from the animals, plants, and critters in the local ecosystem. A common practice among nature connection programs is to give participants a nature name, which they can study, observe, learn about, and finally share inspiration. Taking on specific animal characteristics can also be a way to deepen this learning. For example, in a popular predator-prey game, participants have a chance to transform into herbivores (rabbits, squirrels, deer), omnivores (racoons, bears), or carnivores (cougars, eagles) and put into practice what they have been learning by imitating that animal during the game. Encouraging them to move like the animals and really explore how it is to be that animal always brings the possibility for deep learning.

Group Cohesiveness

Building a supportive group atmosphere is one of the most healing aspects of group work, and Yalom suggests that this factor is equivalent to the importance of the client-therapist relationship in individual therapy. Most children and youth in our group programs have histories of negative social experiences, isolation, and bullying. Thus, as with any group program, our focus on the first day is to establish expectations of safety and inclusion, along with play (the fun factor is essential in getting kids to return on their own volition). We build group cohesiveness through several approaches:

- Establishing group safety agreements defined by the youth themselves
- Trust activities that give the group opportunities to build a sense of confidence in each other and the group as a whole
- Opportunities to discover commonalities and similarities in their lived experiences
- Experiencing play and laughter together
- Numerous avenues for sharing and witnessing stories of nature connection and life

Occasionally, developing group cohesion does not come quickly, and extra efforts are needed for ensuring containment, often including group agreements being revisited regularly. We had one New Roots group program for middle school youth that started to derail quickly because three participants with prior friendships were continually breaking group norms. In order to continue managing the group safely, and at the same time recognize that their opposition and hostility was their way of responding to anxiety, we had to split the group into smaller pods and adjust the curriculum to respond to presenting needs. This particular group ended up loving puppets, and so the program turned into nature-based puppetry, with facilitators using puppets to teach about the fight/flight/freeze response and creating puppet characters with each child to represent their "worry part" and their "strong part." Craft supplies were brought into the nature environment, and participants put on puppet shows from behind a log. Why? Because these children needed to run outside for the first thirty minutes in order to re-move the pent-up energy in their bodies from sitting at school all day. They absolutely loved playing tag and were able to focus much better on the psycho-educational aspects after a few rounds of running wildly through the woods.

Another key aspect of group cohesiveness is a sense of belonging and acceptance among members. For therapists, their task is to stay attuned to the relationships among group members, between members and facilitators, and between participants and nature, and to take measures to ensure threats to these relationships are addressed. Selecting natural environments that are conducive to developing strong relationships is an important consideration. For example, ensuring that the natural space has a variety of ecosystems will allow for participants to experience the spaciousness of an open field for running games as well as varied biodiversity for their Sit Spots. One of the school programs we offer does not have a natural setting close by, aside from a soccer field with some trees along its borders. Recognizing the importance of the participants' relationship with nature, we have chosen to organize bus transport to a nearby park that has more diverse ecology to explore. Trying to run the program at the soccer field would be failing to address the need for a strong relationship between participants and nature and thus undermine the effectiveness of the group. Another important consideration is respecting the elements and ensuring that participants' physical needs are being tended to. In the winter months, the Pacific Northwest turns into a fairly dark and rainy place. Not all of our sites allow for fires, and yet we know that attending to physical needs and making spaces inviting is helpful for the deep listening and sharing aspects of nature connection work. Setting up a tarp and bringing along warm drinks is one of numerous ways to ensure that a child's relationship with nature is one of openness and appreciation. Participants sitting dry under a tarp during a heavy downpour can allow for appreciating the rain in a very different way than if they are shivering and primarily focused on how they are going to get dry and warm.

Existential Factors

Yalom is well-known for his significant contributions to the development and articulation of existential psychotherapy. As it relates to the therapeutic factors of groups, he shares how existential factors include

> our confrontation with the human condition—a confrontation that informs us of the harsh existential facts of life: our mortality, our freedom and responsibility for constructing our

own life design, our isolation from being thrown alone into existence, and our search for life meaning despite being unfortunate enough to be thrown into a universe without intrinsic meaning.[8]

Nature-based groups for children and youth can certainly be fertile sites for addressing some of these important and lifelong realities. Recognizing that different degrees of maturity and life experience influence one's relationship with these bigger questions, nature-based groups can certainly create ample opportunities to explore these questions to varying degrees. Yalom's five areas of the existential factor are certainly all addressed to some degree in our practice, specifically when deepening one's relationship with nature:

- Recognizing that life is at times unfair and unjust
- Recognizing that ultimately there is no escape from some of life's pain or from death
- Recognizing that no matter how close I get to other people, I still must face life on my own
- Facing the basic issues of my life and death, and thus living my life more honestly and being less caught up in trivialities
- Learning that I must take ultimate responsibility for the way I live my life, no matter how much guidance and support I get from others

Spending time observing nature and connecting with the web of life naturally reveal these unavoidable truths about our shared existence as living creatures. For this reason, sharing stories from time spent with the land is so critical, as bringing these questions and insights to the group can support reflection and development. In a recent group program, on one of our wanders, we came across a mouse scampering along a log. After the little critter had made it about halfway along, a hawk swooped down, and in an instant the mouse was gone. The group went from excitement and curiosity to shock and awe and then to a place of vulnerability where the reality set in that we all are just as susceptible as that mouse. In this instance, we decided to take some intentional time to honor and appreciate the mouse, the hawk, and the fragility of our own lives. Depending on the group's goals and needs, we certainly could have spent considerable time exploring any of the five areas listed above. The point is that nature is constantly showing us the hard truths about our existence as well as the beauty and gifts of being alive. Really opening up one's eyes and hearts to these teachings can be scary and overwhelming, but doing so among supportive adults and in the safety of a group can be profoundly impactful and life altering.

Conclusion

In this chapter, we have attempted to highlight how nature-based group programs are an essential component of supporting therapeutic change when working with children and youth outdoors. The therapeutic factors of *instillation of hope, universality, imparting information, altruism, development of socializing techniques, imitative behavior, group cohesiveness, and existential factors* were explored, with particular attention to how incorporating relationships with nature can strengthen the potency of that change agent. So many of the struggles of modern life can be linked back to the dislocation from social, cultural, and environmental connection. Being able to offer a young person the chance to reconnect with nature and themselves among a supportive and accepting community is a key component of addressing many of the underlying causes that are bringing them to counseling in the first place. Thus, nature-based groups are an essential part of our practice.

11

Ethics in Nature-based Therapy

*By ethical conduct toward all creatures,
we enter into a spiritual relationship with the universe.*
ALBERT SCHWEITZER

As with any human service endeavor, ethics are of the upmost importance. To us, an ethical practice is vital to maintain safety for our clients and integrity for our profession. This chapter explores how ethics are considered relative to nature-based therapy practice and frameworks, as others before us have already explored.[1] Ultimately, we are dealing with the reality of a therapeutic practice "out of the office."

The word *ethics* originates from the ancient Greek *ethos*, meaning character, or moral nature. An expression of one's ethics shows up in their behaviors, attitudes, and beliefs. These manifestations then demonstrate one's character or customs. It is how you are seen and judged societally in your context. We can adopt an ethical stance (i.e., principles), *and* we can be guided by ethical rules (i.e., codes), to deal with ethical issues.

First, our ethical stance is comprised of values we hold dearly. These values would supersede decisions or actions taken in practice if they were compromised. An example for us is how we uphold an ethical stance on *relational-centering* in serving our clients. We place the value of relationships, in building and maintaining them, as central to our work regardless of circumstances, expressed best by activist, therapist, and counselor educator Vicki Reynolds:

I have worked alongside diverse therapists and community workers who use a wide range of therapeutic and community work approaches. There are many paths to liberation and no theory or practice is harm-free. The quest is not to find the perfect intervention, but to examine our ethical positioning and hold our practice to enacting these ethics. This requires that clients are centered and that we are effective in creating relationships of dignity and respect across the chasms of difference and privilege that divide us.[2]

Reynolds speaks to the efforts necessary to achieve this ethical stance, which include socially locating oneself, developing a collective ethic among co-workers, establishing structures to support a safe-enough space, holding clients at the heart of supervision, maintaining accountability for one's own transgressions, and supporting a culture of critique. She reminds us that ethics are a fluid process, not static entities, and that we need to be attuned to the immediate needs and circumstances of our clients versus getting hung up on deciding whether things are right and wrong. In this regard, your ethical stance may come up against a "do not" ethical rule. The following example may help illustrate this.

Case Example

A 15-year-old male living in government care was struggling with relationships with the adults in his life as they claimed he was not trustworthy or willing to follow the rules of his current group home. The idea that he would get to go outdoor rock climbing as part of counseling piqued this young adventure seeker's interest. After completing a couple of climbs, he asked if I (Dave) wanted to climb. Because there was no one else present to manage the rope, the options were to either decline his offer or teach him how and place my trust in him. Traditional codes of ethics may see this situation in a black-and-white manner. The relationship was not adequately established to discern if there was any potential risk for harm should the experience not go well—say, if he didn't follow the rules and therefore had to be given consequences so early on in the therapeutic process. At the same time, there was an intuitive understanding that he really wanted to be given authentic responsibility and be trusted in a meaningful way. A quick assessment of the situation confirmed that I was able to ensure my own safety (the route was well within my skill level, and I could grab the belay rope to prevent a fall if necessary), and I accepted the invitation to climb. The youth rose to the challenge, received positive feedback regarding his technique, and the situation ended up being a major contributing factor in developing our therapeutic relationship.

Other examples of our collective ethical stance in nature-based therapy are inclusion and acceptance of diverse ways of being and knowing in the world; decentering the counselor and instead acknowledging clients as experts of their own lives and problems; recognition that children and nature have value in their own right, not for what they will become or their potential future use; and the importance of authenticity and creating an open culture of feedback.

Now, what about ethical dilemmas? When do you know you are in one? And what can you do to address the dilemmas you find yourself in? How can codes help? In general, your ethical stance is much broader than any set of rules. Ethical rules, as set out by professions in a code, are generally aimed at protecting clients from unethical practitioner behavior. They provide guidance to practitioners, can enhance a professional status (in that a code is being adhered to), and can provide the professional association with the ability to hold practitioners to account for inappropriate behaviors or actions. So, you have training and qualification as a practitioner, and you have a professional association with practice guidelines and a code of ethics. Human service work can be messy and complicated and will eventually produce scenarios in which you will be forced to make decisions when you are unsure which course of action is correct. That is the litmus test right there, to know if you are actually in an ethical dilemma. If you have more than one option to resolve a situation and no option fits nicely into ethical practice, you have a dilemma. If any one option is acceptable within your code of practice ethics, you do not have a dilemma. The notion of ethical dilemmas is actually quite often overused and misused. One simple example of an ethical dilemma in nature-based therapy involves the practice of gift giving. It is common to make things from natural materials when engaged in outdoor practice, and at some point, you will find your client's hand stretching over toward you holding something they just made (e.g., a natural cordage bracelet, a woven basket, or a carved stick). In this case, it may be their first time or something they have done numerous times, and they want to gift it away. The dilemma is that you want to honor your relationship, and declining the gift may be taken as a personal rejection and weaken the relationship. However, being in a professional relationship also means maintaining and role-modeling healthy boundaries, so the decision as to what to do is not clear and involves careful consideration.

Of course, context is critical in this regard, since it can vary. In the realm of therapy, specifically in North America, ethics have been moved from being individual expressions into administered and enforced rules set by professional associations, colleges, and regulatory bodies. They manifest in codes of conduct and standards of practice, and most of you reading this book will likely be able to identify by which "ethics" you are held responsible. It is important, however, to not confuse ethical practice—and codes of practice—for ethics, in the manner which we describe our ethical stance above. For the purposes of this chapter, we will be sharing examples and perspectives closely aligned with two specific bodies of oversight: the British Columbia Association of Clinical Counselors (BCACC) for registered clinical counselors and the Council of Canadian Child and Youth Care Associations (CCCYCA) for our child and family support workers. You and your organizations will have titles and professions in alignment relative to your context. Associations set and maintain codes of ethics upon which practice is guided. Our practice includes counselors and child and family support workers, and while often working in collaboration, both roles carry some distinct responsibilities as defined by the scope of practice set out by the respective associations. While these associations are aligned with our work, it is incumbent upon you as practitioners to ensure ethical practice relative to your specific organization, scope, mandate, and client needs.

We must also remind our readers that ethical codes generally are protecting those we serve from harm due to unethical practice. So, in

turn, ethical codes are not indicative or expressive of best practices but
tend rather to include scripts of ideal practice philosophies and the necessary list of "do nots." United Kingdom sociology and social policy lecturer Sarah Banks[3] reminds us to not take codes of ethics too literally;
she points out that some have gone so far as to call them rhetorical and
regulatory devices, rather than guides to help us deal with our ethical
dilemmas. This chapter is framed by four central principles found in
the ethical codes of practice set by many counseling and psychological
service colleges and associations, in this case, the BCACC:

- Principle I: Respect for the Dignity of All Persons and Peoples
- Principle II: Responsible Caring
- Principle III: Integrity in Relationships
- Principle IV: Responsibility to Society

Each of these principles will be explored relative to nature-based
therapy practice, yet not all codes will be addressed. We will include
examples where we can to accentuate our practice interpretations of
the ethical codes, as they may differ from conventional indoor practices. It is recognized that each reader may be governed by a particular
professional code of ethics, operating standards of practice set out by
your organization's policy, and/or other qualification practice guidelines. The exercise of really thinking through your practices relative to
your professional association or college principles is critical. In short,
if your qualifications do not connect you to an ethical framework, then
you should consider finding one to guide your decision-making and
practice.

Principle I: Respect for the Dignity of All Persons and Peoples (and Places)

Free and informed consent is truly at the heart of any therapeutic practice. We are very clear about working with those who choose freely to
"walk" with us. Even this small narrative shift from working with clients to walking with them suggests an "alongside" approach in their
journey to well-being. So, what about when parents force their children to attend? Not an uncommon reality, especially with families in
crisis and parents seeing few to no options as to where their child may

engage. If you have not picked up on this already, nature-based therapy tends to attract children and youth who typically are not interested in conventional talk therapy.

We acknowledge and accept that parental coercion exists and is a common factor influencing client engagement. Ideally, therapeutic relationships are between a client and counselor who both are choosing to engage in service. Is that the norm with children, youth, and families? No, not always. In our experience, most young people experiencing challenges would rather avoid the perceived discomfort of addressing what is going on than confront it head on, especially with someone they do not know. Distraction via screens, spending time with friends, or playing sports helps them to get a break from having to think about their problems and makes sense as a coping strategy. Furthermore, being told by their parents that they need to see someone can contribute to stories of themselves as "the bad kid" or suggest that something is wrong with them. For many, it's hard enough having a parent constantly upset with their choices, and to now be told they must go see someone can feel like further punishment. A strategy we often take is to inform clients that problems neither arise, nor are they located, inside individuals but rather are relational in nature and therefore need to be addressed in such an ecological manner. We ask questions that help to conceptualize the current challenge relationally, such as, How has your relationship been with your family members lately? and If the problems arising in your family were to shift, how would this impact your relationships with one another?

Another consideration regarding informed consent is the reality that distinctions between formal therapeutic conversations and social time can become highly blurred in outdoor settings and may contribute to counselors feeling less bound by ethical and legal aspects of ongoing informed consent, confidentiality, and boundaries. It has been recommended that therapists take appropriate measures to ensure clarity with clients regarding what the outdoor experience entails, including the therapeutic elements.[4] Often, a whole session may be dedicated to discussing the outdoor excursion, followed by the creation of an informed consent contract. Furthermore, Stephen Becker,[5] a pediatric psychologist based in Cincinnati, Ohio, stresses the critical importance of discussing boundaries with clients and co-facilitators prior to any wilderness excursion, as the context is so different from traditional settings, and notes that while on expeditions, being continually mindful of both professional and personal boundaries is vital to ensure preventing harm to individuals and groups.

Counselors have a responsibility to honor clients' autonomy and provide sufficient information such that a competent client can freely decide if they wish to comply with the therapists' recommendations for counseling. Recognizing that nature-based counseling is not your standard therapeutic fare, achieving informed consent requires thoroughness, creativity, and a tenacious spirit to prevent subtly coercing clients to sign up for activities they are not entirely comfortable with. Remember that informed consent is not an event but a process that will encourage continued dialogue with clients as they navigate the novel terrain of an outdoor counseling experience (Shultz, et al., 2007).[6]

Taking informed consent one step further, and following suggestions from Michael Cohen in his book *Reconnecting with Nature*,[7] we encourage asking permission of nature for our presence and activities. We may seek permission or guidance for harvesting materials, and we express gratitude, thankfulness, and love for supporting us and our clients. To animate nature as co-therapist can be a powerful project between client, counselor, and nature, and one in which bonds are made and commitments of care can be established.

Privacy and confidentiality are considered another cornerstone for creating safe and trusting counseling relationships, and as such, it is recommended to discuss this before establishing the counseling relationship. British ecotherapists Martin Jordan and Hayley Marshall[8] provided essential considerations for ethically taking therapy outdoors. They reminded their readers of the historically important role the therapeutic frame has played in establishing the ground rules that govern the therapeutic process. They suggest that conducting therapy outside of the contained and predictable four walls of an office may be considered a transgression of traditional boundaries, bringing up issues regarding confidentiality, timing of therapeutic work, weather, containment, and power dynamics, and it therefore requires additional considerations. They suggest that "the frame represents a way of understanding the relationships and spaces that become therapeutic, and in this sense, can be reconstructed in a more fluid and dynamic way in the outdoors."[9] As mentioned above, their paper supports the importance of adequately contracting with clients before heading outside, as much as possible, so there are agreements about possible scenarios, such as what will happen if they run into people, when the therapeutic work will commence (right from the parking lot or at a destination), what weather factors would warrant a change of plans, and how the sessions will unfold (who leads the way and how to navigate moving in and out of therapeutic conversations). Moving from the counselor-controlled office to outdoor environments where the space is not owned or controlled by either party creates a flattening of power relations as well as an increased sense of mutuality, which can lead naturally to feelings of informality, friendship, and increased sense of involvement in the client's life. Knowing that there will always be an element of unpredictability inherent in outdoor work, they optimistically suggest that "the therapist, through use of an attentive, inquiring, contracting process can help to hold the client at the edge of their experience in a way that may be uncomfortable but will not become overwhelming."[10]

Nature-based therapy includes the natural environment as an active participant in the therapeutic process. For this reason, we extend our practice of **respecting the dignity of all persons and peoples to also include all places**. In communicating with clients, we include language that shows respect for the traditional unceded Indigenous lands where we have the great honor and privilege to be working. Further, we recognize the limitations of tokenized land acknowledgements and instead endeavor to first build authentic and generous relationships with both the land and the First Peoples ourselves. We visit, listen, and learn about the nearby nature forests, beaches, mountains, and established parks. We learn the history of the Indigenous communities who either once met or continue to meet in these places for harvesting and ceremony, or how original names have been anglicized or ignored, and we try our best to assist in reclaiming first names of places. We strive to educate ourselves on the impacts of settler colonialism for the local nations as well as their ongoing historical resistance.

Regarding original place names, one local example in Victoria, British Columbia, is the Anglo-settler name of a local height of land called Mount Douglas (by our sea-level standards at an oxygen-depleting altitude of 738 feet). This summit is called *Pkols* by the First Nations of the local region, the W̱SÁNEĆ and Lekwungen, and holds significant cultural, spiritual, and historical meaning. Included in the history of this peak is the colonial legacy of Captain James Douglas whom the peak was named after. Accessing these storied landscapes allows for conversations about how people treat each other and the land. The legitimacy of land "ownership" in our region is tenuous, and litigation continues to this day. This example highlights our efforts to bring stories of the land, and of its First Peoples, into our visitation of these places. The lived embodied experience of nature-based therapy is here met with a cognitive understanding of place, which further develops our own and our clients' ecological stories.

Principle II: Responsible Caring

In light of the considerations raised by ecopsychology and the growing body of research examining the health benefits of contact with nature, the position that therapists take regarding human–nature relations and its application can be considered important variables influencing therapeutic outcomes. Thus, counselors who ignore human–nature relations and the potential therapeutic benefits of nature could be failing to tap into a valuable healing relationship and perhaps may even be colluding with the problems their clients are seeking solace from. Could it be that therapists working with people struggling with ADHD and not considering the informative research regarding the restorative effects of time in nature are neglecting a potent treatment option? Or what about work with inner-city youth that fails to acknowledge the repercussions of a complete lack of contact with nature, despite compelling research linking time in nature as a critical factor in healthy emotional, cognitive, and spiritual development of young people? Finally, what about those clients who are struggling with depression, anxiety, and/or substance use, yet to whom no acknowledgment or mention is made of the potential contribution that destructive human–nature relations may be having in the manifestation of their symptoms? The point is not to insist that ecotherapies should be mandatory for every client. Rather, it is to raise the question: What are the consequences if counselors fail to acknowledge the insights from ecopsychology and assess for its appropriate application?

Evidence-based Treatment Versus Practice-based Evidence

In order to honor the moral principles of beneficence and nonmaleficence, nature-based counselors are obligated to ensure that the treatment options they present are relatively safe and that a sense of their effectiveness can be communicated. Thus, how one determines the efficacy of their approaches is an important ethical issue.

Clinicians working within government or managed-care settings are well aware of the importance placed on empirically (or evidence-) based treatments (EBT). Due to a lack of randomized controlled studies, nature-based modalities do not fall within these treatment options, nor are they likely to any time soon. Some argue that this needs to occur if the field is to be taken seriously by professional organizations, whereas others fear that doing so would threaten the very foundations of the field. However, nature-based therapy approaches can be considered evidence-informed practices as most variations draw on a large body of existing research.[11]

Practice-informed evidence is another perspective that has emerged and has promising potential with regard to answering the previous question. The work of American psychologist Scott Miller and his colleagues[12] has contributed enormously to an understanding of the factors accounting for successful outcomes during therapy. Their research on the factors influencing therapeutic change indicates that models and techniques only account for 15 percent, whereas client–therapist relationship (30 percent), client/extratherapeutic (40 percent), and placebo/hope/expectancy (15 percent) account for the remainder. These findings shift attention away from models and techniques (typically the independent variables in EBT) and toward the remaining factors. Of particular importance to this discussion is the client–therapist relationship, or alliance, as this is a factor of great importance for nature-based counseling. Research repeatedly suggests that the client–therapist alliance is enhanced in outdoor contexts and, as discussed earlier, brings with it added ethical challenges. However, if the therapeutic relationship accounts for 30 percent of change outcomes, it certainly is an important factor.

Another intriguing aspect regarding therapeutic alliances for nature-based counseling is the introduction of another player, nature. As detailed throughout this book, nature is not just a backdrop but instead a central player in the change process of nature-based counseling; consideration for this point raises further questions regarding how the therapeutic relationship is regarded during a nature-based counseling experience. Clearly client–therapist dualisms fall from the wayside. Consider a quote from the Therapeutic Adventure Professional Group's (TAPG) best practices website: "Attention to the physical space is imperative—a client who is hot, cold, or wet may struggle to engage effectively" (np.).[13] Addressing this point from an ecopsychological perspective would be to state that not only would the client be uncomfortable but their relationship with a crucial co-facilitator could be in jeopardy.

Recognizing the importance and uniqueness of client–therapist–nature relationships brings forth numerous questions regarding their influence on therapeutic results. In the interest of respecting the integrity of clients and promoting their welfare, are counselors responsible for ensuring that positive relational bonds are made with nature during therapy? How exactly would this be done? How would therapists intervene if necessary? These questions raise issues pertaining to the competency of the therapist.

Competence, Training, and Supervision

Due to the number of outdoor therapy variations, issues pertaining to competence are especially relevant as, in addition to traditional training, practitioners may be required to have training in other areas. Calls for dual-trained practitioners, where clinicians are required to possess outdoor skills, experience in nature-connection practices, in addition to their counseling training, have been suggested as preferable methods for addressing competency in outdoor therapy programs.

There is little doubt that, in order to practice ethically, nature-based therapists must ensure they are adequately educated on ecotherapy and ecopsychology theory and techniques for facilitating experiential nature-based activities prior to leaving the comfortable confines of their offices. Conversely, seeking out partnerships with other service providers who have the desired skill sets and resources may be another appropriate action, despite the additional ethical concerns it raises (e.g., confidentiality).

There are very few accredited degree programs at the master's or doctoral level in North America that directly train counselors in nature-based therapy approaches. Nature-based therapists wishing to meet ethical standards for boundaries to competence need to receive formal training in counseling, or an allied helping profession, and then supplement that with training in their desired ecotherapy specialty—including continuing education certificates, specialized workshops and intensives offered by mentors, and personal reading and inquiry. John Scull,[14] a retired psychologist living on Vancouver Island, BC, recommends that therapists wishing to move their practice outdoors ensure they have done some of their own work with experienced ecopsychologists before commencing their client work. The TAPG code of ethics states that "in those areas where generally recognized standards for preparatory training do not yet exist, professionals take reasonable steps to ensure the competence of their work and to promote the welfare of participants."[15] Training specifically in ecotherapy is challenging as, without any representing professional associations, there really is no cohesiveness or agreement regarding what exactly ecotherapy encompasses. This is a matter of professional identity, which is known to be an important aspect for any successful movement toward public protection, public recognition, and licensure.[16]

Finally, with no national or international established set of competencies and few clear routes for training, the possibility for adequate supervision and consultation becomes an important ethical concern. Recognizing that many ethical dilemmas arise when practitioners work in isolation, it is imperative that nature-based counselors seek out allied professionals who have a reasonable level of knowledge and skill in their area and arrange for supervision or consultations when doubts or uncertainties arise during their work. A key question remains: By what standards does someone qualify as a competent professional? If there is no consensus regarding training and best practices within the field, then what standards should determine suitable candidates for supervisors? These questions will continue to raise concerns due to the complexity involved in establishing a professional identity.

Principle III: Integrity in Relationships

Aspire to the highest integrity possible and accept responsibility for the consequences of our actions. Leaving the confines of the office clearly adds elements of risk, compared with standard indoor therapeutic exchanges. The unpredictability and wildness of nature is considered by many to be a core aspect of ecotherapy.[17] Expanding on this topic, the founder of the Nature-Therapy Center in Israel, Ronen Berger, states, "[Nature therapy] takes place outdoors, in nature, in a place that does not necessarily have human-made boundaries, is open to the world's influences, and is not owned by the therapist."[18] He recommends that clinicians assess for populations who "have a need for clear boundaries, hierarchy, and a high level of control"[19] and make the necessary adjustments to their activities and location to ensure client safety.

Although most nature-based therapies do not focus on the facilitation of risk and challenges in the same way that adventure therapy does, potential for physical, psychological, and emotional harm still exits. For example, many outdoor therapists utilize fire, a source of life and sustenance. Robert Greenway, one of the first contributing authors to the field of ecopsychology, coined the term the *wilderness effect* to describe the psycho-spiritual shifts that occur when engaged in wilderness travel and activities. He explains that "a group sitting around a fire often prompts someone to remark, 'we've been here before.' The archetypal setting links us to earlier cultures, earlier times, and the very essence of life."[20] Although sitting around a fire is mesmerizing and full of healing potential, the fact remains that fire can be extremely dangerous and must be interacted with respectfully.

Using fire, encounters with wild animals, and walking within forested trails are examples of nearby nature-based activities that inherently contain elements of risk. Clinicians are caught in a balancing act, where promoting client beneficence comes into conflict with responsibilities to do no harm. Managing these risks becomes an important responsibility for nature-based therapists, and steps must be taken to become aware of potential risks and adequately prepare for them. One effective strategy in dealing with risk associated with nature-based therapies involves establishing risk management plans, although it has been pointed out that much of this debate may be about managing liability versus promoting safety.[21] In evaluating risk in wilderness therapy, Russell and Harper encouraged programs to "examine and identify what risks they are managing, implement the policies and procedures needed to reduce risks, then write and implement risk management plans."[22] These same strategies can be employed by therapists to effectively deal with risk in planned and efficient ways and may be guided through the process of accreditation or adhering to standards set out by recognized professional associations. Client agency and the notion of "choice," especially related to the element of "challenge by choice" in practice, should be further explored by those interested in nature-based therapy.[23] Reading critically on this topic is worth the investment for practitioners who want to better understand what it means to work experientially, and ethically, with clients in meaningfully balancing challenge and support.

Another aspect warranting attention is the experiential nature of ecotherapy. Clients may find themselves moving too quickly or encountering experiences in the environment that are psychologically or emotionally harmful. Ronen Berger[24] commented on this topic by recounting a situation where a client heard the unexpected sounds of a military training drill while working outside the hospital she had been admitted to for PTSD symptoms. The unexpected noise began to trigger memories from her own war experiences, igniting a vicious downward spiral. This story brings attention to the dangers of not being aware of the different ways the environment can adversely influence clients. In addition, simply participating in experiential activities can cause some clients to venture into uncomfortable and potentially harmful psychological and emotional places. Considering psychological depth, adventure therapy theorist and practitioner Michael Gass explains how "[experiential] activities can be too powerful a therapeutic intervention for some [clients] since activities may raise certain issues too quickly in therapy."[25]

In response, Ringer and Gillis[26] suggest that psychological goals should be established prior to ecotherapeutic activities and that staying on track with these goals is the therapist's responsibility. Further, they explain that honoring clients' rights for autonomy include "maintaining the psychological depth above or at the level of contracted agreement (explicit or implied)."[27] This may involve consistently checking in with clients and ensuring that options for stepping back and watching or withdrawing from any activities are established beforehand. Similarly, the TAPG considers "challenge by choice" a critical element of best practice, which involves promoting the client's right of always having a choice to participate in any aspect of the therapeutic process.[28]

Committing to truthfulness and accuracy in communications is an essential component of professional therapeutic practice. Most one-to-one nature-based counseling occurs in isolation from other practitioners (trees, birds, and squirrels do not count in this case), therefore the need for personal integrity and a culture of openness regarding reporting to supervision and owning mistakes is critical for ethical practice. When working with vulnerable children and youth, the risk of allegations becomes a real possibility, and thus practitioners must be highly aware of client needs, practice ethically, and make sure to not put oneself in a position where a false accusation may be made and cannot be defended. A way to navigate this risk is to start sessions either in the office or at more public locations and, even better, to include the parent in sessions, especially at the beginning. As a general rule, we encourage working in teams, at the least in pairs, when possible. Consideration and care must be taken into account for biological needs because a sudden call to the washroom when it is just two of you in the forest is not an ideal situation. Additionally, experiential activities and challenges requiring maintaining physical safety (scrambling up some rocks, crossing a fallen tree, etc.) may necessitate more physical contact than office-based sessions; again, avoiding the element of surprise is key, and instead, discussing these scenarios prior to their occurrence is recommended.

Avoiding dual relationships. Nature-based therapy occurs, as we have described, in settings and through activities that may cloud the lines between when therapy is occurring and when it is not. In this reality, a client may be in a social setting with the counselor—say, while setting up an activity for a group of youth to take part in or playing a game while waiting for a parent to pick them up—and not consider this part of the therapy. In this case, is the counselor something other than therapist? As emphasized above, continually reminding oneself of the responsibility to maintain high levels of professionalism needs to be adhered to despite the informal feel of some aspects of the work. It is recommended that "information that is irrelevant to either the client or group's treatment goals, progress, or safety should not be shared, and relevant information should be discussed in a professional manner at all times."[29]

Another potential dilemma regarding dual relationships is that there is currently a limited number of nature-based counselors available to offer these services, resulting in situations where clients who would normally be referred to another practitioner may have nowhere else to go. Examples in our practice have included siblings or another family member deciding to also seek out services after seeing the positive impacts firsthand or a personal friend wanting to refer their child for nature-based services. Deciding on a course of action requires addressing each situation as it arises and also remembering to revisit one's ethical stances in making such decisions.

Principle IV: Responsibility to Society (and the Planet)

Challenging self and others to be personally accountable to the values and ethical principles of the profession and a commitment to continuous improvement. Therapists, on average, get worse over time. This was the conclusion of a recent and quite robust study of 170 therapists and their combined 6,500 clients.[30] How can this be the case? These researchers suggest it may be due to a lack of integrated learning and development from ongoing evaluation. While not groundbreaking news, investing in deliberate practice, including seeking and working with feedback, was the key element linked to improvement in therapeutic practice.[31] Some therapists adopt the principle of continuous improvement more than others. An American colleague, Will Dobud, who runs an adventure and wilderness therapy practice in Australia, provides some insight into his efforts to improve his practice.

> In 2012 I moved to Australia and opened a small private practice in Adelaide, South Australia, and began offering regular coun- seling sessions and 14-day expeditions for at-risk youth. I was rigorous in how I evaluated our programs and each of our treat- ment effectiveness. As we gathered data, we started to uncover a trend. Some of us were more effective outside the office than in, and some vice versa. The data indicated I'm a better thera- pist in the outdoors and that I needed to become a better "couch therapist." By routinely monitoring my outcomes, I found that clients I worked with in the canoe, on a climbing wall, or moun- tain bike were more engaged, reported greater improvement of well-being, and actually began booking their own sessions. We also found that some of our other therapists were the opposite; their outcomes were better in the office. We have used this data to focus our training and supervision in an effort to improve in areas we need to improve in.[32]

Dobud suggests that implementing solution-focused assumptions and following outcome and alliance data can drastically change program- ming and improve outcomes in therapeutic settings, as privilege is placed on the client's voice and choice. He provides a model of practice demonstrating a strong ethical commitment to continuous improve- ment for himself and his staff team. His work highlights the importance of creating rigorous self- and program evaluations and not making as- sumptions about the effectiveness of our work. Further, by collecting practice-based feedback and bringing it to group supervision, nature- based counselors can learn about elements of practice that are working and identify areas for continued growth.

Respect for peoples revisited: Demonstrate respect for the diver- sity of persons, peoples, and cultures. Historically, nature-based rec- reation and nature appreciation activities have been criticized in North America for serving primarily a privileged homogenous white popu- lation. Much of our suggested "nearby nature" equates to managed natural areas, including municipal through to national parks. While the critique often relates to the design and development of parks, and a particular academic research paradigm of leisure and recreation describing the use of said parks, the picture remains fairly consistent today: those accessing outdoor spaces and outdoor activities are less diverse than the populations living in the region around the park. That said, the human service field we work in is often not representative of the local population by any measures of diversity either. So, is nature-based therapy falling into the same pattern as parks use? And if so, why? And what can we do to responsibly address questions of diversity in our practice?

The etymology of the word *park*, from Old English, is that of a paddock or enclosed space, much like a forest isn't! That enclosure traditionally denoted inclusion and exclusion from use of the space. In this regard, and in our Western Eurocentric realities in North America, parks were in fact developed from a protectionist standpoint, and while not explicitly exclusionary in their promotion, many have become so. Park planners and many leisure researchers have argued that parks hold deterministic values, in that if properly attended, parks can improve lives, uplift spirits, and make for a healthier, happier society. How do these ideals sit if parks are accessed by only certain portions of the population? How do we adopt an ecologically sound relationship with park spaces that bear little resemblance to the previous natural habitat of the area? Wetlands were filled in, streams were dammed, and many species and people have been displaced. This places parks in that realm of *indirect nature* in that it has been manufactured. Does this matter? Do our clients know or recognize the differences? Maybe. Either way, we need to be aware of it because it is an ideal metaphor for the daily struggles of many people in terms of power and autonomy, often due to their social location and society's response to it.[33]

So, what do we mean when we say we need to promote diversity in nature-based therapy? Consider this activity with our clients in which we start by inviting them to look inward and get a sense of how they are doing in that particular moment. We then request they share a movement that captures the essence of their inner landscape. What they express is unique to them and different each time. After acknowledging their expression, a moment is taken to look around at the surrounding outer landscape and notice all the different ways nature is expressing herself: the various shapes of trees, stages of living and dying, and abundance of diverse organisms. The presence of rich biodiversity teaches how each organism is distinct yet important and reinforces an embodied knowing that we too are all different yet can be accepted just the way we are. A healthy ecosystem teaches about *sacred balance*, a vision for a world where humans are in right relation with the rest of the living world, recognizing their deep reliance and embeddedness with the air, water, and soil.

An environment where one species is dominating or has an advantage that sets it apart from the others teaches about the harmful impacts of unchecked domination. If you have ever walked in a Pacific Northwest Douglas fir forest that has been introduced to English ivy, you likely have seen the devastation from the vine carpeting the forest floor and suffocating the trees and understory. Or similarly, the introduction of Scotch broom (which can grow prolifically in this region) in a Garry oak meadow and how the landscape turns from a multiplicity of species to a dense monocrop of broom. The point is not to dig into the debate surrounding invasive species and the management of ecosystems but rather to highlight the detrimental impacts of colonizing forces on diversity and how, when these factors go unchecked, they drastically alter physical environments, closing spaces for alternates, in much the same way as the dominant societal structures operate to marginalize certain groups while bolstering others.

With this metaphor in mind, it is useful to name and contemplate some of the dominant forces that are restricting the diversity of nature-based therapy. A thorough investigation of each of these forces is a considerable and important task. For the purpose of this conversation regarding raising awareness of ethical issues for nature-based practitioners, what will be offered is a small window into some of the important considerations. We recognize that much more work needs to be done on each of these topics (plus there are many more to be named than what we have selected) for the field of nature-based therapy to develop its potential as a truly diverse and socially just field. We hope that this chapter can act as a catalyst for the necessary conversations across related outdoor therapy practices.

Addressing Settler Colonialism

We have already named the profound and ongoing impacts of settler colonialism on the relation between Indigenous people and non-Indigenous settler people and on relations to land and sovereignty. Specifically, how the unjust phenomenon of settler colonialism contin-ues to maintain the dispossession of land, disconnection from culture, and erasure of Indigenous people from the history of the colonized space. Alysha Jones and David Segal's article on *unsettling* ecopsychology takes a strong position on this topic regarding the field.[34]

On the whole, ecopsychology as a field of study and practice does not acknowledge and engage with settler colonialism, its intense impacts on people and land, and its relevance for the field. In many cases, ecopsychologists practice on land that settlers have dispossessed from Indigenous peoples. The logical extension of this critique is to all land-based, nature-based, wilderness, and outdoor programs and practitioners; we are all implicated. According to Jones and Segal, "Addressing settler colonialism as a significant gap in ecopsychology represents an opportunity and invitation for the field to enter into the awkward and challenging task of discussing the unearned advantage (or privilege) to practice ecopsychology on Indigenous lands, as well as challenge the colonial context in which practice occurs."[35]

One of the first steps in the unsettling process is to acknowledge and investigate how nature-based therapy's "culturally situated narratives and knowledge practices may unintentionally reproduce settler colonialism and erase Indigenous histories and voices."[36] Jones and Segal suggest unsettling practices such as questioning whose traditional territory nature-based practice occurs on, what the specific protocols are in that territory, and how is it that they themselves have gained access to the land, in this way and at this time. Further, they recommend asking questions about one's own heritage, as they identify the desire to create an authentic place-based identity among settlers as one of the factors that may be driving the continued harmful dispossession of land and appropriation of Indigenous practices. Finally, serious contemplation regarding how to support the protection and return of traditional lands for Indigenous people is a core component of an unsettling practice. Their article references a personal conversation with Canadian political theorist James Tully regarding the importance of such actions and his comments on the topic:

> By learning about Indigenous resurgence projects and seeking to ensure Indigenous peoples have access to their territories to carry out their traditional cultural practices, settler ecopsychologists would be "joining in on a long history of Indigenous people who have been able to survive genocide, regenerate their lifeways and earthways, and influence at least some settlers to join in and stand beside them."[37]

These are only a few of the unsettling practices that may be helpful in raising awareness and transforming relations regarding the ongoing impacts of settler colonialism operating out of awareness in the field of nature-based therapy. It is recommended that practitioners make efforts to educate themselves on the particular history of relations between Indigenous peoples and settlers in their own countries, inform themselves of the lived realities of Indigenous peoples by seeking out their voices through scholarship and building genuine relationships, and finally investigate how they may be able to support local Indigenous-led initiatives regarding addressing the ongoing injustices and reconnection with land.

Ecofeminist Critique: Addressing Patriarchy

Questions of ethical practice have been asked in the related fields of adventure and wilderness therapy. Denise Mitten, professor and long-time outdoor adventure educator and leader, has written compellingly on ethical considerations in adventure therapy specifically for female clients and other marginalized populations.[38] Aligning herself with ecofeminism, she describes the projects as an effort to "change the subordination of nature, poor people, children, indigenous people, and women. The goal of ecofeminism is to increase the health and welfare of humans and nature." In her 1994 article, she shared a historical reality of patriarchal design and leadership on the adventure education and therapy fields, from stories of "founding fathers" through program aims based on building "boys to men." These themes, stemming from militaristic roots, have diminished little in the intervening decades, and Mitten's critique is equally valid today. The major issue lies in the nature of the programs developed primarily by men and for males in that their use or application to females, transgender, or other populations, may not be appropriate, or as Mitten clearly points out, ethical. It appears to us that the strength of the patriarchal narratives was, and remains today, strong, and this early critique did not receive the attention it deserved.

So, what comprised Mitten's critique of adventure therapy? We have to recall that an adventure therapy approach, compared to a nature-based approach, often includes risk and challenging activities and/or longer trips of multiple days to weeks and involves technical knowledge and skills. The two major issues identified with this approach for women were (1) a leader/therapist and client power imbalance and (2) the role of nature in healing. The first was highlighted by the use of technical skill and knowledge, the group influence on individual behavior, and the possible belief that everyone needs to be compliant for the group's success. Each of these variables has the potential to override an individual client's capacity to speak for themselves and to their needs. Client insecurity entering the adventure arena, coupled with the disempowerment of possibly not having the technical knowledge or skills that, in this Western culture, that boys have grown up learning, and then adding the group influence over personal decision-making can all add up to the potential for further trauma or harm. These place a significant amount of responsibility on the leader/therapist to ensure that client care is at the forefront of their practice.

In 1994, Mitten questioned whether enough had been done to address concerns of power imbalance in outdoor therapies. To consider that the leader/therapist may be providing the technical knowledge of route finding, rope handling, or the management of other technical or safety equipment; choosing the activities of the day; leading the conversations; holding expert status; and having the professional obligation for the group, it is not hard to see how this power differential may be an area of great concern for practitioners. Let us not forget, in the case of female clients, that the leaders may also be male and older, and an all-too-common perception of adventure leaders is that of the hero-guide. Not more than a generalization, but in our minds, this is not far off the norm for outdoor leadership even today; it is a male-dominated field, and stereotypical gender roles still play out in leadership teams.

The second issue raised by Mitten is that of the role that nature can play in therapuetic healing processes. This, of course, is contrasted with the traditional risk, challenge, and physicality of the adventure model. Since this 1994 paper, we have seen considerable developments of more ecopsychological and nature-based approaches, along with advances in understandings of adventure and wilderness therapy (as we have shared in this book). Mitten offered an early challenge to the conversation about whether risk, perceived or real, was justified as a therapeutic practice, and whether the folk pedagogy of "You will overcome your fear" or "You will feel like a hero" held water or would even be useful to clients when they returned home. She questioned directly whether the means justified the ends, again, specifically thinking of the female clinical client who may have been manipulated with untruths in her life. Mitten's recommendations seem simple and effective: allow the client to learn about the activity, its real, and perceived risks, and then provide the opportunity for her to choose to complete the activity or not. As Mitten explained, a woman who may have experienced abuse cannot be told to trust (e.g., as in a trust fall where other clients will catch you); rather she learns to trust through the process of building relationships, and equally, she should be allowed to simply say no to an activity without the leader or the group pushing her to participate and having her capitulate due to peer pressure or fear of upsetting the ones with power.

In a recent conversation with Mitten, she relayed results of her body image study, which suggest benefits in addressing patriarchal relationships in nature-based therapy in general and specifically for women:

Through time in nature, women are able to rebuff the patriarchal beliefs that contribute to the diminishing and objectifying
of women and nature. This seems to illustrate that if someone doesn't try to conquer nature, then nature's acceptance
of oneself is healing. There seems to be a correlation between
women feeling accepted in natural environments and being able
to become internally stronger, resulting in feeling better about
their body image.[39]

Undoubtedly, there is a tremendous amount of work to be done in
understanding and addressing the ways that patriarchal relations
are showing up in nature-based therapy as well as being resisted and
transformed, such as in the work by Mitten and other ecofeminists. We
are grateful for the work of so many dedicated writers, activists, and
changemakers and recognize that the work is really just beginning in
our field.

White Privilege, Ableism, and LGBTQ+

In the groundbreaking edited anthology *Ecopsychology and the Deconstruction of Whiteness*, released in 1995, Carl Anthony, an African
American social justice activist, asked an important and eye-opening
question: "Why is it so easy for people to think like mountains and not
to think like people of color?"[40] He went on to raise concern for the
field's inherent bias toward Eurocentric and predominantly white perspectives. His critique was fundamental to the field starting to address
issues of white privilege operating largely out of awareness in both
academic circles and outdoor programming occurring at the time.
Likewise, the social model of disability was introduced in the mid-'70s
and developed by people living with disabilities in an attempt to shift
perspectives on how they are seen and related to by mainstream society. The social model shifts attention away from the individual being
the source of impairment and to how society is organized as the cause.
For example, if a building has a step to its entrance and no ramp, the
problem lies in the design of the building, not a person's inability to
walk. The model recognizes that all humans at some point in their
lives will face some sort of physical or cognitive challenges, and there-

fore, it is the responsibility of the society to address this reality, not the individual.

This model has been taken up by the Victoria-based non-profit Power To Be Adventure Therapy Society (PTB, featured in chapter 9), and they have made it their goal since 1998 to remove barriers for people to connect with nature. They recognize that people are adapting all the time to meet their needs and have come up with some inspiring and creative ways to ensure that everyone who comes their way, irrespective of their ability, can access the healing power of nature. Finally, in Boulder, Colorado, there is a unique and much-needed program called Queer Nature run by So Sinopoulos-Lloyd and Pınar Sinopoulos-Lloyd, who are queer-identified and passionate about nature connection. On their website, they state how they "recognize that many people, including LGBTQ+ people, have for various reasons not had easy cultural access to outdoors pursuits, especially 'survival skills' like bushcraft, tactical skills, and (ethical) hunting."[41] Their program "envisions and implements ecological literacy and wilderness self-reliance skills as vital and often overlooked parts of the healing and wholing of populations who have been silenced, marginalized, and even represented as 'unnatural.'"[42] An article in their hometown newspaper tells the story of a young man who, as a gay teenager, did not feel safe to join the nature connection programs being offered locally. The lack of a safe space led him to disconnect from the natural world and lose his sense of belonging. He relates how finding Queer Nature has allowed him to rediscover his love for the natural world and let go of his belief that the wilderness was not a place he could access.

These three stories, specifically, Carl Anthony's call for attention to the reality and marginalization of non-white people in the field of ecopsychology, PTB's commitment to the removal of barriers, and the creation of Queer Nature, are examples of positive responses to the mainstream structures threatening to limit diversity in nature-based reconnection work. They are inspiring models of how the field of nature-based therapy can address some of the normative structures existing in the dominant culture that restrict access and marginalize certain groups and instead promote a diverse and vibrant ecology of people accessing nature-based services.

Ethical Concerns Raised in Outdoor Therapies

Numerous deaths and reports of unethical treatment of youth in residential treatment of youth, including wilderness therapy programs, surfaced in the news and popular media in the early 2000s. Action was taken at governmental levels, resulting in reports of incidents including negligence on the part of program staff, inappropriate standards of practice, and in some cases, unhealthy organizational philosophies. The broad inclusion of programs under review by forensic auditors Kutz and O'Connell in 2007 for the US Government Accountability Office (GOA) included interventions best described as boot camps or boarding schools, while others were simply referred to as residential treatment.[43] The GAO report recognized the need for "last effort" services such as those provided by residential treatment options for "troubled youth" who may have already exhausted numerous interventions and resources in their family and home community, leaving this form of residential treatment as an option for difficult cases of emotional, behavioral, and substance abuse issues. In that regard, they recognize the purpose programs such as these may serve in extreme situations. They also point out, however, that in many states (although they don't mention which ones), parents are legally entitled to send kids into treatment (1) without the child's input, (2) against their will, (3) by hiring a "transport" service to (at times physically) remove the child from the home and place them in treatment programs, and (4) make these decisions based on discussions with program administrators and sometimes educational consultants (who are expected to be free of conflict of interest with programs they help refer youth to). Wrapped up in this short narrative are many potential ethical dilemmas.

While we are not writing a book on wilderness therapy, this approach has informed our work, and we three have work histories with longer expedition-type outdoor programs. Wilderness therapy has also been challenged for a lack of theoretical explanation for what appear to be very positive treatment outcomes, a lack of accessibility to this type of intervention due to costs, the difficulty of integrating families in treatment, and establishing meaningful transitions to home or aftercare services near home.[44] What is relatable to our nature-based therapy practice is that we do occasionally use overnight and multi-day trips and, doing so, engage in practices similar to wilderness therapy. What we are not engaged in is working with involuntary clients and families; no one is forced to attend. Although we have acknowledged that parental coercion to have children attend may be present, any client may choose to end the counseling relationship at any point. For those working with involuntary clients, you will need to consider your professional code of ethics and take responsibility for your actions relative to your profession.

As ethical practitioners and researchers, we ask our colleagues to ensure your practices are guided by an ethic of care, child and family rights, and professionalism. Ultimately, in the name of client care, it is our obligation.

Developing a Nature-based Therapy Practice

As noted in the disclaimer at the front of this book, becoming familiar with the ideas and materials in this book is no replacement for training and qualifications. We assume many of you are already qualified practitioners in human service fields. We also know that what we are presenting is not complicated or high-risk in terms of activities or physical risk; nor are we engaging with complex systems of safety, such as those found in rock climbing or sea kayaking. This can be pretty simple stuff; however, that does not make it easy to do.

Instead of writing a chapter on what specific steps you need to take to create your own nature-based therapy practice, we have decided to simply ask questions, knowing that, by asking a question, other questions emerge. We believe that if you are serious about engaging your clients with nature in a caring, ethically, and meaningful way, then you will review these questions with a critical eye relative to your own practice, competencies, and availability of resource.

Last, one common request we get is to provide training on developing a nature-based practice. We enjoy sharing knowledge and often learn much from those we provide training to. We also encourage finding like-minded local practitioners to share ideas and supervision with, which is a great start. If you can find other practitioners or organizations that engage in nature-based approaches, you will take a significant step toward developing your practice too.

Questions to Ask Yourself When Developing a Nature-based Therapy Practice

Are you going to be working independently or in a group?

- Do you have a like-minded team?
- If you work alone, who in your community could you partner with?
- Will you be running group programs? (We suggest to always have a minimum of 2 facilitators in with children.)
- Can you share costs for equipment, insurance, etc.?

What is your clinical training and scope of practice in the mental health field?

- What is your education level that gives you training as a counselor/therapist working with children, youth, and families?
- Are you registered or certified with a governing body of clinical counselors, psychologists, social workers, etc.?
  - Are you familiar with your profession's code of ethics?
  - What is your scope of practice?
- What is your plan for ongoing training and supervision?
  - Do you have mentors within the field of nature-based therapy for ongoing consultation and supervision?

What is your training for working with children and youth in a nature/outdoor context?

- Have you studied ecopsychology, outdoor education, or related fields?
- Have you gained experience and learning opportunities in nature connection and outdoor education?
- Do you have certification in wilderness first aid or equivalent levels of first aid?
- Do you have a background and/or certification(s) in outdoor skills training or guiding (not required, but important to determine your scope of practice)?
- What is your level of knowledge and connection to local places, geology, flora, and fauna, etc.?

How are you nurturing your own personal connection with the natural world?

- How often do you get out to spend time in nature?
- What are your favorite wild spaces to visit in your community?
- What aspects of the natural world do you want to learn more about?
- What daily practices and routines help you maintain and deepen your connection to the web of life?
- Do you know about the traditional lands and Indigenous peoples of your area? Have you started to establish relationships and understand and support their resurgence efforts?

Do you have adequate liability insurance in place to cover yourself or your group?

- Does your professional liability insurance acknowledge the nature-based elements of your practice? And does your commercial general liability cover all activities you expect to be doing with clients?
  - What activities will be included in your practice? (walking, hiking, scrambling, fires, carving, etc.)
  - Do any of your offerings include specialized adventure activities? (rock climbing, kayaking, etc.)
  - Do you have collaborative partners in outdoor or adventure programming sector who can cover you and your clients when working in partnership?
- Do you have risk management policies that outline the outdoor activities you are able to engage with responsibly?
  - What certifications are required?
  - Have you completed a risk/hazard assessment and mitigation plans in the event of an emergency?
  - Do you have a plan as to how to manage incidents when away from the office?

What locations are you able to access for individual or group client work?

- What are the public parks and wild spaces that you are able to work in? Have you recieved permission to access these lands?

- Which locations are accessible to your clients?
  - What type of landscapes do you have access to (forest, beach, field, grassland)?
  - Are there sensitive ecosystems that you need to be aware of?
  - How busy are these park areas? When are they most populated? Are dogs often present?
  - What wild animals live in these areas? What are the hazards?
- Are there any private lands that you can access for meeting with clients?
  - Are fires permissible on this land?
  - Can you harvest plants, be off trail, and build with natural materials?
  - Are there domestic animals you can connect with (horses, dogs, goats, chickens, etc.)?
  - Do you have access to gardens?
- Where can you host group programs?
  - Are there bathrooms accessible in the location?
  - Is there shelter in the case of extreme weather?

What gear and supplies do you need to acquire?

- Do you have a contact sheet for local emergency services, your co-workers, your client's family or guardians?
- Do you have first aid training and supplies? Cell phone for emergencies?
- Do you have supplies for the activities you might plan (balls, ropes, field manuals, blindfolds, carving knives, paper and pen, etc.)?
- Do you have supplies for managing weather conditions (tarp, hot drinks, extra layers, camping stove/fire box, etc.)?
- Do you have access to an indoor office space for holding sessions when that is requested and appropriate?

What community partnerships and collaborations do you have?

- Have you built relationships with the local First Nation communities to learn more about how you can offer your work in ways that are respectful in honoring their lands and culture practices?

- For group programs, community partnerships can greatly enhance the quality, accessibility, and impact of our programs; what relationships have you built in your community?
- Have you connected with school counselors and administrators regarding what you can offer?
- Do you have relationships with the city or parks and recreation organizations? How can they support your programs or help to provide locations and resources?
- What outdoor adventure organizations are in your area? Can they collaborate by providing gear, guiding expertise, co-facilitation, etc.?
- Are there non-profit organizations that can collaborate with you to better serve clients and families in need?

APPENDIX B

Suggested Clothing and Equipment/Materials List

Here is a sample list of gear we suggest that you have on hand in your pack or close-by vehicle, to help manage safety and comfort in varying weather conditions (for both yourself and the client). As the therapist, you need to make sure that you are managing your own physical and emotional comfort appropriately so that you can focus on the needs of your clients. This list is by no means a substitute for training and experience, it is our offering for your consideration:

- A waterproof tarp and ropes to hang it
- Spare warm hat (toque for you Canadians) and gloves
- Spare warm layers (e.g., fleece)
- Waterproof coat (for wet climates) and a spare one for clients
- Rain pants or warmer shell pants (even if the client does not wear rain/snow pants, we recommend you always have them available to keep yourself dry and able to fully play/sit on the ground)
- Sun protection (hat, sunglasses, sunscreen)—we recommend wearing sunglasses sparingly to increase eye contact with clients
- Thermos of hot tea and mugs on cold days (or bring a camp stove and make tea together)
- Blanket, tarp, or insulated pads for sitting on damp ground
- Protective footwear suitable for the specific terrain
- Snacks and water bottle
- First aid kit always in your backpack
- Multiple communication devices (cell phone, whistle)
- Digital camera (for documentation of client records, with consent)
- Writing materials for recording notes, plus waterproof case

- Fixed-blade carving knife and extra(s) for clients, once properly trained to use them
- Materials for games and projects
- Resource books on local flora and fauna
- Emergency contacts numbers (for your clients, as well as local resources)

Notes

Notes to the Reader

1. R. W. Kimmerer (2013). *Braiding Sweetgrass: Indigenous Wisdom, Scientific Knowledge and the Teachings of Plants*. Minneapolis, MN: Milkweed Editions.

Chapter 1: An Introduction to Nature-based Therapy

1. P. Bogard (2013). *The End of Night: Searching for Natural Darkness in an Age of Artificial Light*. London: Little Brown & Co.
2. R. Carson (1962/2002). *Silent Spring*. Boston: Houghton Mifflin Harcourt.
3. P. H. Kahn Jr., (2002). "Children's Affiliations with Nature: Structure, Development, and the Problem of Environmental Generational Amnesia." In *Children and Nature: Psychological, Sociocultural, and Evolutionary Investigations*, P. H. Kahn and S. R. Kellert, Eds., pp. 93–116.
4. "Scottish GPs to Begin Prescribing Rambling and Birdwatching." Retrieved October 15, 2018, from theguardian.com/uk-news/2018/oct/05 /scottish-gps-nhs-begin-prescribing-rambling-birdwatching
5. M. Van den Bosch and T. Gill (2018). *The Oxford Textbook of Nature and Public Health: The Role of Nature in Improving the Health of a Population*. New York: Oxford University Press.
6. D. Suzuki (2007). *The Sacred Balance: Rediscovering Our Place in Nature*, updated and expanded. Vancouver, BC: Greystone Books.
7. A. Faber Taylor and F. E. Kuo (2009). "Children with Attention Deficits Concentrate Better After Walk in the Park." *Journal of Attention Disorders*, 12(5), 402–409.
8. A. Schwarz (2017). *ADHD Nation: Children, Doctors, Big Pharma, and the Making of an American Epidemic*. New York: Simon and Schuster.
9. T. P. Pasanen, L. Tyrväinen, and K. M. Korpela (2014). "The Relationship Between Perceived Health and Physical Activity Indoors, Outdoors in Built Environments, and Outdoors in Nature." *Applied Psychology: Health and Well-Being*, 6(3), 324–346.

10. J. Barton and J. Pretty (2010). "What Is the Best Dose of Nature and Green Exercise for Improving Mental Health? A Multi-study Analysis." *Environmental Science & Technology*, 44(10), 3947–3955.

11. Ibid., p. 3951.

12. R. M. Flett, R. W. Moore, K. A. Pfeiffer, J. Belonga, and J. Navarre (2010). "Connecting Children and Family with Nature-based Physical Activity." *American Journal of Health Education*, 41(5), 292–300.

13. Ibid., p. 292.

14. T. Hartig, R. Mitchell, S. De Vries, and H. Frumkin (2014). "Nature and Health." *Annual Review of Public Health*, 35, 207–228; C. Ward Thompson and P. A. Aspinall (2011). "Natural Environments and Their Impact on Activity, Health, and Quality of Life." *Applied Psychology: Health and Well-Being*, 3(3), 230–260.

Chapter 2: Outdoor Therapies: A Choice of Paths to Follow

1. S. P. Becker and K. C. Russell (2016). "Wilderness Therapy." In R. J. R. Levesque (Ed.), *Encyclopedia of Adolescence* (2nd edition). New York: Springer.

2. M. A. Clifford (2018). *Forest Bathing: Experience the Healing Power of Nature*. Newburyport, MA: Conari Press.

3. Ibid., p. xix.

4. L. Buzzell and C. Chalquist (2009). *Ecotherapy: Healing with Nature in Mind*. San Francisco: Sierra Club Books; H. Clinebell (2013). *Ecotherapy: Healing Ourselves, Healing the Earth*. New York: Routledge; M. Jordan (2014). *Nature and Therapy: Understanding Counselling and Psychotherapy in Outdoor Spaces*. London: Routledge; M. Jordan and J. Hinds (2016). *Ecotherapy: Theory, Research and Practice*. London: Macmillan International Higher Education; A. McGeeney (2016). *With Nature in Mind: The Ecotherapy Manual for Mental Health Professionals*. London: Jessica Kingsley; T. E. Roszak, M. E. Gomes, and A. D. Kanner (1995). *Ecopsychology: Restoring the Earth, Healing the Mind*. San Francisco: Sierra Club Books.

5. K. Hayes, G. Blashki, J. Wiseman, S. Burke, and L. Reifels (2018). "Climate Change and Mental Health: Risks, Impacts and Priority Actions." *International Journal of Mental Health Systems*, 12(1), 28.

6. S. Westland (2014). *Field Exercises: How Veterans Are Healing Themselves Through Farming and Outdoor Activities*. Gabriola Island, BC: New Society Publishers.

7. A. Selby and A. Smith-Osborne (2013). "A Systematic Review of Effectiveness of Complementary and Adjunct Therapies and Interventions Involving Equines." *Health Psychology*, 32(4), 418.

8. M. A. Gass, H. L. Gillis, and K. C. Russell (2012). *Adventure Therapy: Theory,*

Research, and Practice. New York: Routledge; N. J. Harper, L. Peeters, and C. Carpenter (2015). "Adventure Therapy." In R. Black and K. S. Bricker (Eds.), *Adventure Programming and Travel in the 21st Century*, pp. 221–236. State College, PA: Venture Publishers.

9. Ibid.

10. M. Jordan (2014). *Nature and Therapy*.

11. M. Jordan and J. Hinds (2016). *Ecotherapy*.

12. M. Swingle (2016). *i-Minds: How Cell Phones, Computers, Gaming, and Social Media Are Changing Our Brains, Our Behavior, and the Evolution of Our Species*. Gabriola Island, BC: New Society Publishers.

13. A. W. Bailey, G. Allen, J. Herndon, and C. Demastus (2018). "Cognitive Benefits of Walking in Natural Versus Built Environments." *World Leisure Journal*, 60(4), 293–305.

14. I. C. Tang, Y. P. Tsai, Y. J. Lin, J. H. Chen, C. H. Hsieh, S. H. Hung, William Sullivan, Hsing-Fen Tang, and C. Y. Chang (2017). "Using Functional Magnetic Resonance Imaging (fMRI) to Analyze Brain Region Activity When Viewing Landscapes." *Landscape and Urban Planning*, 162, 137–144.

15. C. Maller, M. Townsend, A. Pryor, P. Brown, and L. St. Leger (2006). "Healthy Nature Healthy People: 'Contact with Nature' as an Upstream Health Promotion Intervention for Populations." *Health Promotion International*, 21(1), 45–54.

16. C. Piccininni, V. Michaelson, I. Janssen, and W. Pickett (2018). "Outdoor Play and Nature Connectedness as Potential Correlates of Internalized Mental Health Symptoms Among Canadian Adolescents." *Preventive Medicine*, 112, 168–175.

17. natureconservancy.ca/en/

18. T. Gill (2014). "The Benefits of Children's Engagement with Nature: A Systematic Literature Review." *Children Youth and Environments*, 24(2), 10–34.

19. S. Robson and V. Rowe (2012). "Observing Young Children's Creative Thinking: Engagement, Involvement and Persistence." *International Journal of Early Years Education*, 20(4), 349–364.

20. K. L. Bagot, F. C. L. Allen, and S. Toukhasati (2015). "Perceived Restorativeness of Children's School Playground Environments: Nature, Playground Features and Play Period Experiences." *Journal of Environmental Psychology*, 41, 1–9.

21. M. J. Duncan, N. D. Clarke, S. L. Birch, J. Tallis, J. Hankey, E. Bryant, and E. L. Eyre, (2014). "The Effect of Green Exercise on Blood Pressure, Heart Rate and Mood State in Primary School Children." *International Journal of Environmental Research and Public Health*, 11(4), 3678–3688.

22. K. McArdle, T. Harrison, and D. Harrison (2013). "Does a Nurturing Approach That Uses an Outdoor Play Environment Build Resilience in

Children from a Challenging Background?" *Journal of Adventure Education & Outdoor Learning*, 13(3), 238–254.

23. L. Chawla, K. Keena, I. Pevec, and E. Stanley (2014). "Green Schoolyards As Havens from Stress and Resources for Resilience in Childhood and Adolescence." *Health & Place*, 1–13.

24. E. Elliot, K. Ten Eycke, S. Chan, U. Müller (2014). "Taking Kindergartners Outdoors: Documenting Their Explorations and Assessing the Impact on Their Ecological Awareness." *Children, Youth and Environments*, 24(2), 102–122.

25. M. Ungar (2012). "Too Safe for Their Own Good: How the Right Amount of Risk and Responsibility Helps Children and Teens Become Resilient. Keynote Address." The 6th International Adventure Therapy Conference. Hrubá Skála, Czech Republic.

Chapter 3: Why Nature-based Therapy for Children, Youth, and Families?

1. M. K. Stone and Z. Barlow (2005). *Ecological literacy: Educating Our Children for a Sustainable World*. San Francisco: Sierra Club Books.

2. K. R. Merikangas, J. P. He, M. Burstein, S. A. Swanson, S. Avenevoli, L. Cui, and J. Swendsen (2010). "Lifetime Prevalence of Mental Disorders in US Adolescents: Results from the National Comorbidity Survey Replication–Adolescent Supplement (NCS-A)." *Journal of the American Academy of Child & Adolescent Psychiatry*, 49(10), 980–989; K. R. Merikangas, J. P. He, D. Brody, P. W. Fisher, K. Bourdon, and D. S. Koretz (2010). "Prevalence and Treatment of Mental Disorders Among US Children in the 2001–2004 NHANES." *Pediatrics*, 125(1), 75–81.

3. Erich Fromm (1955) *The Sane Society*. New York: Rinehart & Co.

4. P. Shepard (2011). *Nature and Madness*. Athens, GA: University of Georgia Press.

5. D. J. Siegel (2014). *Brainstorm: The Purpose and Power of the Teenage Brain*. New York: Tarcher.

6. T. Hartig, R. Mitchell, S. De Vries, and H. Frumkin (2014). "Nature and Health." *Annual Review of Public Health*, 35, 207–228.

7. C. Lim, A. M. Donovan, N. J. Harper, and P. J. Naylor (2017). "Nature Elements and Fundamental Motor Skill Development Opportunities at Five Elementary School Districts in British Columbia." *International Journal of Environmental Research and Public Health*, 14(10), 1279.

8. J. D. Barnes et al. (2016). "Results from Canada's 2016 ParticipACTION report card on physical activity for children and youth." *Journal of Physical Activity and Health*, 13(11 Suppl 2), S110-S116.

9. M. S. Tremblay, J. D. Barnes, S. A. González, P. T. Katzmarzyk, V. O. Onywera, J. J. Reilly, and Global Matrix 2.0 Research Team. (2016). "Global Matrix

2.0: Report Card Grades on the Physical Activity of Children and Youth Comparing 38 Countries." *Journal of Physical Activity and Health*, 13(11 Suppl 2), S343-S366.

10. M. Brussoni et al. (2015). "What Is the Relationship Between Risky Outdoor Play and Health in Children? A Systematic Review." *International Journal of Environmental Research and Public Health*, 12(6), 6423–6454.

11. C. Lim, A. M. Donovan, N. J. Harper, and P. J. Naylor (2017). "Nature Elements and Fundamental Motor Skill Development Opportunities at Five Elementary School Districts in British Columbia." *International Journal of Environmental Research and Public Health*, 14(10), 1279.

12. E. Lawton, E. Brymer, P. Clough, and A. Denovan (2017). "The Relationship Between the Physical Activity Environment, Nature Relatedness, Anxiety, and the Psychological Well-being Benefits of Regular Exercisers." *Frontiers in Psychology*, 8, 1058.

13. V. Ulset, F. Vitaro, M. Brendgen, M. Bekkhus, and A. I. Borge (2017). "Time Spent Outdoors During Preschool: Links with Children's Cognitive and Behavioral Development." *Journal of Environmental Psychology*, 52, 69–80.

14. T. Hartig et al. (2014). "Nature and Health."

15. T. Gill (2014). "The Benefits of Children's Engagement with Nature: A Systematic Literature Review." *Children Youth and Environments*, 24(2), p. 19.

16. J. Dewey (1958). *Experience and Nature* (Vol. 471). Courier Corporation.

17. S. R. Kellert (1997). *The Value of Life: Biological Diversity and Human Society*. Washington, DC: Island Press, p. 6.

18. E. Wilson (1992). *Biophilia*. Cambridge: Harvard University Press, 1, 79.

19. R. Kaplan and S. Kaplan (1989). *The Experience of Nature: A Psychological Perspective*. Cambridge University Press.

20. N. M. Wells and G. W. Evans (2003). "Nearby Nature: A Buffer of Life Stress Among Rural Children." *Environment and Behavior*, 35(3), 311–330.

21. B. J. Park, Y. Tsunetsugu, T. Kasetani, T. Kagawa, and Y. Miyazaki (2010). "The Physiological Effects of Shinrin-yoku (Taking in the Forest Atmosphere or Forest Bathing): Evidence from Field Experiments in 24 Forests Across Japan." *Environmental Health and Preventive Medicine*, 15(1),18–26.

22. T. S. Schilhab, M. P. Stevenson, and P. Bentsen (2018). "Contrasting Screen-time and Green-time: A Case for Using Smart Technology and Nature to Optimize Learning Processes." *Frontiers in Psychology*, 9, 773.

23. S. Kaplan (1995). "The Restorative Benefits of Nature: Toward an Integrative Framework." *Journal of Environmental Psychology*, 15(3), 169–182; R. Kaplan and S. Kaplan (2005). "Preference, Restoration, and Meaningful Action in the Context of Nearby Nature." *Urban Place: Reconnecting with the Natural World*, 271–298.

24. Ibid.

25. R. S. Ulrich (1983). "Aesthetic and Affective Response to Natural Environment." In *Behavior and the Natural Environment*, Irwin Altman and Joachim F. Wohlwill (Eds.). Boston: Springer, pp. 85–125.

26. J. J. Gibson (1966). *The Senses Considered as Perceptual Systems*. Oxford: Houghton Mifflin.

27. J. G. Greeno (1994). "Gibson's Affordances." *Psychological Review*, 101(2), 336–342.

28. J. J. Gibson and E. J. Gibson (1955). "Perceptual Learning: Differentiation or Enrichment?" *Psychological Review*, 62(1), p. 34.

29. C. G. Jung (1964). *Modern Man in Search of a Soul*. London: Routledge.

30. R. Otto (1958). *The Idea of the Holy*, Vol. 14. Oxford University Press.

Chapter 4: Making the Choice to Take Therapy Outside

1. D. Abrams (1996). *The Spell of the Sensuous*. New York: Pantheon.

2. J. Macy (1991). *World as Lover, World as Self: Courage for Global Justice and Ecological Renewal*. Berkeley: Parallax Press.

3. A. Næss (1987). "Self-realization: An Ecological Approach to Being in the World." *Trumpeter Journal of Ecosophy*, 4(3).

4. K. Wilber (1997). "An Integral Theory of Consciousness." *Journal of Consciousness Studies*, 4(1), 71–92.

5. H. Clinebell (2013). *Ecotherapy: Healing Ourselves, Healing the Earth*. London: Routledge.

6. John Scull (2008). "Ecopsychology: Where Does It Fit in Psychology in 2009." *Trumpeter Journal of Ecosophy*, 24(3), 68–84.

7. S. R. Kellert and E. O. Wilson (Eds.). (1995). *The Biophilia Hypothesis*. Washington, DC: Island Press.

8. S. R. Kellert (2012). Building for Life: Designing and Understanding the Human-nature Connection. Washington, DC: Island Press, p. 20

9. Ibid., p. 65.

10. Ibid.

11. Ibid., p. 66.

12. Ibid., p. 81.

13. Ibid., p. 85.

Chapter 5: Nature-based Play, Regulation, and Healthy Neurophysiology

1. D. Fosha, D. J. Siegel, and M. Solomon (Eds.). (2009). *The Healing Power of Emotion: Affective Neuroscience, Development & Clinical Practice*. New York: W. W. Norton.

2. S. W. Porges (1995). "Orienting in a Defensive World: Mammalian Modifications of Our Evolutionary Heritage, A Polyvagal Theory." *Psychophysiology*, 32(4), 301–318.

3. Ibid., p. xvi.
4. Ibid., p. 6.
5. P. Ogden, K. Minton, and C. Pain (2006). *Trauma and the Body: A Sensori-motor Approach to Psychotherapy*. New York: W. W. Norton.
6. A. Schore (2012). *The Science of the Art of Psychotherapy: The Latest Work from a Pioneer in the Study of the Development*. New York: W. W. Norton.
7. Personal communication, October 13, 2018, Kaya Lyons.
8. Ibid.
9. L. Kuypers (2011). *The Zones of Regulation: A Curriculum Designed to Foster Self-Regulation and Emotional Control*. San Jose, CA: Think Social Publishing.
10. Ibid.
11. Ibid.
12. R. Wilson and L. Lyons (2013). *Anxious Kids, Anxious Parents: 7 Ways to Stop the Worry Cycle and Raise Courageous and Independent Children*. Deerfield Beach, FL: Health Communications.
13. Ibid.
14. D. Seigel (2011). *Flipping Your Lid*. Retrieved December 12, 2017. heartmindonline.org/resources/daniel-siegel-flipping-your-lid
15. D. Goleman (1996). *Emotional Intelligence: Why It Can Matter More Than IQ*. New York: Bantam Books.
16. L. S. Vygotsky (1978). *Mind in Society: The Development of Higher Psychological Processes*. Cambridge: Harvard University Press; D. Wood, J. Bruner, and G. Ross (1976). "The Role of Tutoring in Problem Solving." *Journal of Child Psychology and Child Psychiatry*, 17, 89–100.
17. P. Ogden, K. Minton, and C. Pain (2006). *Trauma and the Body: A Sensori-motor Approach to Psychotherapy*. New York: W. W. Norton.
18. S. W. Porges (2017). *The Pocket Guide to the Polyvagal Theory: The Transformative Power of Feeling Safe*. Norton Series on Interpersonal Neurobiology. New York: W. W. Norton, p. 9.
19. Ibid., p. 43.
20. K. L. Kain and S. J. Terrell (2018). *Nurturing Resilience: Helping Clients Move Forward from Developmental Trauma, An Integrative Somatic Approach*. Berkeley: North Atlantic Books.
21. S. W. Porges. *The Pocket Guide to the Polyvagal Theory*.
22. S. Stanley (2016). *Relational and Body-centered Practices for Healing Trauma: Lifting the Burdens of the Past*. New York: Routledge, p. 39.
23. F. E. Kuo and A. E. Taylor (2004). "A Potential Natural Treatment for Attention Deficit/Hyperactivity Disorder: Evidence from a National Study." *American Journal of Public Health*, 94(9), 1580–1586.
24. D. Ackerman (2011). *Deep Play*. New York: Vintage.
25. K. L. Kain and S. J. Terrell. *Nurturing Resilience*.

Chapter 6: Outdoor Risky Play in Nature-based Therapy

1. A. Mantler and A. C. Logan (2015). "Natural Environments and Mental Health." *Advances in Integrative Medicine*, 2(1), p. 5.
2. E. B. H. Sandseter and L. E. O. Kennair (2011). "Children's Risky Play from an Evolutionary Perspective: The Anti-Phobic Effects of Thrilling Experiences." *Evolutionary Psychology*, 9(2), 257–284.
3. Ibid.
4. S Robson and V. Rowe (2012). "Observing Young Children's Creative Thinking: Engagement, Involvement and Persistence." *International Journal of Early Years Education*, 20(4), 349–364.
5. A. Mantler and A. C. Logan, (2015). "Natural Environments and Mental Health." *Advances in Integrative Medicine*, 2(1), 5–12.
6. U. Beck (1992). *Risk Society: Towards a New Modernity*. London: Sage.
7. A. Giddens (1999). "Risk and Responsibility." *The Modern Law Review*, 62(1), 1–10.
8. N. J. Harper (2017). "Outdoor Risky Play and Healthy Child Development in the Shadow of the 'Risk Society': A Forest and Nature School Perspective." *Child & Youth Services*, 38(4), 318–334.
9. E. B. H. Sandseter (2009). "Affordances for Risky Play in Preschool: The Importance of Features in the Play Environment." *Early Childhood Education Journal*, 36(5), 439–446.
10. Ibid.
11. For example, M. Brussoni et al. (2012). "Risky Play and Children's Safety: Balancing Priorities for Optimal Child Development." *International Journal of Environmental Research and Public Health*, 9(9), 3134–3148; S. Herrington et al. (2012). 7 *C's: An Informational Guide to Young Children's Outdoor Play Spaces*. Consortium for Health, Learning and Development (CHILD). University of British Columbia.
12. J. D. Barnes et al. (2016). "Results from Canada's 2016 ParticipACTION Report Card on Physical Activity for Children and Youth." *Journal of Physical Activity and Health*, 13(11) Suppl. 2, S110-S116.
13. C. Gray et al. (2015). "What Is the Relationship Between Outdoor Time and Physical Activity, Sedentary Behaviour, and Physical Fitness in Children? A Systematic Review." *International Journal of Environmental Research and Public Health*, 12(6), 6455–6474; M. Brussoni et al. (2015). "What Is the Relationship Between Risky Outdoor Play and Health in Children? A Systematic Review." *International Journal of Environmental Research and Public Health*, 12(6), 6423–6454. M. S. Tremblay et al. (2015). "Position Statement on Active Outdoor Play." *International Journal of Environmental Research and Public Health*, 12(6), 6475–6505.
14. M. S. Tremblay et al. "Position Statement on Active Outdoor Play."

15. P. Gray (2011). "The Decline of Play and the Rise of Psychopathology in Children and Adolescents." *American Journal of Play*, 3(4), 443–463.

16. A. J. Hanscom (2016). *Balanced and Barefoot: How Unrestricted Outdoor Play Makes for Strong, Confident, and Capable Children*. Oakland, CA: New Harbinger Publications.

17. T. Waller et al. (Eds.). (2017). *The SAGE Handbook of Outdoor Play and Learning*. London: Sage.

18. B. Dietze and D. Kashin (2019). *Outdoor and Nature Play in Early Childhood Education*. North York, ON: Pearson Canada.

19. J. M. Swank and S. M. Shin (2015). "Nature-based Child-centered Play Therapy: An Innovative Counseling Approach." *International Journal of Play Therapy*, 24(3), 151–161.

20. Ibid., p. 153.

21. R, Poulton and R. G. Menzies (2002). "Non-associative Fear Acquisition: A Review of the Evidence from Retrospective and Longitudinal Research." *Behaviour Research and Therapy*, 40(2), 127–149.

22. S. W. Porges (2011). *The Polyvagal Theory: Neurophysiological Foundations of Emotions, Attachment, Communication, and Self-Regulation*. Norton Series on Interpersonal Neurobiology. New York: W. W. Norton.

23. G. Maté and G. Neufeld (2019). *Hold on to Your Kids: Why Parents Need to Matter More Than Peers*. New York: Random House.

24. S. Stanley (2016). *Relational and Body-centered Practices for Healing Trauma: Lifting the Burdens of the Past*. New York: Routledge, p. 39.

25. D. J. Siegel and T. P. Bryson (2011). *The Whole-brain Child: 12 Revolutionary Strategies to Nurture Your Child's Developing Mind*. New York: Bantam Books.

26. S. W. Porges. *The Polyvagal Theory*.

27. M. Ungar (2009). *Too Safe for Their Own Good: How Risk and Responsibility Help Teens Thrive*. Toronto: McClelland & Stewart.

Chapter 7: Nature as Co-therapist

1. M. Jordan and J. Hinds (2016). *Ecotherapy: Theory, Research and Practice*. London: Macmillan International Higher Education.

2. A. T. Jones and D. S. Segal (2018). "Unsettling Ecopsychology: Addressing Settler Colonialism in Ecopsychology Practice." *Ecopsychology*, 10(3), 127–136.

3. J. Macy (1991). *World As Lover, World As Self: Courage for Justice and Ecological Renewal*. Berkeley: Parallax Press.

4. R. Louv (2005). *Last Child in the Woods: Saving Our Kids from Nature Deficit Disorder*. New York: Algonquin Books.

5. F. Williams (2017). *The Nature Fix: Why Nature Makes Us Happier, Healthier, and More Creative*. New York: W. W. Norton.

6. J. Cornell (1979). *Sharing Nature with Children*. Nevada City: Dawn Publications; (1989). *Sharing Nature with Children II*. Nevada City: Dawn Publications.

7. Ibid., 1989.

8. J. Young, E. Haas, and E. McGown (2010). *Coyote's Guide to Connecting with Nature*. Washington, DC: OWLLink Media.

9. G. Ehrlich (1985/2017). *The Solace of Open Spaces: Essays*. Open Road Media.

10. J. Kabat-Zinn (2009). *Wherever You Go, There You Are: Mindfulness Meditation in Everyday Life*. New York: Hachette Books.

11. S. Dimidjian and Z. V. Segal (2015). "Prospects for a Clinical Science of Mindfulness-based Intervention." *American Psychologist*, 70(7), 593.

12. G. W. Burns (1998). *Nature-guided Therapy: Brief Integrative Strategies for Health and Well-being*. London: Taylor & Francis.

13. Ibid., p. 73.

14. Ibid., p. 87.

15. D. J. Siegel (2015). *Brainstorm: The Power and Purpose of the Teenage Brain*. Seattle, WA: Penguin.

16. Carson, R. (1956) The Sense of Wonder: A Celebration of Nature for Parents and Children. New York, Harper Perennial.

17. J. Young et al. *Coyote's Guide to Connecting with Nature*.

18. R. Bateman (2007). *Backyard Birds*. Markham, ON: Scholastic Canada/Madison Press.

19. J. Young et al. *Coyote's Guide to Connecting with Nature*, p. 69.

20. A. N. Schore (2015). *Affect Regulation and the Origin of the Self: The Neurobiology of Emotional Development*. New York: Routledge.

21. N. J. Harper, L. Peeters, and C. Carpenter (2015). "Adventure Therapy." In R. Black and K. S. Bricker (Eds.), *Adventure Programming and Travel in the 21st Century*. State College, PA: Venture Publishing, pp. 221–236.

22. G. Hartford (2011). "Practical Implications for the Development of Applied Metaphor in Adventure Therapy." *Journal of Adventure Education & Outdoor Learning*, 11(2), 145–160.

23. M. J. Cohen (2007). *Reconnecting with Nature*, 3rd Ed. Apple Valley, MN: EcoPress.

24. M. White and D. Epston (1990). *Narrative Means to Therapeutic Ends*. New York: W. W. Norton.

25. *New York Times*. (2018). "Is Loneliness a Health Epidemic?" Retrieved October 21, 2018. nytimes.com/2018/02/09/opinion/sunday/loneliness-health.html

26. T. Brach (2004). *Radical Acceptance: Embracing Your Life with the Heart of a Buddha*. New York: Bantam Dell.

27. R. May (1991). *The Cry for Myth*. New York: W. W. Norton.

28. Ibid., p. 15.

29. B. Swimme and T. Berry (1992). *The Universe Story*. London: Arkana.

30. T. Berry (2011). *The Great Work: Our Way into the Future*. New York: Crown.

31. A. Van Gennep (1960). *The Rites of Passage*. Chicago: University of Chicago Press.

32. J. Campbell (1949). *The Hero with a Thousand Faces*. Princeton, NJ: Princeton University.

33. R. L. Grimes (2000). *Deeply into the Bone: Reinventing Rites of Passage*. Berkeley: University of California Press.

34. D. French (1998). "The Power of Choice: A Critique of Joseph Campbell's 'Monomyth,' Northrop Frye's Theory of Myth, Mark Twain's Orthodoxy to Heresy, and C. G. Jung's God-image." Doctoral dissertation, Pacifica Graduate Institute of Santa Barbara.

35. J. Norris (2011). "Crossing the Threshold Mindfully: Exploring Rites of Passage Models in Adventure Therapy." *Journal of Adventure Education & Outdoor Learning*, 11(2), 109–126.

36. A. D. Tian, J. Schroeder, G. Häubl, J. L. Risen, M. I. Norton, and F. Gino (2018). "Enacting Rituals to Improve Self-control." *Journal of Personality and Social Psychology*, 114(6), 851.

Chapter 8: Nature-based Therapy for Families

1. J. Bowlby (1977). "The Making and Breaking of Affectional Bonds: II. Some Principles of Psychotherapy: The Fiftieth Maudsley Lecture (expanded version)." *British Journal of Psychiatry*, 130(5), 421–431; A. N. Schore (2015). *Affect Regulation and the Origin of the Self: The Neurobiology of Emotional Development*. London: Routledge.

2. A. Barrows (1995). "The Ecopsychology of Child Development." In T. E. Roszak, M. A. Gomes, and A. D. Kanner (Eds.), *Ecopsychology: Restoring the Earth, Healing the Mind*. San Francisco: Sierra Club Books, p. 109.

3. S. Bandoroff and D. G. Scherer (1994). "Wilderness Family Therapy: An Innovative Treatment Approach for Problem Youth." *Journal of Child and Family Studies*, 3(2), 175–191; N. J. Harper and K. C. Russell (2008). "Family Involvement and Outcome in Adolescent Wilderness Treatment: A Mixed-methods Evaluation." *International Journal of Child and Family Welfare*, 11(1), 19–36.

4. L. Chawla (2007). "Childhood Experiences Associated with Care for the Natural World: A Theoretical Framework for Empirical Results." *Children, Youth and Environments*, 17(4), 144–170.

5. J. Kolari (2016). *Connected Parenting: Transform Your Challenging Child and Build Loving Bonds for Life*. Berkeley, CA: Penguin.

6. G. Neufield and G. Maté (2013). *Hold Onto Your Kids. Why Parents Need to Matter More Than Peers.* Toronto: Vintage Canada.

7. J. Gerstein (1999). *Sticking Together: Experiential Activities for Family Counseling.* London: Taylor & Francis; D. M. Lung, G. Stauffer, T. Alvarez, and J. Conway (2016). *Power of Family: An Experiential Approach to Family Treatment.* Bethany, OK: Wood 'N' Barnes.

8. T. Borton (1970). *Reach, Touch, and Teach: Student Concerns and Process Education.* New York: McGraw-Hill.

Chapter 9: Multi-family Nature-based Therapy

1. J. M. Swank and A. P. Daire (2010). "Multiple Family Adventure-based Therapy Groups: An Innovative Integration of Two Approaches." *Family Journal*, 18(3), 241–247.

2. E. Asen and M. Scholz (2010). *Multi-family Therapy: Concepts and Techniques.* London: Routledge.

3. S. Jennings (2011). *Healthy Attachments and Neuro-Dramatic-Play.* London: Jessica Kingsley Publishers.

4. A. C. Bohart and K. Tallman (2010). "Clients: The Neglected Common Factor in Psychotherapy." *The Heart and Soul of Change: Delivering What Works in Therapy*, 2, 83–111.

5. R. S. Lazarus (1974). "Psychological Stress and Coping in Adaptation and Illness." *International Journal of Psychiatry in Medicine*, 5(4), 321–333.

6. J. E. Burg (2000). "Adventures in Family Therapy." *Journal of Systemic Therapies*, 19(3), 18–30.

7. R. A. Cohen (2011). "Yerkes–Dodson Law." In *Encyclopedia of Clinical Neuropsychology.* New York: Springer, 2737–2738

8. D. M. Lung, G. Stauffer, and T. Alvarez (2008). *Power of One, One, One: Adventure and Experiential Activities for One on One Counseling Sessions.* Bethany OK.: Wood 'N' Barnes.

9. M. A. Gass (1993). *Adventure Therapy: Therapeutic Applications of Adventure Programming.* Dubuque, IA: Kendall/Hunt.

10. John Conway, taken from transcript of interview with the author.

11. N. Harper, D. Segal, and K. Rose (2011). "Family Roots: An Evaluation of a Nature-based Adventure Therapy Group." Poster presented at the Healthy by Nature Forum. Vancouver, BC.

Chapter 10: Group Applications in Nature-based Therapy

1. M. Cech (2010). *Interventions with Children and Youth in Canada.* New York: Oxford University Press.

2. M. Burns (2006). *Healing Spaces: The Therapeutic Milieu in Child and Youth Work.* Kingston, ON: Child Care Press.

3. M. S. Corey, G. Corey, and C. Corey (2013). *Groups: Process and Practice*. Boston, MA: Cengage Learning.

4. Ibid.

5. I. D. Yalom (2005). *The Theory and Practice of Group Psychotherapy*. New York, Basic Books, p. 1.

6. T. Laaksoharju, E. Rappe, and T. Kaivola (2012). "Garden Affordances for Social Learning, Play, and for Building Nature–child Relationship." *Urban Forestry & Urban Greening*, 11(2), 195–203.

7. M. Iacoboni (2009). "Imitation, Empathy, and Mirror Neurons." *Annual Review of Psychology*, 60, 653–670.

8. I. D. Yalom, p. 98.

Chapter 11: Ethics in Nature-based Therapy

1. I. Hooley (2016). "Ethical Considerations for Psychotherapy in Natural Settings." *Ecopsychology*, 8(4), 215–221.

2. V. Reynolds (2014). "Centering Ethics in Group Supervision: Fostering Cultures of Critique and Structuring Safety." *International Journal of Narrative Therapy & Community Work*, 1, p. 3.

3. S. Banks (2003). "From Oaths to Rulebooks: A Critical Examination of Codes of Ethics for the Social Professions." *European Journal of Social Work*, 6(2), 133–144.

4. N. Ray (2005). "Transactions on the Rock Face." Retrieved April 6, 2008. therapytoday.net/archive/dec2005/cover_feature3.html

5. S. P. Becker (2010). "Wilderness Therapy: Ethical Considerations for Mental Health Professionals. *Child & Youth Care Forum*, 39(1), 47–61.

6. W. E. Schulz, G. W. Sheppard, R. Lehr, and B. Shepard (2006). *Counselling Ethics: Issues and Cases*. Ottawa, ON: Canadian Counselling Association.

7. M. Cohen (1999). *Reconnecting with Nature: Finding Wellness Through Restoring Your Bond with the Earth*. Apple Valley, MN: EcoPress.

8. M. Jordan and H. Marshall (2010). "Taking Counselling and Psychotherapy Outside: Destruction or Enrichment of the Therapeutic Frame?" *European Journal of Psychotherapy and Counselling*, 12(4), 345–359.

9. Ibid., p. 352.

10. Ibid.

11. A. C. Bohart (2005). "Evidence-based Psychotherapy Means Evidence-informed, Not Evidence-driven." *Journal of Contemporary Psychotherapy*, 35(1), 39–53.

12. S. D. Miller, M. A. Hubble, D. Chow, and J. Seidel (2015). "Beyond Measures and Monitoring: Realizing the Potential of Feedback-informed Treatment." *Psychotherapy*, 52(4), 449.

13. Therapeutic Adventure Professional Group (TAPG). (2010). "Adventure Therapy Best Practices." Association for Experiential Education. aee.org /at-best-practices

14. J. Scull (2008). "Ecopsychology: Where Does It Fit in Psychology in 2009?" *Trumpeter Journal of Ecosophy*, 24(3), 68–84.

15. TAPG (2010). "Adventure Therapy Best Practices," 1.1.4.

16. W. E. Schulz et al. (2006). *Counselling Ethics*.

17. R. Greenway (1995). "The Wilderness Effect and Ecopsychology." In T. E. Roszak, M. E. Gomes, and A. D. Kanner, (Eds). *Ecopsychology: Restoring the Earth, Healing the Mind*. Sierra Club Books, pp. 122–139.

18. R. Berger (2010). "Nature Therapy: Thoughts About the Limitations of Practice." *Journal of Humanistic Psychology*, 50(1), p. 72.

19. Ibid.

20. R. Greenway, "The Wilderness Effect and Ecopsychology," p. 136.

21. K. C. Russell and N. Harper (2006). "Incident Monitoring in Outdoor Behavioral Healthcare Programs: A Four-year Summary of Restraint, Runaway, Injury, and Illness Rates." *Journal of Therapeutic Schools and Programs*, 1(1), 70–90.

22. Ibid., p. 72.

23. L. Tyson and K. Asmus (2008) "Deepening the Paradigm of Choice: Exploring Choice & Power in Experiential Education." In K. Warren, D. Mitten, and T. A. Loeffler (Eds.), *Theory and Practice of Adventure Education*. Boulder, CO: Association of Experiential Education, pp. 262–281.

24. R. Berger. "Nature Therapy."

25. M. A. Gass (1993). *Adventure Therapy: Therapeutic Applications of Adventure Programming*. Dubuque, IA: Kendall/Hunt, p. 277.

26. M. Ringer and H. L. Gillis Jr. (1995). "Managing Psychological Depth in Adventure Programming." *Journal of Experiential Education*, 18(1), 41–51.

27. Ibid., p. 50.

28. TAPG (2010). "Adventure Therapy Best Practices."

29. S. P. Becker, p. 54.

30. S. B. Goldberg, T. Rousmaniere, S. D. Miller, J. Whipple, S. L. Nielsen, W. T. Hoyt, and B. E. Wampold (2016). "Do Psychotherapists Improve with Time and Experience? A Longitudinal Analysis of Outcomes in a Clinical Setting." *Journal of Counseling Psychology*, 63 (1), 1.

31. D. L. Chow, S. D. Miller, J. A. Seidel, R. T. Kane, J. A. Thornton, and W. P. Andrews (2015). "The Role of Deliberate Practice in the Development of Highly Effective Psychotherapists." *Psychotherapy*, 52(3), 337.

32. Personal communication.

33. J. Byrne and J. Wolch (2009). "Nature, Race, and Parks: Past Research and Future Directions for Geographic Research." *Progress in Human Geography*, 33(6), 743–765.

34. A. T. Jones and D. S. Segal (2018). "Unsettling Ecopsychology: Addressing Settler Colonialism in Ecopsychology Practice." *Ecopsychology*, 10(3), 127–136.
35. Ibid., p. 128.
36. Ibid., p. 129.
37. James Tully, personal communication.
38. D. Mitten (1994). "Ethical Considerations in Adventure Therapy: A Feminist Critique." *Women & Therapy*, 15(3–4), 55–84.
39. Mitten, personal communication.
40. A. C. Anthony (1995). "Ecopsychology and the Deconstruction of Whiteness." In T. E. Roszak, M. E. Gomes, and A. D. Kanner (Eds.). *Ecopsychology: Restoring the Earth, Healing the Mind*. San Francisco: Sierra Club Books, p. 264.
41. Queer Nature, queernature.org/what-we-do/
42. Ibid.
43. G. D. Kutz and A. O'Connell (2007). *Residential Treatment Programs. Concerns Regarding Abuse and Death in Certain Programs for Troubled Youth* (GAO-08-146T). Retrieved from Washington, DC.
44. S. P. Becker and K. C. Russell (2016). "Wilderness Therapy." In R. J. R. Levesque (Ed.), *Encyclopedia of Adolescence*, 2nd ed. New York: Springer; Harper, N. J. (2017). "Wilderness Therapy, Therapeutic Camping and Adventure Education in Child and Youth Care Literature: A Scoping Review." *Children & Youth Services Review*, 83, 68–79; D. A. Scott and L. M. Duerson (2010). "Continuing the Discussion: A Commentary on Wilderness Therapy: Ethical Considerations for Mental Health Professionals." *Child & Youth Care Forum*, 39(1), 63–68.

Index

About the Authors

NEVIN J. HARPER is an associate professor in the School of Child and Youth Care at the University of Victoria, where he teaches group facilitation skills and nature-based approaches to counseling and youth work, and supervises student field practicums. His career has included stretches as a youth worker, educator, researcher, trainer, and guide in the  realm of adventure education and outdoor therapeutic practices. Nevin is the founder of the Canadian Adventure Therapy Symposium and a founding director of the Child & Nature Alliance of Canada. He continues to research, write, speak, and publish on a range of outdoor approaches to human development and therapy and education.

KATHRYN ROSE has been discovering the joys of experiential and nature-based approaches to the promotion of individual and community well-being for over fifteen years. She has focused her passion on developing accessible nature-based therapy programs for youth and families throughout the greater Victoria area and is co-founder of Human-Nature  Counselling. She completed a master's degree in Transpersonal Counselling Psychology, with a specialization in wilderness therapy, from Naropa University in Colorado and is registered with the British Columbia Association of Clinical Counsellors. humannaturecounselling.ca

DAVID SEGAL has been providing therapeutic nature-based counseling for children, youth, and families for over fifteen years. The wisdom and healing offered through connecting with the natural world that first drew him to this field continues to inspire him every day. He completed a master's degree in Child and Youth Care at the University of Victoria  and is registered with the British Columbia Association of Clinical Counsellors. David is the co-founder of Human–Nature Counselling, provides training and supervision for other counselors and youth workers, and has published articles in *Ecopsychology* and the *International Journal of Child, Youth and Family Studies*. humannaturecounselling.ca

ABOUT NEW SOCIETY PUBLISHERS

New Society Publishers is an activist, solutions-oriented publisher focused on publishing books for a world of change. Our books offer tips, tools, and insights from leading experts in sustainable building, homesteading, climate change, environment, conscientious commerce, renewable energy, and more—positive solutions for troubled times.

We're proud to hold to the highest environmental and social standards of any publisher in North America. This is why some of our books might cost a little more. We think it's worth it!

DON'T EAT THIS BOOK (but you could)

- We print all our books in North America, never overseas

- All our books are printed on **100% post-consumer recycled paper**, processed chlorine-free, with low-VOC vegetable-based inks (since 2002)

- Our corporate structure is an innovative employee shareholder agreement, so we're one-third employee-owned (since 2015)

- We're carbon-neutral (since 2006)

- We're certified as a B Corporation (since 2016)

At New Society Publishers, we care deeply about *what* we publish—but also about *how* we do business.

Download our catalog at https://newsociety.com/Our-Catalog or for a printed copy please email info@newsocietypub.com or call 1-800-567-6772 ext 111.

New Society Publishers
ENVIRONMENTAL BENEFITS STATEMENT

For every 5,000 books printed, New Society saves the following resources:[1]

31	Trees
2,838	Pounds of Solid Waste
3,123	Gallons of Water
4,073	Kilowatt Hours of Electricity
5,159	Pounds of Greenhouse Gases
22	Pounds of HAPs, VOCs, and AOX Combined
8	Cubic Yards of Landfill Space

[1] Environmental benefits are calculated based on research done by the Environmental Defense Fund and other members of the Paper Task Force who study the environmental impacts of the paper industry.

Certified B Corporation

FSC
www.fsc.org
MIX
Paper from responsible sources
FSC® C016245

new society
PUBLISHERS
www.newsociety.com